# PUPIL, TEACHER AND FAMILY VOICE IN EDUCATIONAL INSTITUTIONS

Taking a novel approach to the concept of 'voice' within education systems, this insightful text considers the extent to which the values, opinions, beliefs and perspectives of pupils, families, teachers and members of senior management are heard in educational settings, and explores what can be learned from integrating their views and opinions in decision-making processes.

*Pupil, Teacher and Family Voice in Educational Institutions* traces the historical and legal developments which have heralded an increased appreciation of individuals' perspectives in key decision-making processes. Chapters consider how various parties can be encouraged to voice their opinions and beliefs, and address the issues and challenges which may face institutions as they seek to create an atmosphere of open and active consultation and engagement. Drawing on evidence-based research, case studies and personal accounts, chapters reflect upon the concept of 'voice' in diverse settings and acknowledge the sometimes significant divergence between the intended and actual extent to which such opinions, beliefs and perspectives are reflected in day-to-day practice.

Offering in-depth exploration of the concept of 'voice' and the benefits, implications, challenges and practicalities associated with it, this text will be of interest to future and in-service teachers, educational researchers and policy makers.

**Janice Wearmouth** is Professor of Education at the University of Bedfordshire, UK.

**Andrew Goodwyn** is Professor and Head of the School of Education and English Language and Director of the Institute for Research in Education, at the University of Bedfordshire, and Emeritus Professor at the University of Reading, UK.

# PUPIL, TEACHER AND FAMILY VOICE IN EDUCATIONAL INSTITUTIONS

Values, Opinions, Beliefs and Perspectives

Edited by Janice Wearmouth
and Andrew Goodwyn

LONDON AND NEW YORK

First published 2019
by Routledge
2 Park Square, Milton Park, Abingdon, Oxon OX14 4RN

and by Routledge
52 Vanderbilt Avenue, New York, NY 10017

*Routledge is an imprint of the Taylor & Francis Group, an informa business*

© 2019 selection and editorial matter, Janice Wearmouth and Andrew Goodwyn; individual chapters, the contributors

The right of Janice Wearmouth and Andrew Goodwyn to be identified as the authors of the editorial material, and of the authors for their individual chapters, has been asserted in accordance with sections 77 and 78 of the Copyright, Designs and Patents Act 1988.

All rights reserved. No part of this book may be reprinted or reproduced or utilised in any form or by any electronic, mechanical, or other means, now known or hereafter invented, including photocopying and recording, or in any information storage or retrieval system, without permission in writing from the publishers.

*Trademark notice*: Product or corporate names may be trademarks or registered trademarks, and are used only for identification and explanation without intent to infringe.

*British Library Cataloguing in Publication Data*
A catalogue record for this book is available from the British Library

*Library of Congress Cataloging-in-Publication Data*
Names: Wearmouth, Janice, editor. | Goodwyn, Andrew, 1954- editor.
Title: Pupil, teacher and family voice in educational institutions : values, opinions, beliefs and perspectives / Edited by Janice Wearmouth and Andrew Goodwyn.
Description: Abingdon, Oxon ; New York, NY : Routledge, 2019. | Includes bibliographical references and index.
Identifiers: LCCN 2018053194 (print) | LCCN 2019003625 (ebook) | ISBN 9780429505669 (eb) | ISBN 9781138584860 (hbk) | ISBN 9781138584877 (pbk) | ISBN 9780429505669 (ebk)
Subjects: LCSH: Communication in education. | Teacher-student relationships. | Teachers--Attitudes. | Students--Attitudes.
Classification: LCC LB1033.5 (ebook) | LCC LB1033.5 .P86 2019 (print) | DDC 371.102/2--dc23
LC record available at https://lccn.loc.gov/2018053194

ISBN: 978-1-138-58486-0 (hbk)
ISBN: 978-1-138-58487-7 (pbk)
ISBN: 978-0-429-50566-9 (ebk)

Typeset in Bembo
by Taylor & Francis Books
Printed by CPI Group (UK) Ltd, Croydon CR0 4YY

# CONTENTS

*List of illustrations*   *vii*
*List of contributors*   *ix*
*Preface*   *xii*

1 Developments towards the right to be heard in educational contexts   1
  *Dr Will Coster*

2 Lessons learnt by student teachers from the use of children's voice in teaching practice   15
  *Dr Kate Hudson-Glynn*

3 On bilingualism in monolingual English classrooms: Voicing the challenges for bilingual children, their parents and schools   33
  *Dr Maja Jankowska*

4 Bilingual Creative Writing Clubs: Giving voice to bi/multilingual children in English schools and bi/multilingual university students and staff   55
  *Dr Maja Jankowska*

5 Listening to the voices of indigenous Māori students over time: What do they tell us about national education policy?   76
  *Professor Mere Berryman and Elizabeth Eley*

6 Students' and a teacher's views of factors contributing to positive literacy learning identities for all students in an inclusive classroom 92
*Professor Janice Wearmouth*

7 The hidden voice of pre-service teachers in their private social media interactions 109
*Dr James Shea*

8 A voice for advancing the profession of teaching? 123
*Professor Andrew Goodwyn*

9 The first year of headship: A cross-comparison of the experiences, challenges and successes, expressed by newly appointed headteachers during their first year in post 139
*Dr Karen Lindley*

10 Primary headteachers' perceptions of schools' roles in training teachers within a changing landscape of teacher training 158
*Dr Elaine Barron*

11 Lost in translation: A discussion of a small scale study of South Asian non-English speaking parents' experiences of negotiating their children's primary schooling 172
*Anna Graham and Rumisaa Shabir*

12 A mother's experiences in the special educational needs system 191
*Martha Smith*

13 Students', teachers' and families' views on homework 207
*Dr Wendy Edwards and Professor Janice Wearmouth*

*Index* *223*

# ILLUSTRATIONS

**Figures**

| | | |
|---|---|---|
| 2.1 | The research process | 20 |
| 2.2 | The plan, teach, assess, evaluate cycle | 21 |
| 2.3 | 'The Thinking Fish' | 22 |
| 2.4 | Frequency of themes identified from the 'Thinking Fish' | 24 |
| 2.5 | Themes collated from student teachers' reflective logs | 25 |
| 2.6 | Comparison of frequencies of themes most associated with the principles of social constructivism | 26 |
| 2.7 | Visual representation of learning in this project | 29 |
| 2.8 | Visual representation of Littleton and Mercer's (2013) concept of interthinking as a helix showing learning through the ZPD | 30 |
| 2.9 | Visual representation of the potential position of the framework in this study, in the context of a dynamic model of learning through the ZPD | 30 |
| 4.1 | Examples of bilingual books | 62 |
| 4.2 | A trilingual story | 65 |
| 4.3 | A bilingual story in Bulgarian | 65 |
| 4.4 | Work in progress – a child proudly sharing her illustrations | 71 |
| 4.5 | The final product | 71 |
| 6.1 | Examples of the 'Talking Stones' | 96 |
| 6.2 | Wall display referring to Treaty of Waitangi | 101 |
| 6.3 | Shoot for the moon | 101 |
| 6.4 | Example of a wall display with scaffolding for new writing | 102 |
| 6.5 | Hope's stones | 104 |
| 6.6 | Andrew's stones | 105 |

12.1 Chocolate biscuit in magnetic frame 195
12.2 Laminated photograph of the park 196
12.3 Picture of 'Big Food Adventure Book' 198
12.4 Phonics flashcard 199
12.5 Number board 200

## Tables

3.1 Case study 1: standard scores 52
3.2 Case study 1: scale comparisons 52
3.3 Case study 1: composite scores 52
3.4 Case study 2: standard scores 53
3.5 Case study 2: scale comparisons 53
3.6 Case study 2: composite scores 53
3.7 Case study 3: standard scores 54
3.8 Case study 3: scale comparisons 54
3.9 Case study 3: composite scores 54

# CONTRIBUTORS

## Editors

**Janice Wearmouth** is Professor of Education at the University of Bedfordshire, with wide experience of research and publication in the field nationally and internationally. Her current roles include responsibility for all research students in Education at the university, and course leadership of the National Award for Special Educational Needs Co-ordination in the Masters Programme and of two distance-learning postgraduate certificates in education. Prior to joining the University of Bedfordshire, she was the Director of the Centre for Curriculum and Teaching Studies at the Open University, then Professor of Education at Victoria University of Wellington in New Zealand. She has had many years' experience of teaching in mainstream schools also, first on voluntary service in Cameroon and, later, in Bermuda, London, Northamptonshire and Bedfordshire.

**Andrew Goodwyn** is a Professor and Head of the School of Education and English Language and Director of the Institute for Research in Education, at the University of Bedfordshire, and also Emeritus Professor at the University of Reading. Currently he is President of The International Federation for the Teaching of English and a Fellow of the Royal Society of Arts. His research focuses on first language education and on the concept of teacher expertise. He has published extensively including single authored and edited books, contributed to many scholarly journals and given lectures and presentations around the world.

## Authors

**Elaine Barron** has worked in primary education since the 1970s. She held senior leadership posts in schools in the Middle East and in England before becoming Senior Lecturer at the University of Bedfordshire.

**Mere Berryman** is a Professor at the University of Waikato. Her early research involved collaborative work with schools, Māori students, their families and communities through the formation of culturally responsive relationships. This work merged with the inception of Te Kotahitanga and was further built upon in 2014 with Building on Success: Kia Eke Panuku. This iterative professional development initiative aimed to promote Māori students' educational success as Māori.

**Will Coster** is a Senior Lecturer in Education at the University of Bedfordshire. He gained a D.Phil in history at the University of York where he began his research into the history of religion and the family. This provided the basis for work on baptism, childhood, the family and religion in the Tudor and Stuart periods. He has published extensively on attitudes to and ideas about childhood and youth, the family and the history of war, religion and society. He is currently undertaking research on the history of education and disability.

**Wendy Edwards** has taught at primary and secondary levels in the state and independent sectors, with experience in secondary schools as head of departments of Physical Education, Leisure and Tourism, and Religious Education and head of year. Subsequently she changed career to teach on undergraduate and postgraduate programmes in the Department of Teacher Education and Department of Education Studies and managed various routes into teaching at the University of Bedfordshire in 2006. In 2018 she completed her doctorate, investigating 'What is the point of homework and should schools set it?'

**Elizabeth Eley** comes with wide experiences across the education sector. She is currently Associate Director of Poutama Pounamu: Equity, Excellence and Belonging in the University of Waikato. Poutama Pounamu focuses on making a positive difference for Māori students. Her PhD research explores how to enhance the teacher's role as the 'More Knowledgeable Other' within a student's 'Zone of Proximal Development' in order to enhance student classroom learning and experiences.

**Anna Graham** is a Senior Lecturer at the University of Bedfordshire and Pathway Co-ordinator for the MA Education (Social Justice) degree. She has a particular research interest in the educational implications of poverty and social exclusion across family, school and community contexts.

**Kate Hudson-Glynn** was formerly a primary phase teacher, becoming an Advanced Skills Teacher supporting teachers across a large and diverse county. Subsequently she changed career to lecture in initial teacher education, and further developed her understanding of learning and teaching through practice, a Masters and Doctoral study. Currently she leads the newly qualified teacher (NQT) support in the School of Teacher Education. Her research reflects her interest in the importance of children's voice in developing their own learning but also in improving the understanding of those who teach them, especially student teachers.

**Maja Jankowska** is a Senior Lecturer in Psychology at the University of Bedfordshire. Her work has always been inter-disciplinary, crossing the boundaries of psychology, education and cultural studies. Her interests are in qualitative methodology, personal development, processes of identity development, cultural aspects of teaching, learning and therapy, internalisation of education, life-wide and lifelong learning and creativity. A bilingual herself, she is keen to provide opportunities for multicultural and multilingual learners within the Higher Education sector and the wider community. More about her work is available at www.creativebilingual.com

**Karen Lindley** began her career in secondary education, rising from teacher of MFL (French and German) to the position of Vice Principal. Upon completion of her PhD, she changed career, working initially in teacher training at the University of Northampton in 2014, and currently as Senior Lecturer in the Education Studies Department at the University of Bedfordshire. Her research interests include the impact of compulsory redeployment on teachers, particularly with regard to the role of teacher self and identity, and the leadership and management of school change.

**Rumisaa Shabir** is a postgraduate student at the University of Bedfordshire. Her research interests centre on non-English speaking British South Asian families and the strategies and resources they are able to draw upon to negotiate their children's education and welfare needs.

**James Shea** was formerly Head of English in a secondary school, and is now Senior Lecturer in Teacher Education, programme leader for all the PGCE secondary teacher education programmes at the University of Bedfordshire and the subject lead on the English secondary PGCE as well as an experienced external examiner for teacher education courses at other universities. He has long held an interest in the use of technology in education. His doctoral work centred around the use of private social media interactions and how this provides an insight into the hidden voice of pre-service teachers as they go through teacher education.

**Martha Smith** is a public speaker and blogger (https://msparentadvocate.wordpress.com) who is a passionate advocate of the parent voice. By sharing her experiences, Martha aims to improve empathy and understanding between parents of children with additional needs and the professionals they encounter. She lives in Hampshire with her family.

# PREFACE

### 'Voice' in education

In the current volume, the term 'voice' refers to the values, opinions, beliefs and perspectives of pupils, families, teachers and senior management of institutions in the education system[1]. It also refers to the extent to which those values, opinions, beliefs and perspectives are considered and included when important decisions are being made. We acknowledge that, while the concept of voice is given in the singular, the groups to which we give voice in this book are not intended to represent a unified body of beliefs, perspectives and cultural values.

Rhetoric associated with the concept of voice in education has grown increasingly popular in recent decades. This is predicated on the belief that pupils will achieve more, that parents and families will feel more confidence in the institution, and that teachers will be more effective and professionally fulfilled if the senior management listen to, and act upon, the values, opinions and beliefs of the people community associated with it. However, rhetoric is not always the same as what is actually experienced in reality. This book has been designed to explore some of the tensions in this area of education.

### Pupils' and students' voice

Specific reference to the United Nations Convention on the Rights of the Child (UNCRC) has been made in recent policy documentation in England. For example, a requirement to uphold the rights of children in relation to Article 12 was explicitly built into statutory guidance, 'Listening to and involving children and young people' (DfE, 2014). It requires all local authorities and maintained schools to consider how best to provide opportunities for children and young people to be consulted on matters affecting them, and to contribute to decision making. This guidance (p. 2) supports the view that such involvement in decision making

> encourages pupils to become active participants in a democratic society [...] contributes to achievement and attainment – young people involved in participative work benefit in a range of different ways. Increased confidence, self-respect, competence and an improved sense of responsibility have all been reported by young people who contribute in school. Schools also report increased motivation and engagement with learning.

Discussion in some of the chapters in this book highlights how young people have a wealth of ideas about what supports their learning and can be a rich resource in this. However, as Robinson (2014) comments, we should acknowledge the inherent inconsistencies and contradictions in a situation where many school staff recognise the benefits of positive learning partnerships between teachers and their pupils where those pupils are encouraged to express their views, but are also preoccupied with the current standards agenda that may conflict with moves to involve young people in decisions about their own learning.

Within Article 12 of the United Nations Convention on the Rights of the Child (United Nations, 1989), while teachers are accountable for making decisions that are in the best interests of the children with whom they work, they also have a responsibility to respect children's rights and to listen to, and acknowledge, their opinions and perspectives and, hence, develop ways of engaging with the opinions and ideas of all pupils in an authentic way. However, the issue of children's rights is not the sole consideration in considering why we should listen to young people's views in educational contexts. Crucial to understanding pupils' learning and behaviour is familiarity with common frames of reference within which that learning and behaviour is viewed and the place of pupils' voice within this. It is really important to have a clear grasp of the process of learning itself in order to think about, and plan how to, support further learning in a principled way, and address difficulties where appropriate.

Getting the balance right is crucial. Young children's learning and behaviour are mediated through the kind of relationship they have with a practitioner. This relationship both develops over time and is influenced by the practitioner's sense of a child's value and worth. Obvious implications of this view of learning are that all young children, including those who experience difficulties, need a safe space and time for discussion between themselves and the more informed other(s), most often the practitioner(s) teacher(s), and themselves with peers to enable 'interthinking' (Littleton & Mercer, 2013). This is focused talk around new learning to clarify and consolidate their understanding of new concepts and knowledge.

## *Parents' and families' voice*

Parents and families have not always had a statutory entitlement over decision making in their children's education in state-funded educational institutions. For a long time after education for (almost) all children became compulsory, families had obligations rather than entitlements. Currently, however, in a number of different countries across the world there is a formal acceptance that parents and carers have the right to know about decisions taken in schools in relation to their children, and that they themselves are, potentially, an important source of additional support in addressing difficulties in learning and/or behaviour experienced by young people. However, family and school/college contexts are very different. Schools/colleges have a lot of power to affect the lives of children and their families and carers through the kind of consultation arrangements, assessment and provision that they make. Embedded within the particular discourses, approaches and strategies of schools and colleges is a variety of preconceptions about the ability and rights of parents, families and/or communities, from a diversity of backgrounds and cultures, to support the learning and development of their children.

Parents and carers may have very different wishes and priorities for their offspring that may or may not include similar objectives to those of the setting, school or college. Just to give one example, schools in England are accountable for the measured achievement of their young people which, most recently, enables comparison through school league tables that is open to public scrutiny, including during inspections. Necessarily, therefore, there is an increased focus on schools' accountability for quantified summaries of young people's achievements and the need to meet targets set for all. For the family, of course, things may look very different. Most parents or carers are likely to want the very best for their child, as they see it. This may or may not include meeting targets or goals set by the setting, school or college. Home–school/college relationships can be very sensitive, especially when both sides see themselves as trying their very hardest for a child but the child is not thriving, as is illustrated in the narrative account of the mother of an autistic child in one of the chapters included here. It is often not easy to see a situation through another's eyes, especially if the element of respectful discussion or exchange of important information is lacking. What can be really important in all this is to listen and respond to the experiences of families themselves and personal accounts of what can happen in practice, both in a positive and less than positive sense.

A number of different, but related, terms are often used in a rather ill-defined way to describe the relationship between settings, schools or colleges and parents/carers, for example parental 'engagement' and 'partnership' (Hallgarten, 2000). 'Parental engagement' implies actual engagement in the child's learning process (Goodall *et al.*, 2011) that research has shown can have a significantly positive impact on achievement and well-being (Desforges & Abouchaar, 2003; Campbell, 2011; Shah, 2001; Wearmouth & Berryman, 2011). Parent partnership involves a 'full sharing of knowledge, skills and experiences' between families and the setting or school and, ideally, 'must be equal' (Jones, 2004, p. 39). It seems logical, therefore, that settings and schools might aim to encourage parental/family engagement and partnership in order that the information families have as experts about their children combined with the information teachers have about learning and the curriculum may work together in the interests of all young people.

## *Teachers' voice*

It is patently obvious that teachers are the most important resource that a school or other educational institution has at its disposal, and that, without the active support of the teaching staff, efforts to change or reform policy and practice for the benefit of the learners are less likely to be as effective as they might otherwise be. Personal beliefs play an important role in teachers' work. Eliciting teachers' views can enable a sense of the individual and collective discourses that inform teachers' perceptions, judgements and decision making and that motivate and drive teachers' action (Biesta, Priestley & Robinson, 2015). A mismatch between teachers' individual beliefs and values and wider institutional cultures can be highly detrimental to the smooth working of educational institutions.

In this volume, and in relation to the teaching force, we focus on the voices of head teachers, senior management and classroom practitioners. It is vital to acknowledge that the beliefs and practices of all these groups are important for understanding and improving educational processes. They can be seen to mediate the effects of changes in policies, such as the introduction of new curricula, on pupil learning, linked as they are to shaping pupils' learning environments and influencing student motivation and achievement (OECD, 2009).

For those considering how and why to engage with the views and perspectives of pupils and their families, and for policy makers to consider how the formal outcomes of their decision making may be experienced in practice, this book provides the grounding for an understanding of legislation, policy and practice related in particular to children's, families' and teachers' rights to be heard.

Personal accounts of experience are included to enable readers to appreciate some of the challenges and conflicts that can be felt in this area of education.

## Synopsis and summary of chapters

## *Synopsis*

It is important to contextualise the way in which pupils', families' and teachers' voices in education have assumed their current significance so that current issues and challenges thrown into relief in various chapters of this book can be better understood. The book therefore opens with a chapter that draws on the UK context to outline a brief history of the development and changes in the legal rights and entitlements of pupils, families and teachers to have their voices heard from the beginning of compulsory education to the present day. Subsequent chapters focus on what can be learned from listening to the views and opinions of children and young people, (head) teachers and families.

## Summary of chapters

### Chapter 1: Developments towards the right to be heard in educational contexts

### Author: Dr Will Coster, University of Bedfordshire

This chapter takes a chronological approach in discussing legislative and policy changes in the rights of children and families to have their views heard in education contexts. This account, time period by time period, is contextualised with discussion of societal changes and changes in thinking about the person of the child and family in society over time. It begins, for example, with discussion of what pertained in general terms in the nineteenth century through a period of the growth of industrialisation when primary schooling became compulsory for almost all children who were expected to be 'seen and not heard'. In the Forster Act (Elementary Education Act, 1870, p. 471), School Boards were empowered, with the approval of the Education Department, to make byelaws that required 'the parents of children of such age, not less than five years nor more than thirteen years, as may be fixed by the byelaws, to cause such children (unless there is some reasonable excuse) to attend school'. The chapter includes reflection on the way in which, much more recently, parental engagement in children's education has been a key issue in education policy in the UK with discussion of this in, for example, the Plowden Report (DfES, 1967), the Taylor Report (DfES, 1977), the Warnock Report (Warnock, 1978) and then the 1981 Education Act. Plowden (DfES, 1967, p. 41) comments, for example:

> Heads and class teachers should make themselves accessible for informal exchanges, so that, as one parent said, parents know their children's teachers at least as well as they know the milkman. They will then feel confident in entrusting their children to them.

There is consideration of how, within educational contexts, the growing interest in the realisation of children's right to be heard has focused particularly on the implementation of Article 12 of the United Nations (UN) Convention on the Rights of the Child, ratified in 1989, that enshrined the notion of listening to the child's voice as a basic right for all children:

> State parties shall assure to the child who is capable of forming his or her own views the right to express those views freely in all matters affecting the child, the views of the child being given due weight in accordance with the age and maturity of the child.
>
> *(United Nations, 1989, p. 5)*

The chapter concludes with a consideration of current national policy, underpinned by law, as it relates to the expression of students' and families' voice, and some of the issues and conflicts that may become apparent when individual voices seeking to obtain their entitlements challenge institutional interests.

## Chapter 2: Lessons learnt by student teachers from the use of children's voice in teaching practice

### Author: Dr Kate Hudson-Glynn, University of Bedfordshire

Chapter 2 describes a recent research project, based on an assumption drawn from a Vygotskian theory of learning: that learning is socially constructed and that deliberately seeking children's views about their learning and engaging with these views can enable teachers, who in the research discussed here are students, to construct meaningful classroom learning experiences. The distinctiveness of Vygotsky's work lay in the importance he placed on the social context in which learning takes place. Vygotsky (1978, p. 57) proposed that the learning process takes place at:

- the interpersonal, 'between people' level, mainly through interacting with others, especially a more informed other, and
- the intrapersonal, 'within the individual' level, as s/he thinks about and reflects on new concepts and learning and appropriates skills and knowledge.

One of the most well-known concepts for which Vygotsky is famous is that of the zone of proximal development (ZPD), to explain the process of learning in a social context. The ZPD for a young child is, effectively, the next steps in learning and the range of knowledge and skills that s/he is not ready to learn alone but can learn in interaction with more informed and experienced others (Kozulin et al., 2003). A more informed/expert other must be able to elicit, and heed, the voice of the child to 'scaffold', that is, provide structured support for new learning (Wood, Bruner & Ross, 1976) through the ZPD based on his/her knowledge of the young child and his/her current level of knowledge and understanding of a topic.

The research project discussed in this chapter describes how bespoke pedagogical tools, in particular 'Thinking Fish', were used to create dialogic spaces and to scaffold inter- and intra-personal exchanges to enable student teachers to understand children's learning from a socio-cultural perspective. These tools mediated the children's reflection on their learning and then feedback to the student teacher about what they had learnt, how they had learnt it and what would enable them to learn better. This approach therefore enabled an exploration of:

- what pupils thought helped/hindered their learning in classrooms,
- how heeding children's views of barriers to/facilitators of their learning can be used by student teachers for lesson evaluation, planning and reflective practice,
- the extent to which children's views can support student teachers' understanding of children's learning and the development of their pedagogical practices (this includes both curriculum planning and teaching).

As a result there was:

- enhanced student teachers' understanding of how children learn as they adapted their practice in response to children's views,
- enhanced learning by the children owing to their exchanges on the interpersonal plane, with peers in the dialogic space created by the bespoke pedagogical tools.

Consequently:

- the children could express learning needs when appropriate scaffolds enabled them to articulate abstract concepts,
- when the student teachers responded to children talking about learning they could develop their practice,
- the student teachers highlighted the importance of children's voice to support their developing pedagogy,
- the student teachers had a model by which to create dialogic spaces for children's interthinking.

The researcher concluded that mediating the construction of dialogue with the Thinking Fish provided a way into both the process of interthinking for children, and also student teachers' understanding of such interthinking as expressed through their dialogue; in this way, the Thinking Fish may be considered to be the vicarious presence of the teacher.

## Chapter 3: On bilingualism in monolingual English classrooms: Voicing the challenges for bilingual children, their parents and schools

### Author: Dr Maja Jankowska, University of Bedfordshire

Chapter 3 is included to set the scene for the following chapter that describes a research project aiming to enable bilingual primary school children's voices to be heard and valued. It will make clear why the kind of project outlined in Chapter 4 is so important at the present time.

Poland is one of the biggest countries among the accession states and between 2004 and 2008 Poles constituted the largest migrant group (Home Office, 2006). Currently Polish is the second most widely spoken language in England and Wales (Sobkow, 2014; Rawlinson, 2014) with more than half a million people speaking Polish as their first language. It is predicted that the number of Polish–English bilingual children in the UK will continue to grow and that the needs of these children will need to be studied and addressed. This chapter provides some background information on the nature of Polish migration and its key features as it is argued that this knowledge may facilitate better understanding of the Polish–English bilingual pupils within the English system of education. It considers some of the challenges for Polish parents, their bilingual children and the teachers of these children within

English monolingual curriculum and assessment, which seems to be largely outdated and inappropriate for an increasingly diverse population. Case studies are presented to illuminate specific issues and challenges, highlighting how myths about bilingualism are still alive and at play and how they can impact on children's psycho-social development and behaviour as well as put strain on the relationship between schools and parents. Some tentative recommendations will be made and future research directions will be discussed.

## Chapter 4: Bilingual Creative Writing Clubs: Giving voice to bi/multilingual children in English schools and bi/multilingual university students and staff

### Author: Dr Maja Jankowska, University of Bedfordshire

The focus of this chapter is a project, Bilingual Creative Writing Clubs, which aimed to provide a platform for bilingual primary school children's voices to be acknowledged, heard and valued. The idea for the project came from the author's perceived need to address some pressing educational and social issues: that children for whom English is an additional language may be perceived as problematic, at risk of under-achieving and their linguistic talents left untapped.

Although children who use a language other than English are not a minority (especially in urban areas in the UK), English classrooms remain largely monolingual and (perhaps to a lesser extent) also monocultural. Monolingualism is perceived as a norm and there seems to be an expectation that children who are not native English speakers should speedily acquire English so that they can assimilate into the English system of education. Children's native voices are often left outside the school gates and positioned as separate from schools and curricula. There seems to be little acknowledgement and appreciation of languages other than English and the celebration of diversity is often ad hoc and superficial. Moreover, children with English as an additional language (EAL) are often seen as 'problematic' (requiring additional support) and at risk of under-achieving. The focus tends to be on remedial work (improving their English) and little space is given to the exploration of their voices and potential talents.

In this project, the researcher attended to children's voices and provided them with an opportunity to express themselves in both their home and the English language. Both theory and empirical evidence (small but continuously growing) indicate that validating home languages and providing children with opportunities to express themselves in both languages can lead to an increased sense of inclusion, confidence, self-worth and overall well-being.

The data collected within this project indicates that taking part in the Bilingual Creative Writing Clubs project had a statistically significant impact on children's confidence. Becoming a published author (of a bilingual story) provided children with a chance not only to express themselves, but also to experience an immense sense of achievement and pride. The perception of the children as 'under-achievers' was also successfully challenged within the schools' environments.

## Chapter 5: Listening to the voices of indigenous Māori students over time: What do they tell us about national education policy?

### Authors: Associate Professor Mere Berryman and Elizabeth Eley, University of Waikato, New Zealand

Chapter 5 moves beyond the UK to Aotearoa, New Zealand where, for a very long time, there has been a marked discrepancy between the educational attainment of indigenous Māori students and those of non-Māori origins. It explores the aims of a Ministry of Education (MoE) policy designed to enable indigenous Māori students to achieve greater success in schools and what it actually meant to them as the intended beneficiaries of that policy.

In this chapter the authors describe how, over the past decade, Māori secondary school learners have begun to reflect on the central tenet of the Māori education policy: 'Māori enjoying and achieving education success as Māori' (MoE, 2008, 2013). They provide evidence from mixed-methods studies to explore the experiences of Māori students in two secondary school reform initiatives that were funded by New Zealand's Ministry of Education. These were *Te Kotahitanga* (unity of purpose), a school reform initiative that had reached Phase 5 in its development, and *Kia Eke Panuku* (building from). These reform initiatives were undertaken end-on-end using an iterative, research and professional development model.

The authors first outline the results emerging from a quantitative study over four years, from 2009 to 2013, when schools in *Te Kotahitanga* were in their fourth year of the programme (Alton-Lee, 2015). The outcomes of national examinations in these schools show that parity of attainment is possible and, indeed, in pockets, they begin to show the importance of Māori students enjoying these educational achievements whilst retaining their identity as Māori. The second results come from qualitative data, compiled in 2015, from the experiences of senior Māori students (16 to 18 year olds) describing what achieving and enjoying education success as Māori means to them. These students come from *Kia Eke Panuku* (building from), in its second year of implementation in 94 secondary schools. In line with the Ministry's umbrella Māori education strategy, 'Ka Hikitia' (to step up), this evidence tells us what belonging as culturally located can look like in the eyes of the students themselves, rather than through the paternalistic lenses of others.

### Chapter 6: Students' and a teacher's views of factors contributing to positive literacy learning identities for all students in an inclusive classroom

### Author: Professor Janice Wearmouth, University of Bedfordshire

The location of the research study discussed in Chapter 6 was also Aotearoa, New Zealand. It was carried out in the classroom of a primary teacher formally identified by a national body as being an excellent practitioner in supporting young people's literacy acquisition. The aim of this study was to examine students' identities as literacy learners within the context of her pedagogy and the learning environment of her classroom. In particular the intention was to compare high and low literacy achievers' identities as writers and to identify whether any lessons might be learnt from this comparison about ways in which the overall level of literacy achievement among low achievers might be raised. (As in the previous chapter, the term 'student' is used as synonymous with 'pupil' in this chapter, as more commonly used in New Zealand.)

## Chapter 7: The hidden voice of pre-service teachers in their private social media interactions

### Author: Dr James Shea, University of Bedfordshire

Chapter 7 moves on to the area of students' reported experiences at the level of higher education and considers how the first-hand reports of student teachers on their experience of mutual support through the use of private social media during teaching placements can shed light on the discomfort they may experience if their own personal values and those of the schools in which they are placed are in conflict, and also how to mitigate these conflicts.

While historically pre-service secondary subject teachers come together into communities of pre-service teachers as part of their teacher training, there have been two major changes in recent years. The first is the advent of private social media interactions (PSMIs) through mobile technology. The second major change is the introduction of neo-liberal competition into schools and teacher education. Through accessing the voice of pre-service teachers whilst retaining the privacy of their PSMIs it has been found that pre-service teachers now use these PSMIs as part of specialist subgroups to broker and share ideas about teaching to each other synchronously and asynchronously. They also broker ideas about teaching to and from school communities even when the communities themselves are reluctant to share and broker practice. Accessing the hidden voice of pre-service teachers shows that PSMIs help pre-service teachers develop their professional ideas about teaching not just for their course but for their newly qualified teacher (NQT) year as well.

## Chapter 8: A voice for advancing the profession of teaching?

### Author: Professor Andrew Goodwyn, University of Bedfordshire

Chapter 8 focuses on the issue of the vital importance to young people, their educational achievements and, hence, future life chances of the quality of classroom teaching. It is now a global phenomenon that most education systems have recognised that there is a significant problem with keeping the best teachers in the classroom where they make the biggest difference to pupils' lives. There are two major issues. Many very good teachers either simply leave the profession, becoming worn down by constant externally imposed changes, or move out of the classroom to take on management roles. A range of countries are trying to tackle this challenge by creating an alternative career structure that provides recognition, status and reward and keeps the teachers working in their own classrooms but also helping to develop other teachers.

In England, The Advanced Skills Teacher scheme (1997–2013) was summarily abolished with no consultation and with the vague suggestion of a 'Master Teacher' model instead; nothing has come of this proposal. Now The Chartered College of Teaching may have an opportunity to develop a new model.

This chapter tells the story of the Advanced Skills Teachers (ASTs) drawing on extensive research data with ASTs themselves, Local Authority AST coordinators and a range of Senior School Leaders. It gives voice to the experience of ASTs, their passion for teaching and learning, their anger and disappointment at the summary abolition of their hard won status and it also airs the views of Head Teachers and others who were equally concerned about this peremptory policy change. Some of these voices also articulate criticisms of the role and put forward ideas for improvement.

The chapter concludes by putting forward a new conceptual framework – drawn from the research and examples from other systems. It also examines the need to overcome the empty rhetoric of politicians who make much noise about 'world class teachers' but do nothing to develop the profession to achieve such a level. It will also address the narrow prejudice of the media who often deride these models as 'Super Teachers'. What society needs to be able to hear is the voice of its leading teachers who can be the best advocates for the importance of the teaching profession.

## Chapter 9: The first year of headship: A cross-comparison of the experiences, challenges and successes, expressed by newly appointed headteachers during their first year in post

### Author: Dr Karen Lindley, University of Bedfordshire

As the most senior leader in a school with a high degree of power and authority to make things happen, clearly it is very important to take account of what headteachers have to say with regard to important aspects of their job. Chapter 9 moves to a consideration of the challenges facing heads in their first year of their headship.

There is a body of literature which focuses on the topic of newly appointed headteachers (e.g. Weindling & Dimmock, 2006; Hobson *et al.*, 2003; Earley *et al.*, 2011; Earley & Bubb, 2013) with particular reference to the experiences, challenges faced, and preparation and ongoing support for newly appointed headteachers to their new post. However, there seems to be less of a focus on the positives or successes associated with the first year of headship. This chapter therefore explores newly appointed headteachers' reports of their own experiences of both challenges and also successes during their first year in post.

## Chapter 10: Primary headteachers' perceptions of schools' roles in training teachers within a changing landscape of teacher training

### Author: Dr Elaine Barron, University of Bedfordshire

Chapter 10 continues with the theme of the significance of head teachers' views and considers the specific example of their responses to the notion of overall responsibility for guiding and supporting teachers in training in their schools.

Recent changes to provision for teacher training in England have seen a move towards placing greater responsibility for the training of teachers with schools rather than Higher Educational institutions. The rationale appears to be the belief that this will produce the kind of teachers that schools are looking to employ. However, there appears to be little research focused on the opinions of the senior management of schools. This chapter outlines a research study that did just that, exploring the views and experiences of headteachers about the role of schools in the training of teachers, therefore this is particularly pertinent at the current time. When consulted, twelve experienced headteachers believed schools should not take sole responsibility for training teachers as the teachers they sought to employ needed to develop and apply critical thinking skills to their teaching. The headteachers sought to work in an equal partnership with universities to train teachers fit to practise.

## Chapter 11: Lost in translation: A discussion of a small scale study of South Asian non-English speaking parents' experiences of negotiating their children's primary schooling

### Authors: Anna Graham and Rumisaa Shabir, University of Bedfordshire

Education policy in the UK has sought to emphasise the importance of parental engagement with children's primary schooling as central to improving attainment, inclusion and integration. However, rhetoric is not always reflected in lived experience.

Amid renewed debates about the role of schools in engaging families from ethnically diverse communities, this chapter draws on a small scale study of non-English speaking Asian mothers' experiences of communicating with their children's primary teachers. It examines the ways in which language barriers exacerbate cultural dissonance between families, communities and schools and undermine inclusion policies and the values of diversity and difference underpinning professional practice.

## Chapter 12: A mother's experiences in the special educational needs system

### Author: Martha Smith

Crozier and Reay (2005, p. 155) suggest that parents' and families' entitlement to have their voices heard during the formal education of their children is the 'centre piece' in 'twenty first century' education policy making. The right of parents and/ or carers to be consulted at every stage of decision making about their children is enshrined in law across the UK, for example, in the Special Educational Needs and Disability (Northern Ireland) Order, 2005; Children and Families Act, 2014 in England; 1996 Education Act, Part IV in Wales; Education (Additional Support for Learning) (Scotland) Acts, 2004 and 2009. However, entitlement in law is not always synonymous with experience in practice. In 2009, the Lamb Enquiry into special educational needs and parental confidence in the system concluded that 'Failure to comply with statutory obligations speaks of an underlying culture where parents and carers of children with SEN can too readily be seen as the problem and as a result parents lose confidence in schools and professionals' (Lamb, 2009, 1.1).

Chapter 12, written by the mother of a young boy who is autistic, describes her own experiences of bringing up her son, the way in which she taught him to communicate, her and her son's relationship with the various professionals, including teachers, they encountered, and the lessons she learnt along the way. Much of what she describes illustrates some of the issues and challenges facing parents and families of children with special or additional learning at the present time, leaving one to conclude that Lamb (2009, 1.1) might well continue to draw the same conclusions that he did nearly a decade ago: 'As the system stands it often creates "warrior parents" at odds with the school and feeling they have to fight for what should be their children's by right; conflict in place of trust.' However, in the midst of negativity from a number of quarters, there is also optimism and joy in the author's account of her experiences.

The chapter concludes with personal recommendations for practices that will enable many autistic children to be more effectively included in schools, and their families to be more confident that their children will have the opportunity to thrive.

## Chapter 13: Students', teachers' and families' views on homework

### Authors: Dr Wendy Edwards and Professor Janice Wearmouth, University of Bedfordshire

The research outlined in this chapter focuses on the views of students, teachers and families on one particular issue, homework, that affects all three groups, but in different ways. It highlights very important differences in the reported experiences of students, teachers and families that schools and policy makers would do very well to heed, and, in doing so, throws into sharp relief the issue of how problematic it can be to reach a resolution in an area where the stakeholder groups have such different and conflicting opinions.

Research on homework since the nineteenth century shows that there has been very little change in the issues surrounding it for over a hundred years. Governments have discussed it and the media have reported on it and it is still a contentious issue for schools and homes alike. This chapter discusses a research project focused on students', families' and teachers' views, perceptions and experiences of homework that was undertaken in a number of schools in an urban area in the East Midlands in England.

The outcomes of this research indicated important differences between the various groups in their knowledge, views and opinions. Many students and families, although seeing some benefits, opposed the setting of homework as a result of the impact on family time and the stress caused by it. Teachers and governors supported the setting of homework and the important contribution they claimed it makes to students' overall performance in school. There were differences between different types of schools and those with lower and higher ability students and the influence that homework has on the stress levels of those students in higher performing schools. Homework was seen as a marketing tool for some schools to use in selling themselves on the competing educational market place.

The chapter concludes with a discussion of the implications of the differences in the views of the stakeholder groups and, in particular, what this means for schools and policy makers in the future.

## Note

1 In some chapters in this book, the word 'student' is used as synonymous with 'pupil'.

## References

Alton-Lee, A. (2015). Ka Hikitia demonstration report: Effectiveness of Te Kotahitanga Phase 5 2010–12. Wellington: Ministry of Education.

Biesta, G., Priestley, M. & Robinson, S. (2015) 'The role of beliefs in teacher agency', *Teachers and Teaching: Theory and Practice*, 21(6), 624–640.

Campbell, C. (2011) *How to involve hard to reach parents: Encouraging meaningful parental involvement with schools*. Nottingham: National College of Teaching and Learning.

Crozier, G. & Reay, D. (2005) *Activating participation: Parents and teachers working towards partnership*. London: Trentham Books.Department for Education (DfE) (2014) Listening to and involving children and young people. London: DfE.

DfES (1967) Plowden Report. Children and their primary schools, a report of the Central Advisory Council for Education (England), vol. 1. London: HMSO.

DfES (1977) The Taylor Report. A new partnership for our schools. London: HMSO.

Desforges, C. & Abouchaar, A. (2003). The impact of parental involvement, parental support and family education on pupil achievement and adjustment: A literature review. Nottingham: DfES.

Earley, P. & Bubb, S. (2013) 'A day in the life of new headteachers: Learning from observation'. *Educational Management Administration and Leadership*, 41(6), 782–799.

Earley, P., Nelson, R., Higham, R., Bubb, S., Porritt, V., & Coates, M. (2011) Experiences of new headteachers in cities (Executive summary). Nottingham: National College for School Leadership.

Elementary Education Act (Forster Act) (1870). Available at: www.educationengland.org.uk/documents/acts/1870-elementary-education-act.pdf

Goodall, J., Vorhaus, J., Carpentieri, L., Brooks, G., Akerman, R., & Harris, A. (2011) Review of best practice in parental engagement. London: Institute of Education.

Hallgarten, J. (2000) Parents exist, ok!? Issues and visions for the parent-school relationship. London: IPPR.

Hobson, A., Brown, E., Ashby, P., Keys, W., Sharp, C., & Benefield, P. (2003) Issues for Early Headship – Problems and Support Strategies. Nottingham: National College for School Leadership.

Home Office (2006) Control of Immigration: Statistics United Kingdom. Norwich, UK: The Stationery Office. https://assets.publishing.service.gov.uk/government/uploads/system/uploads/attachment_data/file/228967/7197.pdf

Jones, C. A. (2004) *Inclusion in the early years* (3rd edn). Maidenhead: McGraw-Hill.

Kozulin, A., Gindis, B., Ageyev, V. & Miller, S. (eds) (2003) *Vygotsky's educational theory in cultural context*. Cambridge: Cambridge University Press.

Lamb, B. (2009) Report to the Secretary of State on the Lamb inquiry review of SEN and disability information. London: DCSF.

Littleton, K. & Mercer, N. (2013) *Interthinking: Putting talk to work*. London: Routledge.

MoE (Ministry of Education). (2008) Ka Hikitia – Managing for success: The Māori education strategy 2008–2012. Wellington: Crown/Ministry of Education.

MoE (Ministry of Education). (2013) Ka Hikitia – Accelerating success 2013–2017. Wellington: Crown/Ministry of Education.

OECD (2009) Creating effective teaching and learning environments: First results from TALIS. Paris: OECD.

Rawlinson, K. (2013, 30 January). Polish is second most spoken language in England. *The Independent*. Retrieved from www.independent.co.uk/news/uk/home-news/polish-is-second-most-spoken-language-in-england-as-census-reveals-140000-residents-cannot-speak-english-at-all-8472447.html

Robinson, C. (2014) *Children, their voices and their experiences of school: What does the evidence tell us?* York: Cambridge Primary Review Trust/Pearson.

Shah, M. (2001) *Working with parents*. Oxford: Heinemann Educational Publishers.

Sobkow, W. (2014, 5 June) Learning Polish, the UK's second most spoken language, is a plus. *The Guardian*. Retrieved from https://www.theguardian.com/education/2014/jun/05/learning-polish-a-plus-ambassador

United Nations (1989) Convention on the Rights of the Child. Available at: https://downloads.unicef.org.uk/wp-content/uploads/2010/05/UNCRC_united_nations_convention_on_the_rights_of_the_child.pdf?_ga=2.176019686.553253286.1526472776-399870493.1526472776 (accessed 16 May 2018).

Vygotsky, L. (1978) *Mind in society: The development of higher psychological processes*. Cambridge, MA: Harvard University Press.

Warnock, H. M. (1978), The Warnock Report, Special Educational Needs Report of the Committee of Enquiry into the Education of Handicapped Children and Young People. London: HMSO.

Wearmouth, J. & Berryman, M. (2011) 'Family and community support for addressing difficulties in literacy' in C. Wyatt-Smith, J. Elkins & E. Gunn (eds) *Multiple perspectives on difficulties in learning literacy and numeracy*. London: Springer.

Weindling, D. & Dimmock, C. (2006) 'Sitting in the "hot seat": New headteachers in the UK'. *Journal of Educational Administration*, 44(4), 326–340.

Wood, D., Bruner, J., & Ross, G. (1976) 'The role of tutoring in problem solving'. *Journal of Child Psychology and Psychiatry*, 17, 89–100.

# 1

# DEVELOPMENTS TOWARDS THE RIGHT TO BE HEARD IN EDUCATIONAL CONTEXTS

*Dr Will Coster*

## Introduction

The concept of student and family voice only dates from the late twentieth century, but the ideas, attitudes and policies that underpin it have been developing since at least the establishment of a national education system in England and Wales in the nineteenth century. This process has not been linear and cannot be isolated from wider developments in education, society and politics. This chapter will discuss these changes, examining the ways in which they have affected the legislative and policy framework that has come to underpin developments in the rights of children and families to have their views heard in educational contexts. It will begin by examining the situation in the nineteenth century, as England and Wales were undergoing rapid social and attitudinal change. It will then discuss the process by which parental concerns and preferences came to be accepted as an important part of the educational process in the twentieth century. Next it will examine the related process by which the idea of student voice has become part of the intellectual and legislative process of education, before concluding by outlining the current situation in England and Wales. This account will be contextualised with a discussion of the societal, philosophical and political changes towards the person of the child and the family over time, and the degree to which the voices of parents and students have genuinely been incorporated into the system and have had a significant impact on the process and experience of education.

## The nineteenth-century background

It is difficult to grasp just how distant schooling in the nineteenth century was from the humane and democratic model of modern education. In short, the concept of student voice has replaced one of children's silence. The much recited proverb that 'children should be seen but not heard' achieved its modern form in an anonymous poem, 'Table rules for little folk', published in 1858. It had antecedents in the fifteenth century and reflected a history of conduct advice that encouraged silence and limited speech of both women and children, but it is often seen as symptomatic of Victorian attitudes towards the young (Kelen, 2016, p. 67). This view was rooted in the concept of original sin, which presented a pessimistic view of the nature of childhood. John Wesley (1703–91), the founder of Methodism, observed of the child, 'make him do as he is bid, if you whip him ten times running to affect it ... break his will now, and his soul will live, and he will probably bless you to all eternity' (Wesley, 1836, p. 320). This was no attempt to consider the student voice, but to silence it and constrain independent thought.

These attitudes can be seen in English public schools, which were the model for later educational foundations. Until the nineteenth century they had been the preserve of the landed-classes, whose boys often left home to be boarded from the age of 7. With industrialisation they were colonised by the children of the new middle classes, of professionals and employers. The leading schools were Eton, Winchester, Harrow, Shrewsbury, Charterhouse and Rugby, but more were promoted from grammar schools or arrived as new foundations, particularly from the 1860s, including Bradfield, Lancing, Haileybury, Marlborough, Radley, Wellington, Uppingham and Sedbergh. They inculcated a particular form of masculinity that stressed obedience and resilience (Fletcher, 2008, p. 196). This was formalised through the practice of 'fagging', by which younger and weaker boys became the servants of the older and more powerful. Cruelty was institutionalised through the practices of flogging by masters, but also by the tossing of boys in a blanket, by 'smoking out', where boys were terrified by having burning paper placed in blocked study doors, and by 'roasting', in which boys were held close to a fire (Chandos, 1984, pp. 80–82). All of this was immortalised in Thomas Hughes' (1857) novel, *Tom Brown's School Days*, but is substantiated through contemporary accounts. As one former boy, who started as a fag, observed in 1803, 'the system of bullying seemed to have banished humanity from most of the boys above me' (Fletcher, 2008, p. 199).

Given the brutality and silencing meted out to the sons of the wealthy, it might be expected that far worse awaited the children of the poor and labouring classes. Most of those from these social groups that received some formal education did so within the parish and petty schools that had grown up out of local initiatives. Some of the able or higher status boys might have gone on to one of the small number of grammar schools. They were dominated by the established church and supplied basic education to those that could afford a modest fee. Parish schools were usually based in one large room, where a master would teach children of all ages and both sexes. In larger towns, boys, girls and infants might be separated, with teachers for each and the master of the boys acting as the headmaster. Outside of this, the hiring of additional adult teachers was almost unknown (Wardle, 1970, p. 64).

With large and diverse classes, physical violence as discipline was widespread, as it was in the home, the workplace and the workhouse (Wood, 2004). The degree to which silence permeated the classroom is difficult to judge. It was mitigated by recitation and reading aloud. Josephine Hoegaerts (2017) argues that, in middle-class education, silence was not simply a mechanism of discipline, but that it facilitated the creation of a 'borderland' that allowed movement between the 'uncivilised noises' of childhood and the 'rational noises' of adulthood, mediated through speech, pronunciation and song. This sidesteps the realities of the classroom and the ways in which these things reinforced the social norms of the ruling classes, but it does suggest that the ultimate aim in elite education was the ability of the student to articulate, albeit within considerable constraints.

There is evidence of a softening of attitudes towards physical punishment from the middle of the century. In 1839 one observer noted that 'people are beginning to suspect that the rod in most, if not all, cases was merely a barbarous expedient to hide the incapacity of the teacher' (Wood, 2004, pp. 66–67). The first serious challenge to the harsh disciplinary system was in the educational reforms introduced by the Quaker, Joseph Lancaster (1778–1838) and the Scottish Episcopalian, Andrew Bell (1753–1832), mediated through the British and Foreign Society (from 1808) and the National Society (from 1811), that, respectively, pursued their agendas (Willis, 2005, p. 7). Their variations of the monitorial system utilised older children as educators of the younger. They offered positive rewards in rank, badges and esteem to encourage participation and good behaviour. They eschewed beatings and encouraged a move away from silent attention to the master to smaller groups within the classroom. The system flourished in the early nineteenth century, before its costs and limitations in a time of expanding need meant that it was overtaken by the process of teacher training and professionalisation. The monitorial system was less physically abusive, but gave little scope for the voices of pupils. It was still backed by a harsh disciplinary regime, particularly in the Lancaster Schools. This was often public and humiliating; being tied in a bag, or tethered were punishments for idle or talkative children (Kirby, 2013, p. 145).

A traditional narrative, based in part in Hughes' book, saw a watershed in the practice of public schools in the mid century, after the headmastership of Thomas Arnold at Rugby, from 1828 to 1842. Arnold's reforms in the organisation and moral conduct of students attempted to break the 'bond of evil' that he saw between boys (Neddam, 2004, p. 309). Fabrice Neddam (2004) has suggested that it floundered on the ingrained culture among the boys. It applied a veneer of morality in 'muscular Christianity', but only displaced the physical bullying into an emphasis on sporting excellence and physicality that retained the features of a system rooted in abrasive masculinity. J. A. Mangan (1987) argues that the 1850s were a watershed, as the success of Darwin's *Origin of Species* led to a change from a system of neglect and indifference to one of deliberate inculcation of a harsh environment that would teach boys the virtues that would sustain society and empire. Successful or not, Arnold became a symbol of a more humane and moral system of schooling that did have long-term effects in 'civilising' and reorganising schools in England (Fletcher, 2008, pp. 199–200). From 1860 corporal punishment had to be 'moderate and reasonable' (Middleton, 2008, p. 254). The limits of this civilising process can be seen in the switch from flogging with birches to the use of canes, particularly in the foundations of the 1860s. This was seen as 'free from cruelty and unkindness', but corporal punishment was underpinned by a belief that teenage boys needed frequent beatings. Prefects and senior boys could administer beatings at will, although they usually had to report them, to a degree replacing the unsupervised hierarchy of bullying with one headed by the masters (Fletcher, 2008, p. 203). Younger boys who stepped outside of the strict limits of acceptable behaviour were harshly punished. The student voice in schools of the nineteenth century and into the twentieth was thus silenced, first by a hierarchy of power and second by a hierarchy of punishment.

Attitudes to discipline had softened by the time of the Forster Act of 1870, which signalled the move to a national system of free elementary schooling (from ages 5 to 13) in England and Wales. It would see an extensive programme of school building. After 1880 attendance was compulsory and some parents and children resisted, requiring the local school boards, responsible for administering the system, to propose by-laws and appoint School Attendance Officers, who could use the minor courts to prosecute parents (West, 1994, p. 167). This was not a system designed to incorporate the voices of children or parents, but, despite the widening of the franchise after 1832, one designed to constrain the poor and the young, particularly as a series of labour laws across the century had removed most children from the workforce. This necessitated some way of occupying, socialising and controlling them. Some, like clergyman Richard Dawes, argued against this use of education as a means of social control, criticising the Anglican-dominated National Society, 'which would establish in every parish a charity school for the education of the poor … keeping the labouring classes, in their education and habits formed in early life, entirely apart from the classes immediately above them' (Dawes, 1850, p. 8). Nevertheless, working-class leaders and radicals saw education as a route to social advancement and power, even if it had to be forced on the working classes (Wardle, 1970, p. 54), creating a consensus for the expansion of the system.

Nineteenth-century education emphasised the silence of children and the acquiescence of parents, enforced through discipline and the legal system. The case of *Gardiner v. Bygrave* (1889) established that masters were largely free to administer corporal punishment, and as a result it continued into the twentieth century (Middleton, 2008, p. 255). However, the need to create an educated and passive workforce, which led to the creation of a national system of elementary schools, had unintended consequences. Engaging both parents and children in the process of education and finding ways to achieve much more with it than basic literacy and numeracy would create a need to incorporate them into the frame, marking a significant departure from the silencing of voices of both groups that had predominated in earlier education.

## The growth of parental engagement in the twentieth century

The removal in 1890 of payment by results that had been introduced in 1862, and the move to increasing standards through training and inspection, significantly changed the character of public education and the teaching profession. The moral stake of parents in those schools can be seen where they challenged the school, particularly over issues of discipline. In his autobiographical account of his childhood in early twentieth-century Glamorgan, G. H. Davis, the biblical scholar, recalled how he had been thrashed after refusing to be punished twice for the same offence, but that an uncle went to the school and frankly and successfully spoke to the headmaster. Other accounts indicate that this was not an isolated case (Middleton, 2008, p. 262). The creation of a national school system had made families participants in the educational process.

The first Hadow Report (Board of Education, 1927) into *The Education of the Adolescent* indicated the beginnings of a consideration of the wishes (and consent) of parents, as the system of secondary education needed to offer continued instruction for larger numbers of children, drawn from deepening social strata. It noted that, 'the progress of education depends, in the long run, on the existence of a belief in its importance sufficiently strong to induce men and women, individually as parents and collectively as citizens, to make sacrifices in order to promote it' (p. 94). However, this was a process of explanation and acquiescence, not of consultation, or of direct parental participation. The second Hadow Report, on elementary education (*The Primary School*; Board of Education, 1931), recommended the extension of local parents' associations, open days, school sports and annual or terminal reports, that had already been adopted by a number of schools, as 'valuable opportunities for contact between teachers and parents' (p. 203). The principles of these reports would underlie the adoption of secondary education for all in the 1944 Butler Act that led to the Tripartite System, designed to engage all classes and both sexes in secondary education. The system had widespread political consensus, but was notable for the use of film and print propaganda to inform the public of its fairness and of new opportunities aimed at gaining support from parents and children (House of Commons, 1950, p. 8).

The election of a Labour government in 1964, and the issuing of Circular 10/65, began the end of the tripartite system and a move to comprehensivisation. The Plowden Report (DfES, 1967) for England, and the Gittins Report (Central Advisory Council for Education, 1967) for Wales, endorsed changes in teaching that had already taken place. It envisioned a different relationship between teachers and parents. Plowden (DfES, 1967, p. 41) argued that:

> Heads and class teachers should make themselves accessible for informal exchanges, so that, as one parent said, parents know their children's teachers at least as well as they know the milkman. They will then feel confident in entrusting their children to them.

This was not a process by which parents (let alone children) had a say in the running of schools, but a one-way process by which teachers would recruit parents into the education of their children. They would encourage them to understand its importance, participate in homework and engage in fundraising and support of the school through a Parent Teacher Association (PTA). It also encouraged the appointment as managers, parents who had children at the school (pp. 414–415).

The Taylor Report (DfES, 1977), which was concerned with school organisation and governance in England and Wales, picked up themes that had emerged in Plowden. It wanted governing bodies to include representatives of the LEA, but also teachers, members of the local community, parents and, as will be explored in the next section, pupils. It noted that increasing work had been done in appointing parent governors, but it also made it clear that these processes were patchy and it recommended an informed democratic process that provided each parent with one vote (pp. 28–29). The need for parent participation was also echoed for children with special educational needs in the Warnock Report (Warnock, 1978), which emphasised the role of 'parents as partners' and the importance of 'dialogue with parents', noting that, 'unless the parents are seen as equal partners in the educational process the purpose of our report will be frustrated' (p. 150). However, this was a one-way form of communication, made up of 'information, advice and practical help' (p. 152). Warnock did not consider that pupils with special educational needs should have a voice in their education.

As Plowden (DfES, 1967, p. 44) acknowledged, given that there was usually one school in an area, parents had little choice about which school their children would attend, but this encouraged more informed choice for parents. This idea of parental choice would become increasingly important. While the Plowden Report was condemned among educational conservatives for its endorsement of progressive teaching methods, the idea of parent participation gained support on all sides in the next decade. Even Rhodes Boyson, one of the authors of the Black Papers that led the attack on progressive teaching methods, and someone who condemned the influence of 'mindless sociologists' and the loss of traditional forms of discipline, endorsed greater parental participation (Boyson, 1973; Boyson, 1975). However, this was meant to be market or financial involvement for those who could afford it, and owed much to both a form of traditionalism in methods and neo-liberal ideas in economics.

The election of a Conservative government under Margaret Thatcher in 1979 meant that the 1980 Education Act based on Taylor was less radical than it might have been (New, 1993, p. 70). Governing bodies of county or controlled schools were to include at least two parent governors, elected by parents. An aided or special agreement school was to include at least one parent governor (Education Act, 1980, c. 20). The increasing role of parents marked a decisive shift from a model of participation by concerned persons, towards a view of their involvement as consumers. The 1986 Act (Education (No. 2) Act, 1986) went further, increasing the representative rights of parents and co-opted governors, but at the relative expense of teacher participation, which became tokenistic. Phil Brown (1990) characterised this as 'the ideology of parentocracy'. This was a complex phenomenon that developed under the premierships of Thatcher and Major and included attempts to commodify education and introduce competition and markets, all underpinned by parental choice, that would raise standards and decrease the power of perceived vested interests such as teachers and the local education authorities (LEAs). The idea of greater involvement by parents was a key principle of the 1988 Education Act and can be seen in the establishment of the Parent's Charter in 1991 (Wagg, 2005, p. 19). Apart from their presence on governing bodies, parents were given a direct relationship with the Ofsted school inspectorate; they interacted with LEAs through parent partnership services (established in 1994) and were given statutory rights to information and to hold school management to account at annual meetings (Green, 2007, p. 227).

The proposal in 1991 to bar teachers from being governors in the role of parents in any school underlined the motive of limiting the perceived power of professionals in the running of schools. However, widespread opposition, particularly from parents, who saw this as an infringement of the right to participate in governance regardless of their other roles, meant that the proposal was abandoned (New, 1993, p. 70). The attempt was symptomatic of a contradictory attitude to parent power. A desire to raise parent participation and influence as a counter to the professional control of schools vied with concerns about the potential for parent governors to frustrate government policy. This became significant in the push for schools to obtain academy status in the 2000s, where parent governors were not now resisting an LEA, but a head wishing to academise, or the perceived encroachment of a large academy chain (Hatcher & Jones, 2006).

Academies were not required to have parent governors, although many retained them when they changed status. This issue led to a proposal by the Conservative Education Secretary Nicky Morgan, in a White Paper in 2016, to abolish the mandatory nature of parent governors in all schools. The paper abandoned the manifesto pledge to force all schools to become academies by 2022, and these measures were not unconnected. The policy was in turn abandoned by her successor Justine Greening, but they were no longer required in academies, and at least one multi-academy chain removed them before the policy was rescinded and did not plan to reinstate them (Richardson, 2016).

The parental voice grew in the twentieth century as ideas of society changed, but also because of the need to engage parents in a widening system and the increased demands of a broadening education for their children. The political consensus that had valued a parental voice in schools fractured once alternative structures were rolled out. It had then served its purpose and became less attractive to a government wishing to change the status of schools to academies. Most schools, including independent academies, have retained parent governors and all state that they value parental input, but the high watermark of the parent voice may have been reached in the early twenty-first century.

## Children's right to be heard in the twentieth century

The rise of the student voice in the twentieth century was due to the two key educational revolutions, one in the early decades of the century and the second in the 1960s and 1970s. The first originated in diverse theories on education, known as the 'new education', which included contributions from abroad by figures such as Dewey, Herbart, Froebel, Sloyd and Ling and Montessori. This was reflected in educational thinking in England as many of these ideas influenced commentators and practitioners. The instructions in the 1905 *Handbook of Suggestions for the Consideration of*

*Teachers and Others Concerned in the Work of Public Elementary Schools* (Board of Education, 1905), which was issued as a blue book by the Board of Education, reflected a rewriting of the entire relationship between teacher and student. It argued that,

> The teacher must know the children and sympathize with them, for it is of the essence of teaching that the mind of the teacher should touch the mind of the pupil. He will seek at each stage to adjust his mind to theirs, to draw upon their experience as a supplement to his own, and so take them, as it were, into partnership for the acquisition of knowledge.
> 
> *(Maclure, 2005, p. 160)*

After World War I, when ideas of democracy and the avoidance of future tragedies through education began to come to the fore, these ideas were taken up by T. Percy Nunn in his *Education: Its Data and First Principles* (1920) (Silver & Silver, 1974, p. 152). Child-centred views of education were popularised by psychologist Susan Isaacs at the Malting House School near Cambridge, between 1924 and 1927, and in her subsequent writings (Gardner, 2017). The application of the idea of the student as a fitting partner in his/her education can also be seen from the 1920s in the alternatives to the authoritarian norms developed in private schools by A. S. Neill at Summerhill (1921–73), W. B. Curry at Dartington School in Devon (1931–57) and Howard Case at Epping House in Hertfordshire (1958–78). Student participation was mediated through the development of whole school meetings, where student perspectives could be expressed (Fielding, 2011, pp. 72–73) and the voice of the youngest child carried the same weight as that of the most experienced adult. The reaction to these changes was often to deem them 'radical' and impractical, particularly at Summerhill, where children were allowed to choose whether to attend lessons (Bailey, 2014, pp. 1–2).

The Second Hadow Report (Board of Education, 1931) gave some encouragement, if not a ringing endorsement, of these views. The new ideas would be reflected in a decisive move to informal styles of teaching in elementary education, which accelerated after 1945 but that was rare in state secondary schools of the tripartite system. An exception in the state sector was the approach pioneered by Alex Bloom at St. George-in-the-East Secondary School, Stepney, from 1945 to 1955 (Fielding, 2005). Plowden depicted a positive view of the best progressive schools and contrasted it with the situation 30 years before, emphasising the move away from authoritarianism and towards an informal, but carefully planned, style of teaching without strict time or special control (DfES, 1967, pp. 266–267). This included an element of choice, within parameters determined by the teacher, seen as necessary to engage the pupil's interest and enthusiasm (p. 268).

The second 'revolution' in education in the 1960s and 1970s arose from the implementation of radical ideas linked to the counterculture and the opportunities and challenges of comprehensivisation. The period saw the rise of the 'student power' movement in universities and was extended to secondary and primary education (Levin, 2000, p. 155). 'Free schools' sprang up in major urban centres across England offering a form of 'libertarian education' (Shotton, 1993). These included the London Free School in Notting Hill, which opened in 1966, the Scotland Road School in Liverpool (1971) and the White Lion Street Free School in Islington (1972) (Wright, 1989). There were others in Bristol, Birmingham, Manchester, Leeds, Nottingham and Brighton. Existing outside of the state system, unlike public schools, their clientele was often working class and a wide range of ages. They avoided the traditional structures of the school system. Often there was no timetable, no compulsory lessons, no uniform or established hierarchy, with teachers known by their first names. The children often made the rules and decided what they wanted to learn. Most of these schools soon folded, not least because there was no system of funding and they charged no fees, relying on donations and gifts, often with the full-time staff relying on benefits. However, a handful continued into the 1980s and 1990s, before they were incorporated into the state structures, or closed in the case of Islington because it would not accept the National Curriculum. A few state schools experimented with these ideas, including Countesthorpe College in Leicestershire (from 1973), William Tyndale School, Islington (1975) and the Sutton Centre in Nottinghamshire (1977) (Griffith, 2000, p. 128).

A watered-down version of these ideas was adopted in comprehensive schools in the state system. This included the erosion of authoritarian discipline and adoption of more 'humane' environments. Uniforms were abandoned or dress codes made less rigorous (Brunsma, 2004, pp. 6–7), teaching became informal, reflected in buildings at both primary and secondary level, facilitating a move from isolated classes to open-plan education (Harwood, 2015, p. 77). In the 1970s many secondary schools adopted the idea of the student council as a means of expressing student views. Most of these bodies fell well short of the democratic ideas of student empowerment of places like Summerhill. In function they varied from advisory to the deliberative, but they often lacked power, which remained in the hands of heads, teachers and administrators (Chapman, 1970; International Bureau of Education, 1970, p. 17).

The Plowden Report, unsurprisingly, avoided mention of student democracy; however, the proposals of the Taylor Report (DfES, 1977) on pupil participation in the governance of schools were radical for the time. Only legal objections prevented the report from suggesting pupil governors, recommending 'that the Secretaries of State should take definitive advice on whether it is possible to change the law to enable pupils to serve as governors at 16' (p. 29). In the absence of such a possibility they recommended that,

> the local education authority should consider making provision for the appointment of pupils, on election by at least the upper classes of the school, to one or more of the places available for parents. Where this is not considered practicable, every effort should be made to involve pupils in the work of the governing body to the utmost extent compatible with the law.
>
> (p. 29)

However, as seen above, the 1980 Education Act focused on the parents (and not the children) as participants and consumers, with Taylor's recommendations on student involvement in decision making being ignored.

Student democracy was always more limited in schools than in universities, where, because of the adult status of students and the relative power of the Student's Union, it became ingrained into university structures. As the political climate changed in the latter 1970s, in the words of Benjamin Levin, in schools 'we saw a steady retreat from the idea that students had a right to involvement in decision-making, and a steady increase in the view of students as the passive – and often insufficiently thankful – recipients of others' nostrums' (Levin, 2000, p. 156). Instead, the focus was on the role of education to prepare students for their economic role in a changing world. However, this began to change again in the latter 1980s as the idea of children's rights took off. The United Nations (UN) *Convention on the Rights of the Child* (United Nations, 1989) Article 12 enshrined the notion of listening to the child's voice as a basic right for all children, encouraging that:

> States Parties shall assure to the child who is capable of forming his or her own views the right to express those views freely in all matters affecting the child, the views of the child being given due weight in accordance with the age and maturity of the child.

The application of the Enlightenment idea of rights to children was to have profound effects on the status of the student voice in schools, finding its way into attempts to reform children's status in the wake of scandals over child exploitation and protection.

## Developments in the twenty-first century

Geoff Whitty and Emma Wisby identified four main drivers of the rise of the student voice (Whitty & Wisby, 2007, p. 5). First are children's rights, encapsulated in the *Every Child Matters* (ECM) initiative (DfES, 2003), in which one of the three goals to which schools had to show that they were aiming was that children had to 'make a positive contribution' to the life of the school. Second is the active citizenship that was pursued by the New Labour government of Tony Blair. The final two are the school improvement and a personalisation agenda that have been shared by all recent governments. The rise of the idea of the student voice can be seen in schools in areas such as involvement in research, surveys, questionnaires and focus groups, but as Whitty and Wisby (2007) noted, 'school councils are a particularly tangible and visible manifestation of its presence' (p. 5) and this resulted in a revival. In the 1990s, studies indicated that around 50 per cent of secondary schools in England had a school council. Roughly a decade later, 95 per cent of schools in England had one, in both the maintained and independent sectors, with particular expansion in primary schools (Whitty & Wisby, 2007).

In Wales, the School Councils (Wales) Regulations (2005) made school councils a statutory requirement in maintained primary and secondary schools. They must meet regularly, and members are elected by fellow pupils by means of a secret ballot. A council can nominate up to two of their members to serve as associate members on the school's Board of Governors. In England school councils are not mandatory, but the Department for Education (DfE) informally encourages their establishment, with a spokesperson noting that, 'we want schools to consider the views of pupils on matters that affect them. Schools should determine for themselves the most effective way to do this' (Bennett, 2012). The question of how democratic or influential these councils are has led to accusations of lip-service being paid to these aims. The Citizenship Education Longitudinal Study (Kerr *et al.*, 2003) found that only 57 per cent of teachers and 27 per cent of students thought that the whole school was involved in discussion and decision making. Whitty and Wisby (2007) found a range of experiences, from genuine attempts to incorporate student voices, to mere talking shops or token organisations.

In most maintained schools, there are at least two elected parent governors. It is also clear that many co-opted parent governors are, or even more commonly have been, parents at a school and parent governorship can be seen as an apprenticeship. In 2016, in the wake of the 'Trojan Horse' controversy in Birmingham and fear of 'rogue governors', it became possible for the governing body to vote to remove parent governors; although this is meant to be only in exceptional circumstances, it does mark a move back to the power of professionals (Richardson, 2017). The 'free schools' programme, the flagship education policy of the coalition government, from 2010 was aimed at parents opening their own, innovative schools, but a report from the Sutton Trust and NFER (2018) found that increasingly they are the result of academy chain initiatives. The situation with student governors has gone some way to meet the aspirations of the Taylor report. From 2003 students under the age of 18 could become associate governors for up to four years. There is no compulsion to appoint them, they lack the legal responsibilities of adult governors and have limited voting rights, being unable to affect decisions on admissions, appointment of governors, budget or financial decisions, although they can vote in committees (DfE, 2017).

In universities student voice became more significant due to the commodification of higher education that began in the 1970s and intensified in the 1990s. This is evident in the creation of a single university system, attempts to stimulate a 'market' in higher education, the introduction of tuition fees for students under the New Labour government in 1998, and their subsequent increase by a factor of three under the coalition government in 2004 (Foskett, 2010). The introduction of the annual National Student Survey, the results of which are incorporated into various league tables of universities, and in 2017 the creation of the *Teaching Excellence and Student Outcomes Framework*, which incorporates student satisfaction survey results, both point to increasing consideration of the student voice. This is added to internal processes that consider student satisfaction and feedback on modules and courses, and an emphasis on students as 'change agents', as outlined by the 1994 group of universities

'Enhancing the Student Experience' statement in 2007 (Furedi, 2010, p. 32). This emphasis on students as valued consumers has led to complaints from academic teachers that their status is challenged by the overriding consideration of student concerns over their professional judgements (Morley, 2003, p. 146).

## Conclusion

The development of the concept of the parent and student voice has been a long and complex process. Although lauded as a 'good thing' by politicians, academics and educators alike, it is not a neutral thing, as voices are part of a wider matrix of power relations. The consideration of one set of voices is often at the expense of the 'voice', or power, of other parties. As is clear from the rise (and fall) of parent power, this can be intentional, but parental and student voices always contain a potential to become a Frankenstein's monster in education and, because of their nature, can often prompt actions or prevent change against the wishes of another interest group. Thus, notable features of parental and student voices are the ways in which they are limited, kept away from the centres of power, or constrained if they are seen as a threat to existing interests or ideologies. This is of course all in the nature of democracy, where voting, in elections or referenda, always has the potential to derail vested interests or the position of professionals and elites, but voting systems also limit and constrain that capacity. They give the illusion of popular power, while preventing real change or reform. As with democracy, so with the voices of parents and students, which exist between the rock of tokenism and the hard place of challenging other interests.

## References

Bennett, T. (2012) 'School councils: Shut up, we're listening', *Guardian*, 12 March 2012. Available at: https://www.research.ed.ac.uk/portal/files/31081018/HASAS_Research_Briefing_2_April_2010.pdf (accessed 20 May 2018).
Board of Education (1905) *Handbook of suggestions for the consideration of teachers and others concerned in the work of public elementary schools*, London: HMSO.
Board of Education (1927) The Hadow Report. Report of the Consultative Committee on the education of the adolescent, London: HMSO.
Board of Education (1931) The Hadow Report. Report of the Consultative Committee on the primary school, London: HMSO.
Boyson, R. (1973) 'Who is conning whom?', *Spectator*, 22 September, 12.
Boyson, R. (1975) *The crisis in education*, London: Woburn Press.
Brown, P. (1990) '"The 'third wave": Education and the ideology of parentocracy', *British Journal of Sociology of Education*, 11(1), 65–85.
Brunsma, D. L. (2004) *The school uniform movement and what it tells us about American education*, Lanham, MD: Scarecrow Press.
Central Advisory Council for Education (Wales) (Gittins Report) (1967) Primary education in Wales, London: HMSO.
Chandos, J. (1984) *Boys together: English public schools, 1800–64*, London: Hutchinson.
Chapman, J. (1970) 'Origins and development of school councils', *New Era*, 51, 268–279, 316–332.

Dawes, R. (1850) *Remarks occasioned by the present crusade against the education plans of the Committee of Council on Education*, London: Groombridge and Sons.

DfE (2017) The constitution of governing bodies of maintained schools statutory guidance for governing bodies of maintained schools and local authorities in England. Available at: https://assets.publishing.service.gov.uk/government/uploads/system/uploads/attachment_data/file/640562/The_constitution_of_governing_bodies_of_maintained_schools_2017.pdf (accessed 15 May 2018).

DfES (1967) Plowden Report. Children and their primary schools. A report of the Central Advisory Council for Education (England), vol. 1, London: HMSO.

DfES (2003) Every child matters. London: The Stationery Office, Cm5860.

DfES (1977) The Taylor Report. A new partnership for our schools. London: HMSO.

Education (No. 2) Act (1986). Available at: https://www.legislation.gov.uk/ukpga/1986/61/contents (accessed 18 May 2018).

Education Act (1980), c. 20. Available at: https://www.legislation.gov.uk/ukpga/1980/20/contents (accessed 18 May 2018).

Fielding, M. (2005) 'Alex Bloom, "Pioneer of radical state education"', *Forum*, 47(2/3), 119–134.

Fielding, M. (2011) 'Patterns of partnership: Student voice, intergenerational learning and demographic fellowship', in N. Mockler, J. Sachs, eds, *Rethinking educational practice through reflexive inquiry: Essays in honour of Susan Groundwater-Smith*, London: Springer Science & Business Media.

Fletcher, A. (2008) *Growing up in England, the experience of childhood*, New Haven, CT: Yale University Press.

Foskett, N. (2010) 'Markets, government, funding and the marketisation of higher education in the UK', in M. Molesworth, R. Scullion and E. Nixon, eds, *The marketisation of higher education*, London: Routledge, 25–38.

Furedi, F. (2010) 'Introduction to the marketisation of higher education and the student as consumer', in M. Molesworth, R. Scullion and E. Nixon, eds, *The marketisation of higher education*, London: Routledge, 1–7.

Gardner, D. E. M. (2017) *Susan Isaacs: The first biography*, London: Routledge (1st edn., 1969).

House of Commons (1950) *Parliamentary papers, House of Commons and command*, vol. 10, London: HMSO.

Green, C. (2007) *The privatization of state education: Public partners, private dealings*, London: Routledge.

Griffith, R. (2000) *National curriculum — National disaster? Education and citizenship*, London: Psychology Press.

Harwood, E. (2015) *Space, hope and brutalism: English architecture, 1945–1975*, London: Yale University Press.

Hatcher, R. & Jones, K. (2006) 'Researching resistance: Campaigns against academies in England', *British Journal of Educational Studies*, 54(3), 329–351.

Hoegaerts, J. (2017) 'Silence as borderland: A semiotic approach to the "silent" pupil in nineteenth-century vocal education', *Paedagogica Historica*, 53(5), 514–527.

International Bureau of Education (1970) Educational Trends in 1970: An International Survey, Paris and Geneva: Unesco. Available at: https://unesdoc.unesco.org/ark:/48223/pf0000000673 (accessed 11 December 2018).

Kelen, C. (2016) 'Child autonomy and child governance' in C. Kelen and B. Sundmark, eds, *Children's literature: Where children rule*, London: Routledge.

Kerr, D., Cleaver, E., Ireland, E., & Blenkinsop, S. (2003) *Citizenship education longitudinal study: First cross-sectional survey* 2001–2002, London: DfES.

Kirby, P. (2013) *Child workers and industrial health in Britain, 1780–1850*, London: Boydell & Brewer.

Levin, B. (2000) 'Putting students at the centre in education reform', *Journal of Educational Change*, 1(2), 155–172.

Maclure, S. (2005) ed., *Educational documents: 1816 to the present day*, London: Taylor & Francis.

Mangan, J. A. (1987) 'Social Darwinism and upper class education in late Victorian and Edwardian England', in J. A. Mangan and J. Walvin, eds, *Manliness and morality: Middle-class masculinity in Britain and America 1800–1940*, Manchester: Manchester University Press.

Middleton, J. (2008) 'The experience of corporal punishment in schools, 1890–1940', *History of Education*, 37(2), 253–275.

Morley, L. (2003) *Quality and power in higher education*, New York, NY: McGraw-Hill Education.

Neddam, F. (2004) 'Constructing masculinities under Thomas Arnold of Rugby (1828–1842): Gender, educational policy and school life in an early-Victorian public school', *Gender and Education*, 16(3), 303–326.

New, S. J. (1993) 'The token teacher: Representations of professional educators in school governing bodies', *International Studies in Sociology of Education*, 3(1), 69–89.

Richardson, H. (2016) 'Parent governor role won't be scrapped – Greening', BBC News, September 2016. Available at: www.bbc.co.uk/news/education-37362301 (accessed 20 May 2018).

Richardson, H. (2017) 'Schools to get new powers to sack "maverick governors"', 6 May 2017. Available at: www.bbc.co.uk/news/education-39795037 (accessed 20 May 2018).

Shotton, J. (1993) *No master high or low: Libertarian education and schooling in Britain 1890–1990*, London: Libertarian Education.

Silver, P. & Silver, H. (1974) *The education of the poor: The history of the national school 1824–1974*, London: Routledge.

The School Councils (Wales) Regulations (2005), no. 3200 (W. 236). Available at: www.legislation.gov.uk/wsi/2005/3200/contents/made (accessed 18 May 2018).

Sutton Trust and NFER (2018) Free for all? Analysing free schools in England, 2018. Available at: https://www.suttontrust.com/wp-content/uploads/2018/05/FreeForAll-SuttonTrustNFER-1.pdf (accessed 31 May 2018).

United Nations (1989) Convention on the rights of the child. Available at: https://downloads.unicef.org.uk/wp-content/uploads/2010/05/UNCRC_united_nations_convention_on_the_rights_of_the_child.pdf?_ga=2.176019686.553253286.1526472776399870493.1526472776 (accessed 16 May 2018).

Wagg, S. (2005) 'Don't try to understand them: Politics, childhood and the new education market', in J. Pilcher, and S. Wagg, eds, *Thatcher's children? Politics, childhood and society in the 1980s and 1990s*, London: Routledge.

Wardle, D. (1970) *English popular education, 1780–1870*, Cambridge: Cambridge University Press.

Warnock, H. M. (1978) *The Warnock report, special educational needs report of the Committee of Enquiry into the education of handicapped children and young people*, London: HMSO.

Wesley, J. (1836) *Sermons on several occasions, vol. 2*, London: B. Waugh and T. Mason.

West, E. G. (1994) *Education and the state: A study in political economy*, 3rd edn, London: Liberty Fund.

Whitty, G. & Wisby, E. (2007) Real decision making? School councils in action, London: Institute of Education, University of London. Available at: https://dera.ioe.ac.uk/6611/2/DCSF-RR001.pdf (accessed 11 December 2018).

Willis, R. (2005) *The struggle for the General Teaching Council*, London: Psychology Press.

Wood, J. C. (2004) *Violence and crime in nineteenth-century England: The shadow of our refinement*, London: Routledge.

Wright, N. (1989) *Free school: The white lion experience*, London: Libertarian Education.

# 2

# LESSONS LEARNT BY STUDENT TEACHERS FROM THE USE OF CHILDREN'S VOICE IN TEACHING PRACTICE

*Dr Kate Hudson-Glynn*

## Introduction

McIntyre, Pedder and Rudduck (2005) describe children as 'expert witnesses' to their own learning and asserted that their views should be considered as valid in discussing such learning. It is pertinent, therefore, to take the view that Initial Teacher Education (ITE) is the place to prepare teachers for this understanding. Chapter 2 describes a recent research project, based on an assumption drawn from a Vygotskian theory of learning (Vygotsky, 1978), that learning is socially constructed and that deliberately seeking children's views about their learning and engaging with these views can enable teachers, who in the research discussed here are students on teaching practice, to construct meaningful classroom learning experiences. The chapter explores the following questions:

- What do pupils think helps/hinders their learning in classrooms?
- How can heeding children's views of barriers to/facilitators of their learning be used by student teachers for lesson evaluation, planning and reflective practice?
- To what extent can children's views support student teachers' understanding of children's learning and the development of their pedagogical practices (this includes both curriculum planning and teaching)?
- How does this impact upon the development and learning of ITE students as student teachers engaged in reflective practice?

## Context of the study

Teaching is a complex activity. It is very clear that, to be effective practitioners, teachers need to understand the process of children's learning. Surprisingly, perhaps, such understanding is not emphasised in the Teachers' Standards (DfE, 2012) in England, where the current research project was carried out. The notion of taking account of children's voice is not included in these Standards. Rather, the focus is on student teachers developing towards, and demonstrating specific skill sets to, pre-specified standards of competence, with an assumption that children will make progress in their learning as a result of this form of teacher training. This approach is further emphasised in the current school-based preferred models of ITE where greatest focus is placed on student teachers gaining experience of practice in the classroom alongside an experienced professional (this begs the question, of course, of what students learn if the role model is a bad one). The emphasis in all teacher training should be on teachers providing opportunities for children to reflect on their own learning. However, thinking about learning (metacognition) is an abstract concept and the experienced teacher appointed to mentor the student teacher may not fully understand the process of learning him/herself. Where this is the case there may be limited opportunity to understand children's learning by both the student teacher and the children themselves. In addition the new Standards for the mentors of students on teaching practice in schools (DfE, 2016) do not emphasise a role in helping student teachers to understand children's learning, further limiting the possibility of students acquiring knowledge about the learning process.

## Underpinning pedagogy

A principal premise of social constructivist theory is that learning is a social process (Vygotsky, 1986), and that social interaction precedes cognition. An awareness and understanding of one's own surroundings is acquired through speech and action working in tandem. First, understanding is internalised as a result of practical external activity. Next follows an elaboration of personal understanding through interpersonal processes between people in the context and the learner. Finally intrapersonal (within-the-person) cognitive change takes place, enabling the learner to move forward (Vygotsky, 1978). An important aspect of this is demonstrated in the notion of the Zone of Proximal Development (ZPD) (Quay, 2003; Mahn, 1999).

Learning and development are interrelated. The ZPD is the distance between the actual development of the learner and what can be achieved in collaboration with a More Knowing Other (MKO). The concept of transition through the ZPD (Chaiklin, 2003) supports Vygotsky's notions of psychological development and how the maturing functions progress, from the learning activity and interaction in a social environment with an MKO to internalisation (appropriation). In collaboration with an MKO the learner is able to do something that their level of psychological maturity would not have enabled them to complete on their own. The learning in the ZPD today will be the actual development of the learner tomorrow (Vygotsky, 1978). The ZPD therefore is a theoretical basis for pedagogical interventions (Chaiklin, 2003) and it is essential that time is given to this process (Eun, 2008).

Important to an understanding of the learning process in the ZPD is the notion of 'scaffolding'. Scaffolding originates from the work of Wood, Bruner and Ross (1976), who posit that it is the cognitive support required by, and tailored to, each learner which is gradually withdrawn over time until learning is appropriated as the learner becomes autonomous. In this scenario the teacher mediates, or scaffolds, the learning (Warwick *et al.*, 2010) by providing the necessary cognitive support through dialogue and the way the task is set up. A social constructivist view of learning mirrors this idea with the MKO scaffolding/mediating learning on the inter- and intrapersonal planes using dialogue before learning is internalised and automatised (Vygotsky, 1978, Kozulin *et al.*, 2003).

An example of reciprocal scaffolding can be identified in ITE where each student teacher, on teaching practice, has an assigned MKO in the classroom: the mentor. In this situation an MKO could be a mentor, student teacher or child depending on the learning taking place. The mentor scaffolds the learning of the student teacher through their ZPD, on the interpersonal plane by discussion, feedback, questioning, modelling and so on, so the student teacher can reflect and internalise their learning. At the same time the mentor learns about, and from, the student teacher so the learning is reciprocal. For their part, the student teacher, as the children's MKO, engages with the child's learning and scaffolds them through their ZPD. The student teacher learns about, and from, the child and, as such, the learning relationship is also reciprocal. Social constructivist theory assumes the significance of the social interaction of all parties. It is important that the relationship between mentor and student teacher and/or student teacher and child enables a learning environment that satisfies needs in order to facilitate learning and elaborate intrapersonal understanding.

Recently, Warwick, Mercer and Kershner (2013) have suggested that there are two types of scaffolding that a teacher may use to mediate learning: direct and indirect scaffolding. Direct scaffolding is as suggested in the original definition by Wood, Bruner and Ross (1976). However, indirect scaffolding is the result of the vicarious influence of the teacher (Warwick *et al.*, 2010). This is a resource or task with restricted freedoms, which is provided by the teacher to allow the learner to concentrate on fewer variables thus enabling a deeper connection with, or interpretation of the task. Again this aligns with a social constructivist view of learning as these indirect or vicarious scaffolds are cultural tools; that is, artefacts which mediate learning (Kozulin *et al.*, 2003). The teacher is not absent from the process (Warwick *et al.*, 2010), but rather mediates learning through cultural artefacts, thus their presence is vicarious.

Both direct and indirect forms of scaffolding help learners to apply frames of reference that they are inexperienced at using (Mercer, 2008). Scaffolding creates a shared dialogic space, which promotes the active construction of learning and learner agency (Warwick *et al.*, 2010). Both the MKO (direct scaffolding) and cultural artefacts (indirect scaffolding) were used in the research project discussed in this chapter. As such, the term 'scaffolding' represents both direct and indirect mediation by the teacher of the learning, and refers to the various ways in which a teacher supports cognitive and meta-cognitive activity that engages learners in learning (Warwick *et al.*, 2010).

The culture of a classroom involves language, which, as Dewey (1910) suggested, is a set of abstract symbols representing meaning. Each symbol makes meaning distinct and enables meaning to be constructed by others through talk. Education transforms language into an intellectual tool to convey and assist with knowledge (Dewey, 2010). Social constructivist thinking posits that language is a symbolic system, which is employed as a psychological tool to support thinking (Kozulin et al., 2003). Language is a means of representing events and things, and thought is internalised language (Kozulin et al., 2003; Vygotsky, 1986). Language is the tool that supports and transforms thinking and understanding (mental functioning) so that ideas may be appropriated and reality constructed (Kozulin et al., 2003). Language is used by individuals to express thinking on the intra- and interpersonal planes (Kozulin et al., 2003). If this relationship between talk for learning and metacognitive processes is to be accepted, language becomes a teachers' foremost tool (Light & Littleton, 1999; Mercer & Littleton, 2007). Therefore, it is important to give time to discourse in a child's learning.

Children require support structures to enable their thinking (McGregor, 2007). These structures can be conceptualised as 'scaffolds' (Wood, Bruner & Ross, 1976). In the classroom, if the teacher scaffolds children's learning with a framework of meta-language, the children are better able to think about and describe their learning (Light & Littleton, 1999). Scaffolding with, for example, the use of meta-language can help children to talk effectively about their learning (McGregor, 2007; Mercer & Sams, 2006). In many instances in classrooms the scaffolder can be the teacher as the MKO. Here the role is to reinforce learning, model ideas and maintain motivation on the task (Mercer & Littleton, 2007). The scaffold can be, for example, a framework designed to guide the talk for learning, such as a scaffold of prompts, which directs thinking and discussion.

A number of researchers have used scaffolds to support the articulation of children's thinking. An example of this is a tool called the 'Ishikawa' (Turner, 2002, cited in Hopkins, 2008), which was adapted for use in the research study reported in this chapter. This was a fishbone structure chosen to engage children's interest as well as to annotate their responses. Each 'bone' on the fish carried a particular theme for questioning the children about their learning, which would provide potentially meaningful insights into their thinking about the classroom and was rooted in research by McCallum, Hargreaves and Gipps (2000) and McIntyre, Pedder and Rudduck (2005), as well as Macbeath, Frost and Pedder (2009), who were interested in eliciting information through listening to children's voices. The themes included learning activities, the roles of the teacher and other children, and so on, and were focused around a key research question, for example, 'What makes lessons enjoyable?' The themes on the bones then provided themes for analysis. Some of these supports for children's thinking about their learning have been integrated into the current research study in the classroom.

In understanding learners by listening to their views, student teachers can make children's learning, through their teaching, more focused as there is a shared understanding and language between learner and teacher (McIntyre, Pedder & Rudduck, 2005; Rudduck & Flutter, 2004; Flutter & Rudduck, 2004). The student teacher has to be able to support children's learning in the ZPD in the role of the

MKO. A pedagogy that takes children's views into account enables a very clear focus on the learning and teaching relationship. The children are, after all, providing an 'expert' or 'insider' view of what the learning means to them (Rudduck & Flutter, 2004, Flutter & Rudduck, 2004).

## Approach to the research

An underpinning assumption of the research study was that everyone can learn, but they will need an MKO to elaborate their understandings. Tharp and Gallimore (1998) illustrate one way of understanding the process of Vygotsky's model of socially constructed learning through identifying stages of learning. The ZPD is the area in which learning takes place. Stage 1 of the ZPD is the space where interpersonal dialogue occurs with an MKO. Stage 2 of the ZPD is the space where intrapersonal reflections occur leading to internalisation/appropriation The MKO mediates (scaffolds) the ZPD by using the tool of language. For student teachers starting out on their careers this provides a clearly structured role for them in the development of children's learning. It also suggests a means by which this may be achievable using talk for learning. Through this model understanding is actively constructed.

The study reported here was constructed as a case study containing a spiral of research and evaluation with multiple methods chosen to elicit insights about both the participants and the context. The approach to data collection and analysis was largely constructivist as is compatible with the pedagogical underpinning of the classroom practices of the participant student teachers. Bespoke pedagogical tools, also designed from a social constructivist perspective, were utilised both to scaffold the participants' practice and as research tools.

## Research design

### Participants

The participants were:

- students training to be primary teachers and registered on a Postgraduate Certificate in Education course at a University in England. Out of a cohort of 115 student teachers, 32 participated;
- groups of six children, chosen by each of the student teachers as a purposive, stratified, criteria-based and convenience sample;
- the student teachers' mentors during their teaching practice.

### Research process

The process for the research is outlined in Figure 2.1. There was concurrent activity from each of the participants, each adopting normal classroom working practice.

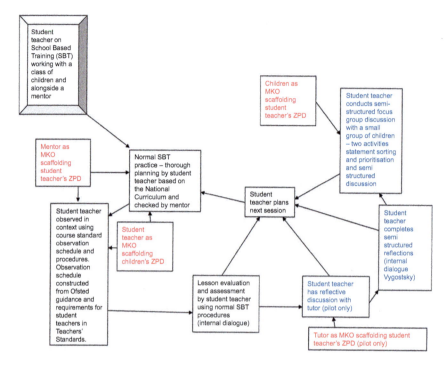

**FIGURE 2.1** The research process

During their teaching practice:

- the student teachers planned, taught, assessed and reflected upon learning for the children;
- the mentors observed the student teachers and provided feedback;
- the children completed the work planned and fed back to the student teachers about their learning.

Figure 2.2 illustrates how the plan, teach, assess, evaluate and feedback cycle was enacted through the week. It indicates that this cycle is the iterative approach followed by teachers as they prepare to teach children. Typically the first step for a student teacher is to plan a lesson and then teach it. During the teaching a mentor will observe the student teacher and provide them with feedback afterwards. Following this, the student teacher will then reflect on their learning and teaching, the feedback provided by the mentor and then plan the next subsequent lesson.

Through the research process the mentors acted as the MKOs to the student teachers. They had been trained by the University to observe the student teachers' practice, provide feedback and targets as well as make assessments as to the quality of the that practice.

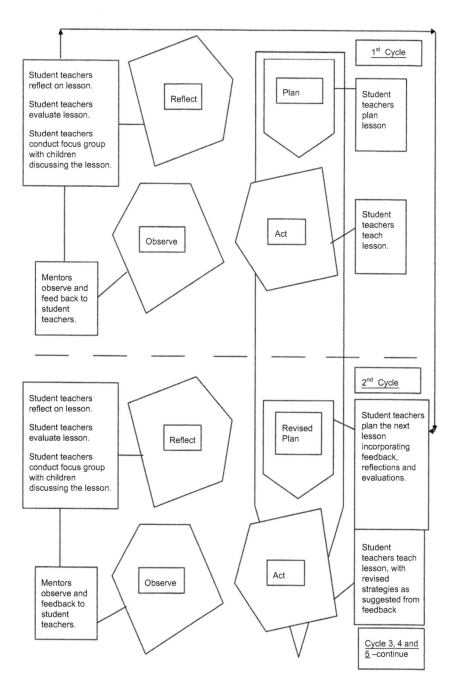

**FIGURE 2.2** The plan, teach, assess, evaluate cycle
Adapted from Kemmis & McTaggart, 1981, p. 14, cited in Open University, 2001, p. 137

## Bespoke pedagogical tools

### i. 'The Thinking Fish'

Integral to this research was gathering the views of children about their learning. As noted above, thinking about learning is an abstract concept and scaffolding in the form of a shared language was needed in order to support children to discuss their views about their learning. As such, the 'Thinking Fish' (Figure 2.3) was designed by adapting Hopkins' (2008) Ishikawa fish bone tool and then implemented.

At the end of each lesson, the children were met by their respective student teachers in focus groups of approximately six, as advocated by Macbeath, Frost and Pedder (2009). The 'Thinking Fish' was a way to capture the understanding of children about their own learning – a scaffold (Wood, Bruner & Ross, 1978). Each student teacher provided the 'Thinking Fish' and responsive assistance to their focus group as the children became the MKOs to their student teacher and provided feedback about their own learning, and their student teacher's teaching, using the shared language of the 'Thinking Fish' scaffold. This process involved the children responding to two questions and annotating the 'Thinking Fish' accordingly. The questions related directly to the lesson the student teacher had just taught to them:

- What went well, in that lesson, for your learning?
- What could be improved in the future for your learning?

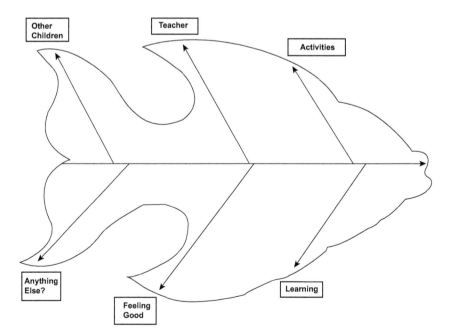

**FIGURE 2.3** 'The Thinking Fish'

## ii. Classroom observation tool

During the taught component of the lesson, the mentors completed observations of the student teachers' teaching. In support of this they had scaffolded observation prompts. The observations were graded in competencies and overall in accordance with the University's PGCE course requirement at the time.

## iii. Students teachers' reflective logs

After the taught session, the mentor feedback and the 'Thinking Fish' feedback with the children, the student teachers completed scaffolded reflective logs about their own practice, a further course requirement, which included lesson planning and evaluations as a result of the combined feedback they had received, and that provided a trail of reflective intrapersonal thinking.

All of these sources of data were reviewed and ideas were connected. This enabled the triangulation between tools and the views of the participants. Analysis was transparent, thematic and analytical and so content/thematic analysis including frequency counts of themes was employed. In addition a small amount of quantitative analysis was completed that was related to the mentor grading of the quality of the teaching and associated with the lesson observations. Data were further triangulated against Tharp and Gallimore's (1998) framework of stages of progress in the appropriation of learning. This was a way of making sense of the data as well as scaffolding the interpretation.

## Findings

Over time children developed an increased awareness of their own learning. In addition the children scaffolded the understanding of the student teachers about children's learning. The student teachers' practice changed as a result of intrapersonal reflection from activity with the 'Thinking Fish' and their understanding of children's learning increased. Planning showed incorporation of children's feedback in teaching next steps and there was a change in the student teachers' focus from that of teaching to that of children's learning. The process was reciprocal and was collaborative learning for the student teacher and the children. The feedback from the mentors and the children aligned. Dialogic learning in both intra- and interpersonal spaces at all levels for all participants was valued and student teachers reflected that they were professionals who listen to children about their learning.

The data from the 'Thinking Fish' were analysed thematically and frequency counts of the themes identified were taken. Figure 2.4 shows this frequency count.

The 'Thinking Fish' scaffolded the language for children to articulate their understanding about their learning. Themes identified from the focus group data most associated with a social constructivist view of learning included, notably, the role of the MKO, the discussion on the interpersonal plane (talk for learning) and the need for scaffolding. Talk for learning through the 'Thinking Fish' activities

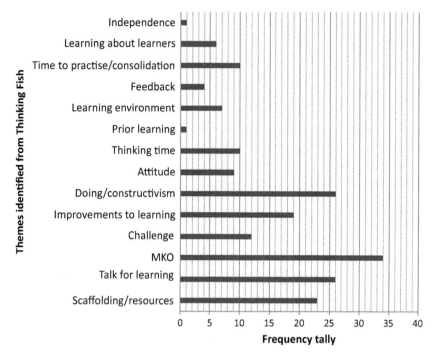

**FIGURE 2.4** Frequency of themes identified from the 'Thinking Fish'

had connected with the children's metacognitive processes, their 'metalearning', through their 'interthinking' with their peers (Littleton & Mercer, 2013) and they recognised the development of their own learning. Learning progressed for the children, as indicated through their intrapersonal reflections, and this was enabled by the learning environment that had been created by the student teachers.

## Themes identified from the student teachers' reflective logs

The data from the reflective logs were analysed thematically and frequency counts of the themes identified were taken. Figure 2.5 shows the frequency count of these themes.

The scaffolded prompts for reflection for the student teachers, both in the inter- and intrapersonal space were important. Figure 2.5 shows how, through the scaffolded reflection process, the development of understanding of the student teachers changed. Overall the average proportional gain in grades for the quality of the students' teaching they observed recorded by the mentor was 15 per cent, with the proportional gain in the following areas being the greatest: resources including adults (scaffolding/MKO), individual needs (learning) and talk for learning (social constructivist view of learning). It is also worth highlighting the change to the aspects of differentiation, adaptation of practice and understanding of the needs of the children as the progress in understanding in these aspects was the greatest and the most relevant to a social constructivist view of learning.

Lessons learnt by student teachers from children 25

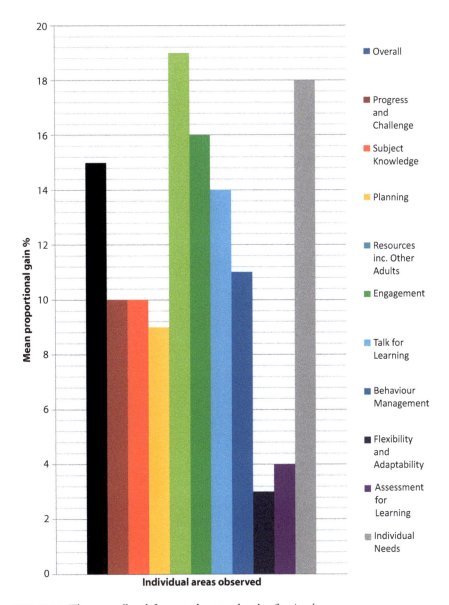

**FIGURE 2.5** Themes collated from student teachers' reflective logs

During the process the focus of the student teachers shifted from the importance of them taking on the role of the teacher to ensuring the learning of the children. This evidenced that the student teachers had a renewed understanding of their role as teacher as the MKO in the ZPD of the children. However this was reciprocal as the interpersonal scaffolds supported the intrapersonal reflections of the student teachers but also enabled the children to understand how they learnt best as well. This understanding of the student teachers' and children's own learning (meta-learning) demonstrates the value of feedback in the process. If the feedback is positioned in a way that adopts shared language (as scaffolded by the bespoke pedagogical tools) it enables all of the participants to take on board the feedback and act on it. All students understood children's learning better, to a greater or lesser extent.

## Themes identified from the mentors' feedback

The mentors had an important role in scaffolding the understanding of student teachers about children's learning in the interpersonal space through their feedback following their observation of the student teachers teaching the children. The data from the mentors' feedback were analysed thematically and a frequency count of the themes identified was taken. Figure 2.6 shows this frequency count.

The mentors could evidence the progress that the student teachers made but their feedback talked around the principles of social constructivist theory rather than addressing them directly. For example they would discuss how well a student

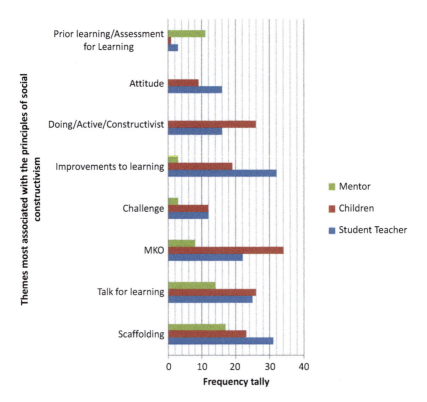

**FIGURE 2.6** Comparison of frequencies of themes most associated with the principles of social constructivism

teacher had deployed adult support to the children for the activities but they would not directly discuss the role of the adult as the MKO and how they were therefore moving children's understanding through their ZPD. In addition there were some contradictions in the feedback, for example the social constructivist approach of using talk for learning in the learning of the children was highlighted as a strength but this was contradicted by comments addressing behaviour in the learning environment as 'too noisy'.

## Discussion

Student teachers better scaffolded learning through the children's ZPD when this social constructivist pedagogy was adopted. The embedding of children's voice as part of the learning process enabled reciprocal learning between the student teacher and the children, which allowed shared meanings about the children's learning to develop. All participants recognised the value of the iterative process of inter–intra personal reflections (metacognition) and the role of the MKO in the interpersonal space to enable thinking aloud; whether the role was the student teacher, the children or the mentor.

There are difficulties connected to the mentors providing contradictory advice around the value of talk for learning and in turn the lack of support for the mentors in the Teachers' Standards to focus feedback towards developing student teachers' understanding of children's learning. Despite this, the value of talk for learning to aid reflection is important.

Myths about the inability of children lacking in experience to comment on their own learning have been dispelled for these participants and an open-mindedness to adopting a more socially constructed learning environment developed. The value of adopting social constructivist principles into pedagogy was evidenced in the transformation of practice. The interpersonal exchanges enabled and scaffolded the interpersonal reflections and, as such, movement through the ZPD was evident.

A number of issues and concerns centred around the observations. There were questions about the mentors' understanding and interpretation of the grade boundaries for the Teachers' Standards and this raised wider issues of inter-rater reliability in the observation of student teachers' practice. Further, the grading of an observation of a dynamic teaching and learning activity using quantitative means reduces the whole value of the activity of teaching to a mechanistic assessment of attainment against a set of competencies. In addition there were questions raised about the mentor interpretation of whether to grade the student teachers as students or as teachers. This is a significant concern given that the same set of Teachers' Standards is applied to student teachers, Newly Qualified Teachers (NQTs) and experienced teachers. This can lead to feedback from the mentor to the student teacher through a transmission, rather than a constructivist approach, to ensure there is evidence of meeting the Teachers' Standards. The mentors should scaffold the interpersonal and subsequent intrapersonal reflections of the student teacher. Moreover the grades themselves create a 'ceiling effect' on the student teachers' ability to be a teacher. The process of teaching is too complex to be graded and the role of the mentor role itself is made more complicated by being both the assessor/grader and the MKO in the student teachers' ZPD.

## Lessons learnt

In brief, findings from a small-scale research study cannot be generalised, but, if replicated, the research project would suggest that:

- Children can express their learning needs when scaffolded with appropriate language.
- Student teachers understand how children learn when scaffolded appropriately.
- Student teachers value and respond to the feedback from the children and their pedagogy develops as a result.
- Student teachers' practice changed and their understanding of children's learning deepened.
- Mentors need to talk to student teachers about children's learning.
- Mentors need professional development about how to provide opportunities for student teachers to listen to children talking about their learning.
- The role of the MKO to learning is critical whoever is adopting that role – children, student teachers or mentors.
- ITE needs should include children's voice as a way of student teachers understanding children's learning.

## Conclusions

The learning process is complex and therefore there is a place for collaborative interthinking in the development of student teachers' understanding of children's learning. This can be scaffolded further through collaborative reflection as part of the observation process. The focus of ITE could be redirected towards *qualifying to help children learn* to further acknowledge that teaching is a complex process and that by providing a scaffolded pedagogy, critical reflection and thinking, an increased emphasis on children's learning is embedded in student teachers' practice. This means that the Teachers' Standards for ITE should also be refocused towards how children learn and the skills required to be able to manage the development of children's learning.

Establishing a context that is appropriate for student teachers to develop an understanding of children's learning is critical. Integral to this are three components: an enabling environment, an MKO and scaffolding (Figure 2.7). Through these an iterative model of social constructivist learning and teaching can be developed and embedded. It is the inter- and intrapersonal exchanges in these dialogic spaces that enable transformation through collaborative reflection (interthinking).

Scaffolding this project was the visual representation of Vygotsky's social constructivist learning theory by Tharp and Gallimore (1998). This provided a way of seeing the components of social constructivist theory enacted as stages of the learning process: for example, the inter- and intrapersonal stages of the ZPD of the student teacher learning with the MKO and then internalising (reflecting) in order to transform practice. However this model implies that the development of learning is sequential. While the student teachers in this project did make progress in their

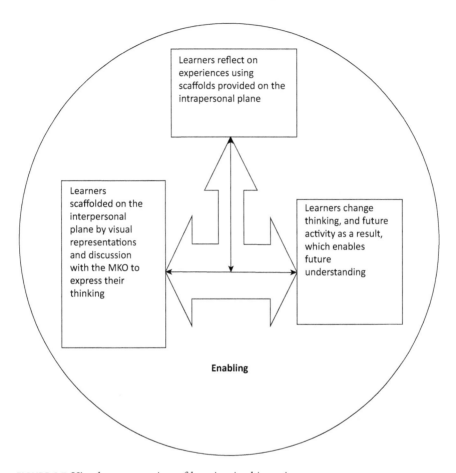

**FIGURE 2.7** Visual representation of learning in this project

understanding of children's learning and their teaching practice, this was not always sequential. Littleton and Mercer (2013) posit that, as a consequence of interthinking, learning can be seen more as a helix (Figure 2.8). This implies an iterative process of transformation through joint reflection.

But learning is a complex process and, while the helix does indeed imply the iterative process of learning, it still implies that learning always moves forward and that there is only one occurrence of each of the components of Vygotsky's theory. For example in any learning situation the MKO will only be required once on the interpersonal plane to scaffold the progress of the learner through their ZPD.

However, with student teachers' developing understanding of children's learning, this was not always the case. The MKO, the children and/or the mentor were required to reiterate or reemphasise ideas through the iterative process of collaborative reflection (interthinking) in the interpersonal space. Therefore it is perhaps better to see Tharp and Gallimore's (1998) model as one slice of the helix of interthinking

**30** Kate Hudson-Glynn

(Littleton & Mercer, 2013), so that the scaffolding that the Tharp and Gallimore (1998) (Figure 2.9) model provides is embedded as part of the process of collaborative reflection for student teachers.

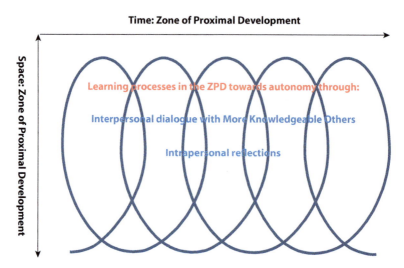

**FIGURE 2.8** Visual representation of Littleton and Mercer's (2013) concept of interthinking as a helix showing learning through the ZPD

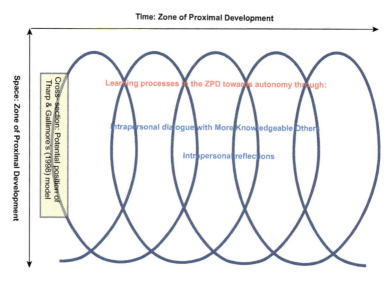

**FIGURE 2.9** Visual representation of the potential position of the framework in this study, in the context of a dynamic model of learning through the ZPD

This could be enacted with beginning teachers in ITE and their NQT year through a model of observation to enables the MKO (mentor) to provide feedback to student teachers about their ability to enact a social constructivist learning pedagogy in their practice to meet the Teachers' Standards.

In this way theory underpins practice and means that the student teachers have a scaffolded way (using shared language – for example the 'Thinking Fish') of interthinking with mentors and children that scaffolds intra- and interpersonal reflection and enables reciprocal learning, transformative learning and teaching.

## References

Chaiklin, S. (2003). 'Locating the zone of proximal development'. In A. Kozulin, B. Gindis, V. Ageyev & S. Miller (eds.), *Vygotsky's educational theory in cultural context*. Cambridge: Cambridge University Press, 38–64.

Dewey, J. (1910) *How we think*. New York: DC Heath and Co.

DfE (2012) Teachers' standards. London: HMSO.

DfE (2016) National Standards for school-based initial teacher training (ITT) mentors. London: HMSO.

Eun, B. (2008) 'Promising practice: Making connections: Grounding professional development in the developmental theories of Vygotsky', *The Teacher Educator*, 43, 134–155.

Flutter, J. & Rudduck, J. (2004) *Consulting pupils: What's in it for schools?* London: Routledge Falmer.

Hopkins, E. (2008) 'Classroom conditions to secure enjoyment and achievement: the pupil's voice. Listening to the voice of "Every Child Matters"', *Education 3–13*, 36(4), 393–401.

Kozulin, A., Gindis, B., Ageyev, V. & Miller, S. (eds.) (2003) *Vygotsky's educational theory in cultural context*. Cambridge: Cambridge University Press.

Light, P. & Littleton, K. (1999) *Social processes in children's learning*. Cambridge: Cambridge University Press.

Littleton, K. & Mercer, N. (2013) *Interthinking*. London: Routledge.

Macbeath, J., Frost, D. & Pedder, D. (2009) The influence and participation of children and young people in their learning (IPiL) project. Available at: www.gtce.org.uk/research/commissioned_research/pupil_learning/influence_participation/ (accessed 16 November 2009).

Mahn, H. (1999) 'Vygotsky's methodological contribution to sociocultural theory', *Remedial and Special Education*, 20(6), 341–350.

McCallum, B., Hargreaves, E. & Gipps, C. (2000) 'Learning: The pupil's voice', *Cambridge Journal of Education*, 30(2), 275–289.

McGregor, D. (2007) *Developing thinking: Developing learning*. Maidenhead: Oxford University Press.

McIntyre, D., Pedder, D. & Rudduck, J. (2005) 'Pupil voice: Comfortable and uncomfortable learnings for teachers', *Research Papers in Education*, 20(2), 149–168.

Mercer, N. (2008) *The guided construction of knowledge: Talk amongst teachers and learners*, 5th edn. Bristol: Multilingual Matters.

Mercer, N. & Littleton, K. (2007) *Dialogue and the development of children's thinking*. London: Routledge.

Mercer, N. & Sams, C. (2006) 'Teaching children how to use language to solve maths problems', *Language and Education*, 20(6), 507–528.

Open University (2001) *Research methods in education handbook*. Milton Keynes: Open University Press.

Quay, J. (2003) 'Experience and participation: Relating theories of learning', *The Journal of Experiential Education*, 26(2), 105–116.

Rudduck, J. & Flutter, J. (2004) *How to improve your school: Giving pupils a voice*. London: Continuum.

Tharp, R. & Gallimore, R. (1998) 'A theory of teaching as assisted performance'. In D. Faulkner, K. Littleton & M. Woodhead (eds.), *Learning relationships in the classroom*. London: Routledge, pp. 94–110.

Turner, S. (2002) *Tools for success: A manager's guide*. New York: McGraw Hill.

Vygotsky, L. (1978) *Mind in society: The development of higher psychological processes*. Cambridge, MA: Harvard University Press.

Vygotsky, L. (1986) *Thought and language*. Cambridge: MIT Press.

Warwick, P., Mercer, N. & Kershner, R. (2013) '"Wait, let's just think about this": Using the interactive whiteboard and talk rules to scaffold learning for co-regulation in collaborative science activities', *Learning, Culture and Social Interaction*, 2, 42–51.

Warwick, P., Mercer, N., Kershner, R. & Staarman, J. (2010) 'In the mind and in the technology: The vicarious presence of the teacher in pupils' learning of science in collaborative group activity at the interactive whiteboard', *Computers and Education*, 55, 350–362.

Wood, D., Bruner, J. & Ross, G. (1976) 'The role of tutoring in problem solving', *Journal of Child Psychology and Psychiatry*, 17, 89–100.

# 3

# ON BILINGUALISM IN MONOLINGUAL ENGLISH CLASSROOMS

Voicing the challenges for bilingual children, their parents and schools

*Dr Maja Jankowska*

## Introduction

This chapter is concerned with the importance of paying attention to and hearing bilingual children's and their parents' voices within the English education system. It highlights the need to engage with bilingual children's and their families' values, opinions, beliefs and perspectives, on an individual basis, without making (often dangerous) assumptions about the cultural and linguistic background, stereotyping or employing unhelpful (still often prevalent) myths surrounding bi- and multilingualism. It also sets the scene for Chapter 4, in which an example of a project aiming to enable bilingual primary children's voices to be heard and valued is described and its research outcomes analysed.

Although this current chapter is based on research conducted with Polish–English bilingual children, families and host schools, and, to some extent, draws on an article published in *Sustainable Multilingualism* (Jankowska, 2014), the findings and recommendations are likely to apply to other bi- and multilingual children, their families and schools. It advocates a more open communication with children and their parents, especially migrant parents, and the need to withhold often unhelpful, if not hurtful, preconceptions about both academic and linguistic abilities of children (and parents), and parents' ability to exercise their rights to know about (and, if necessary, challenge) decisions taken in schools in relation to their children as well as their right to support children's learning (including bilingual education).

The case studies in this chapter highlight that disregarding children's and parents' voice can be a costly mistake, which can not only make home–school relationships sensitive but can also have a negative impact on the children's confidence, self-esteem and overall psychological functioning, as well as their educational achievement.

## Statement of a problem: the norm of monolingualism and the 'standards' agenda

Although children who use a language other than English are not a minority population (especially in urban areas) in the UK, I would argue that English classrooms remain largely monolingual and (to a lesser extent) also monocultural. Monolingualism is still perceived as a norm and there is a strong pressure on children and their families to acquire English as fast as possible and assimilate into the English system of education. Within this system, there seems to be an expectation to give precedence to a dominant/majority language and a lack of recognition for the multitude of cognitive, social and psychological benefits linked to bilingualism (Krashen & McField, 2005). The underlying assumption for this seems to be that 'other languages and cultures interfere with successful learning of [English] and with achievement in the curriculum' (Levine, 1990, p. 1) and therefore learners should focus mainly on English. For instance, Sales, Ryan, Lopez-Rodriguez and D'Angelo's (2008) report on Polish pupils in London schools provides evidence of such attitudes among educators. In the quotation below the teacher not only expects the child to make an effort to speak English but also the Polish mother to speak to her child in their Polish household in English:

> I said I was concerned about A that she was not going to get her level 4 because she is not accessing the curriculum because she is not accessing the language. There was a stubbornness about it. So I said to the mum: 'Do you speak any English at home ever?' and that was not happening.
> 
> *(Sales et al., 2008, p. 20)*

Even though such views have been heavily challenged in the literature (Levine, 1990; Bialystok, 2001; Baker, 2007, among many others) and, as Safford and Drury (2013) explain, the move from segregation to inclusion of bilingual children was enacted as a matter of civil and educational rights, it has been:

> undermined by national education policy which has eroded language support and imposed highly prescriptive content and pedagogy. Bilingual learners have come to be 'included' in a strongly centralised, monolingual national curriculum and assessment system where [...] there is little space for schools to respond to local language and cultural contexts (Leung and Creese 2008) and therefore little space for teaching or assessment practices that take account of bilingual children's learning paths; for instance, the national Early Years Foundation Stage (EYFS) Curriculum sets pre-specified learning targets for children from birth to age five and attaches age phases to descriptors of language development which are native English speaker developmental norms, emphasising that at age five, children should be 'school ready' by reaching a good standard of English language. [...] Large numbers of bilingual children therefore enter mainstream education pre-labelled as underachievers in relation to mother tongue English norms.
> 
> *(Safford & Drury, 2013, pp. 72–73)*

This centralised, monolingual curriculum and assessment seems to be largely inappropriate for an increasingly diverse population, especially in classrooms where English native speakers may indeed be in a minority. Eversley et al. (2010) reported that 41 per cent of state school children in London use another language in addition to English (with Somali, Tamil, Polish and Albanian being the most widely used languages).

## Background to the study: Polish migration to the UK

Since 2004 there has been a rapid increase in Polish migration to the UK and this wave was 'substantial, and largely unplanned' (Sales et al., 2008) with thousands of Polish children entering British schools 'often with little knowledge of English or of the environment into which they have been thrust' (p. 4). Poland is one of the biggest countries among the accession states and, according to the most recent Office for National Statistics (2018) report, Polish is the most common non-British nationality in the UK. An estimated 1 million Polish nationals lived in the UK in 2017 and this accounted for 16 per cent of the total non-British nationals resident in the UK. Polish is the second most widely spoken language in England and Wales (Sobkow, 2014; Rawlinson, 2013) with more than half a million people speaking Polish as their first language.

Sales et al. (2008) highlighted six key features of Polish migration that have significant implications for children's experiences and challenges as they settle in British schools.

- First, the speed of migration has been unprecedented, with some schools going from no Polish pupils to several dozen within a space of two to three years. Moreover, migration has become a normal part of life for many Polish people, and Sales et al. (2008) suggest that this led to them making little preparation for the move. Therefore, they may often be unfamiliar with the language and the host country's system of education, 'so children may be placed into an unfamiliar environment, which they, and their parents, find hard to understand in early stages' (Sales et al., 2008, p. 6).
- Second, literature also points to the often temporary and circular form of migration displayed by the Poles ('commuter migration' (Morokvasic, 2004)), which takes a form of retaining 'a stake in Polish society and the option to return', which, in turn, reduces 'motivation to learn English and to integrate in Britain' (Sales et al., 2008, p. 7).
- Third, due to their EU status, Polish migrants developed 'a sense of entitlement' in Britain and high expectations of services, including education. This, as is evidenced in the case studies below, can become a source of tension and sensitivity between parents and schools.
- Fourth, Polish migrants are reported to lack familiarity with diversity and multiculturalism as contemporary Polish society is predominantly white (98 per cent) and Catholic. Therefore, the children joining British schools may have limited

knowledge and experience of dealing with other cultural and religious groups. This can lead to misunderstandings and xenophobic behaviour.
- Fifth, some parents' economic situation (low status employment, high levels of deskilling, long hours, shift work, insecure contracts, etc.) often impacts on their ability to become involved in their children's education and sometimes to provide an appropriate environment for their children to study.
- Lastly, there is also an issue of geographical dispersion with Polish migrants often working in agriculture and services and their children attending schools in the areas that lack diversity, where Polish pupils become more visible as 'foreign' and may be subject to racial abuse and where schools have little experience in dealing with such matters. Some of these issues are referred to in the case studies below.

It is important to note that the characteristics described above give an illusion of uniformity of the Polish population in the UK. However, the demographic picture is much more complex with many multicultural families (e.g. where only one parent is Polish), families with higher socio-economic status, and bilingual children born in the UK (or brought to the UK early on in life) for whom English (not Polish) is a dominant language.

The primary focus of education policies is that English-only instruction is the best way to improve English-language-learner students' communication with their peers and teachers and many sources report teachers' expectation and emphasis on gaining English and assimilation into the system and the environment. This is a worrying phenomenon. While learning English and understanding the local system is, of course, important, keeping native language and traditions is a well-known psychologically protective factor (Winsler et al., 2014). As children become more integrated into the local culture, they seem to lose the protection and caring features of their home culture. In addition, it has been reported that they also become increasingly reluctant to speak their family's language and unable to preserve their parents' linguistic heritage, which is not only detrimental to academic outcome but also to cognitive flexibility and abstract thinking (Portes & Hao, 1998).

Given that Polish migration may be temporary (with many families keeping their options of returning to Poland open), retaining home language and tradition may be particularly important. However, as indicated above, addressing the needs of bilingual children is not a priority in most British schools. Safford and Drury (2013) highlight that there are no dedicated funds to support bilingual learners in schools in England. Schools can apply for 'pupil premium', the main criterion for which is economic deprivation, but this does not apply to many children. Moreover, bilingual children are measured against monolingual native English speaker norms and can be perceived as underachievers from the very beginning, as the case studies below indicate. Receiving what is termed 'failure feedback', a child may experience reduced confidence in his or her abilities or future success and negative educational trajectory (Eccles, 1999). The negative social comparison and the 'failure feedback' received at schools have distinct implications for pupils who see their own cultural identity as different from that of their peers, which can lead to an increased probability of later dropout and delinquency (Hamre & Pianta, 2001; Wehby, Dodge & Valente, 1993). This problem is of particular significance for young children given the plasticity of their behavioural and emotional well-being during the early school years (Alexander & Entwisle, 1996; La Paro & Pianta, 2000; Saft & Pianta, 2001; Rumbaut, 1994).

## The study

### Aims

This chapter draws on a pilot investigation that was conducted within an area of dense Polish population in England. The aims were to investigate the association between oral and written communication and its impact on how children were being perceived in schools, and that between the language status of children and their behavioural and emotional well-being. A further aim was to establish a community network for future projects aimed at improving the situation of migrant children at schools (see Chapter 4).

This chapter reports on three selected case studies (out of ten completed within the pilot investigation) to give voice to the bilingual children and their parents and illuminate the discussion of issues they face in the English system of education.

### Methodology

This study employed a multi-method approach, with data collected from three sources: parents, teachers and children. The parents' and teachers' opinions about the children were surveyed via questionnaires, specifically constructed for the study (based on measures with good reliability and validity, such as McCulloch, Wiggins, Joshi and Sachdev's (2000) scale of behaviour problems). The teacher questionnaire asked about the child's level of English upon entry to school, current level, any additional support received, academic performance and (compared with typical pupils of the same age) the child's effort, behaviour (in general), how much s/he is learning and how happy s/he is, any concerns about the child as well as the child's best points. It also asked the teacher to judge whether the child had behaviour problems, including external (frequency of arguing, fighting, getting angry, acting impulsively and disturbing ongoing activities) and internal (apparent presence of anxiety, loneliness, low self-esteem and sadness) behaviours. The parent questionnaire also asked similar questions about the child's level of English language, additional support received, academic performance and behaviour. Additionally, it surveyed home language use (dominant languages of all family members and the patterns of languages spoken, e.g. the frequency of use of the child's mother tongue and other language/s). Parents frequently also volunteered information about their interaction with schools and concerns they had about it.

The children's language was assessed using the Oral and Written Language Scales (OWLS-II; Carrow-Woolfolk, 2011) test, which provides a complete and integrated picture of oral and written receptive and expressive language skills across a wide age range (up to 21 years).

## Ethical considerations

The research, ethically approved by the author's university's Psychology Department Ethics Committee, adhered to the British Psychological Society Ethical Code of Conduct. The schools, parents and children received a comprehensive information pack. Consent forms were signed by parents and teachers and assent forms by children participating in the pilot study. In order to protect the family's identity, pseudonyms are used here, and other information is kept to a minimum.

All parents and children were debriefed after the study and offered guidance on where they could find more information about dual language learning and education. Once the author had calculated the scores, these were relayed to the parents and children and thoroughly explained. The scores were not reported back to schools, but parents and children could use them as a basis for discussions with teachers, should they wish to. Some parents welcomed this opportunity and those who used it reported that it was useful.

## Sample

This small pilot study included ten case studies, each based on the questionnaire information provided by parents and teachers, and the author's assessment of the children's language skills. All children were Polish–English bilinguals, but their language status was varied as family backgrounds differed. Diversity in the sample was intentional as the author wanted to explore whether language status and sociocultural context influenced the teachers' perceptions of the children and had an impact on their school experiences.

## Results

### Case study 1: Kamila

Kamila was 13 years, 7 months at the time of assessment. She comes from a Polish migrant family that had arrived in the UK approximately a year prior to the assessment. Kamila learned English in her previous schools in Poland. However, English was learned as a second language, not to a level sufficient to communicate fluently in an English school. Hence, she is a typical sequential bilingual with a strong dominance of a native language (Polish). The family communicates in Polish. The parents reported that their daughter was a high achiever in Polish schools in all areas of the curriculum (particularly in creative writing) and they believed she could continue achieving at the same level in England.

Kamila's mother expressed her strong disappointment with the schooling system in England and felt that her daughter's abilities were not recognised and, consequently, Kamila was not challenged beyond her level. Her mother felt that the teachers were 'not bothered', saying 'it's not quite good because she is not encouraged to do more. Her development and progress are not good enough. She could do so much more'. She gave examples of Kamila getting tasks and homework that were much below her ability levels and below what she was used to doing back in Poland and becoming demotivated by this. Her mother was aware of Kamila's English as an additional language (EAL) status (Kamila was getting one hour per week of additional support at school) and explained that, in her perception, because of Kamila's developing English she was being treated as not cognitively able. The mother was also concerned with her daughter's marked shyness and progressively worrying social withdrawal. She reported that her daughter had one friend (who was Polish) and that she couldn't 'speak with other children'. She also explained that her child did not eat lunch at school at all and went hungry all day. The girl felt too intimidated to eat in the big hall and the headteacher 'forb[ade] [her] to eat lunch during language club' (or any other time/place). The mother was disappointed with the school's attitude – the lack of acknowledgement of these psychological problems and, consequently, the absence of any interventions.

The data reported by the teacher was scarce and evidenced rather shallow knowledge of Kamila and her specific issues. The teacher had 'no concerns' and believed that the girl 'worked really hard and was very keen to improve English' – these were the teacher's only comments. In terms of her academic performance Kamila was judged to be 'average' in most subjects (although the data are incomplete) and 'above average' in numeracy. Compared with typical pupils of the same age the teacher felt that Kamila was: working somewhat more than others, behaving much better, learning much more and about average happy. The teacher marked 'not true' for each of 26 items on the scale of behaviour problems. On the same scale the mother reported several worrying behaviours, including: being rather high strung, nervous or tense, too fearful or anxious, arguing too much, being disobedient, not being sorry after she misbehaves, having trouble getting along with others, being impulsive and acting without thinking, being restless and overly active, being stubborn, sullen and irritable, having a very strong temper and losing it easily but also being withdrawn from contact with others. The mother also reported that Kamila sometimes felt worthless or inferior, cheated or told lies, was unhappy, sad or depressed, cried too much, clung to adults, was too dependent on others, demanded attention and was not liked by other children.

From conversations with this family it appeared that Kamila was withdrawn, quiet and almost 'invisible' at school and hence her problems and inhibitions were not being noticed. At home, however, she vented her anger and disappointment, frequently causing conflicts and expressing her wish to return to Poland. Her parents despaired, not knowing how to help her.

Her mother expressed immense frustration, powerless and lack of voice and agency regarding her daughter's school situation. Her own English was limited, and she felt helpless and misunderstood/fobbed off in her attempts to communicate with the school. Kamila's father, whose 'voice', potentially, could be heard more (owing to his English proficiency) was not able to attend school meetings as he often worked long hours and/or away from home.

In relation to the language assessment:

- Table 3.1 in the Appendix at the end of this chapter presents Kamila's main scores.
- Table 3.2 presents the scale comparisons (difference between the four main language skills).
- Table 3.3 presents the composite scores.

On the listening comprehension (LC) scale, Kamila obtained a standard score of 94 with a percentile rank of 30. This score is within an average range for same-age peers (one standard deviation above and below the mean).

On the Oral Expression (OE) scale she obtained a below average score of 79 with a percentile rank of 8, indicating her performance was better than that of only 8 per cent of her peers.

She scored 99 on the Reading Comprehension (RC) scale with a percentile rank of 47 (average score). However, Kamila obtained a standard score of 137 on the Written Expression (WE) scale with a percentile rank of 99, a very superior score when compared with those of same-age peers, and one achieved by fewer than 2.2 per cent of peers. This score is striking, given that writing is the most complex and sophisticated skill that language learners have to develop, and many children achieve their lowest scores on the written expression scale within a normal population of same-age children.

OWLS-II indicated a large gap between oral and written expression (58 standard points). This is not uncommon for sequential bilinguals in whom spoken language may develop later than listening and reading comprehension. Moreover, many sequential bilinguals find it easier to express their ideas in writing than orally because while writing they have more time to formulate their thoughts and pay attention to grammar, style, form and spelling. There is a danger, however, in that because oral language is something that teachers, peers and other people notice first they may make a superficial judgement of an individual's cognitive ability based on the oral proficiency. While this young teenager made several grammar and other mistakes in speech, it was obvious that it was not because she did not have the knowledge and ability to formulate her thoughts well in English.

Unfortunately, it seemed that her oral language skills significantly affected this teenage girl's confidence and self-esteem. She reacted withdrawal and extreme shyness and refused to communicate with other children at school, which further thwarted her chances of practising oral expression. She also remained largely 'invisible' to her teachers who were not only unaware of the psychological issues and behavioural problems but also her unique talents (writing) and overall high intellectual potential. This, combined with her mother's lack of voice, bargaining power and agency, meant that the child continued to be given tasks below her actual cognitive abilities, and her outstanding writing skills and other talents remained unrecognised.

## Case study 2: Lila

Lila was 6 years and 2 months old at the time of assessment. She was born in the UK and raised in a Polish–English speaking family (Polish mother, English stepfather). The mother reported that the child initially was introduced to Polish in her first eight months of life but then went to English nursery. Soon after, an English-speaking stepfather joined the family. The mother tried to maintain Polish, but she reported that it was becoming increasingly difficult and English was gradually becoming more dominant. The mother perceived the child as having English language dominance. She tried to communicate with the child predominantly in Polish while the stepfather used English only. In all family interactions English was dominant. To prevent language deterioration and enhance the child's bilingualism, the mother decided to engage the child in Saturday Polish school and various Polish community events. She then later also introduced the child to the Polish system of education through online home-schooling.

Initially the mother perceived the child as coping very well with school, on target with everything, making good effort and being slightly above average. The first school experience seemed to be positive and the reception's report was very good. When Lila was in Year 1 (5 years old) the family moved and she went to a new (English) school. The mother reported that she gradually became concerned with the new school and the attitude displayed by Lila's classroom teacher. She recalled the teacher making assumptions that the child was being raised in a Polish migrant family and that Polish was her dominant language, and making comments that 'bilingual children will always lag behind'. The teacher was reported to use gestures and speak very slowly to both the mother (disregarding the mother's relatively high English level proficiency and socio-economic and educational status) and to the child. The mother became aware that the child was being perceived as unable to achieve and was put into the bottom sets. The mother tried to reason with the teacher, but this had little impact on the child's position within the new classroom. This continued for approximately three months, at which point the mother received an Individual Education Plan (IEP) in which the classroom teacher identified Lila as having some learning difficulties ('problems with cognition and learning'). The overall aims were 'to improve the reading age' and 'to improve unaided learning skills'. The alleged difficulties were reported to be related to the child's [assumed] bilingualism. The child was then 5.7 years old and her reading age, comprehension age and spelling age were all on target at 5 years 7 months. The mother, surprised with the teacher's perception that the child had special educational needs, requested re-assessment. She used her expert knowledge to challenge the teacher's assumptions. The child was re-assessed by the SEN coordinator at school and the IEP was cancelled. The next assessment at school was conducted when Lila was 6.2 years old (at the end of Year 1) and, just five months after the initial report of special educational needs, she was reported to be functioning at the following levels (there was no reference to the particular tests used):

- Reading age: 7.0 years.
- Comprehension age: 7.3 years.
- Spelling age: 5.10 years.

This reflected more closely the mother's observation of the child as doing well and above her age in terms of reading, comprehension and mathematics and slightly below average with spelling. While the child could learn to spell simple words, she often forgot the spelling after a few weeks and made mistakes in the words that appeared to have been secure before. This coincided with the introduction of Polish language spelling and grammar and the mother felt that the spelling difficulties may have been related to the child learning to differentiate between the two systems.

The school refused to take part in the research and, consequently, no further data from the teacher was obtained. Despite this, the author has included this case study as it highlights how some myths about bilingualism may be still alive among some teachers and how this can negatively impact on the child's development. Should the parent not have intervened, the child could have gone through the system with the label of SEN and remained in the bottom sets. The mother reported that the relationship with the school remained strained, but she decided to keep the child there only because Lila was settled and had close friends and she did not want to disrupt this with yet another move.

In relation to the language assessment:

- Table 3.4 in the Appendix at the end of this chapter presents Lila's main scores.
- Table 3.5 presents the scale comparisons.
- Table 3.6 presents the composite scores.

On listening comprehension, Lila obtained a standard score of 100 with a percentile rank of 50. This score is within an average range. Her standard score of 118 on Oral Expression and percentile rank 89 is well above average, higher than that of 89 per cent of her peers. She obtained a standard score of 116 on Reading Comprehension with a percentile rank of 86, again well above average and higher than those of 86 per cent of her peers. She obtained a standard score of 102 on the Written Expression with a percentile rank of 55, indicating an average score. Her performance was higher than that of 55 per cent of other children of her age.

Overall, Lila functioned on an average/upper average level of language development. As can be seen in Table 3.4, Lila's strongest points were her oral expression and reading comprehension. All composite scores fall within the normal range. A slightly lower level of ability to express in writing was compensated by a much higher level of oral expression and, similarly, poorer listening skills were compensated by better reading comprehension. This seems to be a natural pattern for many young children, who have only begun to learn to write. As can be seen in Table 3.5 over 25 per cent of children Lila's age have a substantial difference in the level of their functioning in oral and written expression.

In conclusion, at odds with the initial teacher's perception, there were no significant language delays and no reasons for concern in terms of language development.

## Case study 3: Marek

Marek was a boy aged 9 years and 8 months at the time of assessment. He was born in the UK to a Polish–Irish family. The boy was functionally bilingual, with English being more dominant, and communicative Polish. The mother and his four other siblings spoke Polish to each other and maintaining Polish was of particular importance to the mother. She recalled having to provide arguments in her attempt to convince the school that her son's bilingualism was not an issue and that keeping Polish was in fact beneficial. The child had recently been diagnosed with attention deficit/hyperactivity disorder (ADHD) and Asperger's syndrome and there were also signs of dyspraxia. The mother reported that she 'had no choice' but to take the child for a comprehensive assessment and diagnosis to a neuropsychologist in Poland as she felt she was not getting anywhere in terms of obtaining a clear diagnosis and recommendations in the UK. Following this, she received a statement of SEN.

The classroom teacher agreed that the child's dominant language was English, but he was also 'pretty fluent' in Polish. In terms of his academic performance Marek was perceived to be performing 'far below average' in literacy and numeracy and 'below average' in science and history and other social studies. He 'regularly goes out with the LSA for phonics and reading' and he was also 'withdrawn from numeracy lessons' (presumably for extra 1:1 or small group support). In comparison with peers, Marek was reported to work 'much less', behave 'somewhat less' appropriately, learning 'somewhat less' and also being 'somewhat less' happy. The teacher reported several concerns, among them the fact that the homework was 'hardly ever completed', 'he is very rarely read with at home' and 'he is very well supported and cared for at school but a lack of support from home has hindered potential progress'. Among other noted behaviour problems (which can mainly be associated with ADHD and social issues, which may be linked to Asperger's syndrome), the teacher noted that Marek often clung to adults, demanded a lot of attention and was too dependent on others. She added a handwritten note, in which she stated:

From conversations I've had with [...], he says he doesn't get a lot of attention at home (this is evident through the fact that no-one sits with him to help him complete his homework or read with him). I think this is why he craves attention of adults from school.

With regard to the good points, the teacher observed that Marek was 'very enthusiastic about learning', 'keen to show the class interesting books/objects he has found' and that 'he is a friendly and affectionate little boy (most of the time!)'.

From a conversation with the mother, it transpired that she was disappointed with the school's efforts to cater for her son's specific educational needs and expected that much more should be done. She spoke of very difficult family circumstances, which meant the family could not dedicate as much time as they wanted to support Marek (as another family member was the centre of attention at that time) and was bitter about the lack of understanding and support from school.

The language assessment carried out by the author further confirmed Marek's language development delays:

- Table 3.7 in the Appendix at the end of this chapter presents Marek's main scores.
- Table 3.8 presents the scale comparisons.
- Table 3.9 presents the composite scores.

In listening comprehension Marek obtained a below average standard score of 82 with a percentile rank of 10. His performance was higher than that of only 10 per cent of his peers. He obtained a below average standard score of 84 in Oral Expression (OE) scale with a percentile rank of 14, indicating his performance was higher than only 14 per cent of peers. In terms of Reading Comprehension he obtained a below average standard score of 83 with a percentile rank 13, indicating that his score was higher than those of only 13 per cent of other children his age. In the Written Expression he obtained a well below average standard score of 75 with a percentile rank of 5. This was his weakest score and it indicated that his performance was higher than only 5 per cent of other children his age. Completing this scale was particularly challenging as Marek struggled to focus and stay on task. He rushed through and wanted to complete the tasks without paying much attention to instructions.

Overall, Marek functioned on a below average/deficit level of language development. As can be seen in Table 3.7, all his scores placed him in the below average category, with the written expression score being the lowest. The composite scores provided more detailed information about different aspects of language development. Oral language (composed of listening comprehension and oral expression) appeared to be the most developed but still below the average (average range = 85–115). However, two other areas (receptive language and expressive language) were particularly weak (in only respectively 0.1 and 0.4 percentiles). The overall language score indicated the overall language deficiency and suggested that currently the child was performing better than only 1 per cent of children his age in the general population.

Moreover, behavioural observations made by the author confirmed the mother's and the teacher's observations that Marek had difficulties in concentration and retention of information. The boy struggled to follow the instructions and the author often felt that it was not so much the lack of ability to answer some of the simpler items but the lack of attention. The boy also wanted to rush through the items, often would not listen to an instruction or read an item to the end before jumping to an answer. The instructions for OWLS-II clearly state that repetition of the instructions is not allowed, and the author had repeatedly to remind the boy to listen carefully, not to rush and to pause and think. Marek was quite confident of his responses and did not attempt to self-correct or check his responses. There was no sign of anxiety and the boy seemed not to be discouraged by the more difficult items. This is a positive sign that shows certain resiliency and confidence. However, the boy found it difficult to sit for longer stretches of time (required to complete each of the sections) and this also contributed to his tendency to rush. Once he lost concentration, he would become impatient and rush through the following items, which then had a deleterious effect on his scores.

In summary, based on OWLS-II results, this boy was a student with a language delay that is likely to increase in significance as skills along the developmental continuum become more complex.

## Discussion

In the section below there is discussion of some common threads across all the case studies and available literature together with tentative observations.

First, for the most part, a degree of mismatch between the teachers' and the parents' perceptions of the children (in terms of their language and overall cognitive abilities as well as their psycho-social problems) was noted. The case studies also evidenced some discrepancies between the teachers' perceptions of children's language abilities and the actual scores, objectively measured by the OWLS-II. In some cases, these discrepancies were not substantial enough to warrant concerns. However, in others, they may have led to disastrous consequences for the child. Case study 2, for instance, evidenced how the teacher's perception of the child as having 'cognitive problems' led to her placing the child in the bottom sets, drafting the IEP (which suggested removing the child from the main lessons and placing her in the 'remedial' small group intervention) and attaching the label of SEN. These perceptions seem to have been based on the assumption that 'bilinguals will always lag behind', a view that subsequently lowered the teacher's expectations for that child. This was despite the fact that the teacher was in possession of the latest child's assessment, which evidenced that the child was 'on target' in each aspect and was performing appropriately for her age. OWLS-II assessment indicated an even larger discrepancy between the teacher's perception and the child's actual language development.

Two cases evidenced how teachers failed to notice children's exceptional writing abilities. In both cases the children were judged as 'average' by the teachers and 'well above average' by the parents. Kamila and Lila both obtained superior scores on the OWLS-II written expression scale (137 and 133 respectively). In both cases this was even more of an achievement for the children as both came from Polish migrant families and for both of them Polish was a dominant language. In both cases the parents pointed out their disappointment with English schools. They felt that their children were presented with tasks far below their actual cognitive levels and, as a result, the children were bored and demotivated. In Kamila's case, the large score gap between her oral and written expression may have contributed to the teacher's perception of her 'averageness'. Such 'misperceptions' of bilingual pupils may limit the children's chances of moving up to higher sets and accessing 'gifted and talented' programmes. They may certainly affect children's self-perception and self-esteem, demotivate them and contribute to the development of other behavioural problems (in Kamila's case further withdrawal and psycho-social problems; in Lila's case 'misbehaving' due to the experienced boredom and lack of appropriate stimulation). As Lauchlan (2014) explains, it is important to be aware of the impact of the school not valuing the child's minority language 'on the child's lower self-esteem and self-confidence, a reduced belief in the learning ability, lowered academic motivation and poorer school performance' (p. 17).

Based on this preliminary study and the author's extensive engagement with bilingual children, it seems that teachers should be very careful in their assessment and in forming perceptions about bilingual pupils. As Lauchlan (2014) warns:

> an evaluation based on the administration of the test in the child's 'weaker' language may lead to an under-estimation of a child's abilities, or perhaps a misdiagnosis, and generally speaking could provide a false impression, or at least a very partial and biased profile of the capabilities of the child.
>
> (p. 14)

Furthermore, the author also observed the lack of deeper understanding of bilingualism and we recorded instances of well-known myths still at play. A striking example of this was the teacher's belief in Case study 2 that bilingualism causes cognitive delays. Two other schools advocated the view that children with SEN should abandon their mother tongue (Polish) and concentrate on one language only (English). In one case, according to the mother's account the child 'developed spoken language very late and this speech delay was initially linked with behaviour traits attributable to the autistic spectrum' (disregarded later). The family sought the child psychologist's and health professionals' opinions and were advised to concentrate on English language development only. 'The child attended monthly speech therapy sessions at the Child Development Centre and received daily speech development support from his family. All language development activities were undertaken in English', the mother reported. Subsequently, as she explained, her youngest son (unlike his other two siblings) struggled to communicate in Polish. In Marek's case the mother had to strongly put her case for the advantages of bilingual education to the school.

In another case the child went through a classic 'silent stage' and refused to speak at school for nearly a year. The parents did not know what to think about this and were worried that the child may have a disorder, such as autism. They sought the school's help and support, but the school had no advice to offer and the family was left to their own devices.

As Lauchlan (2014) highlights, children with Autistic Spectrum Disorder (ASD) are likely to have problems with language and communication. However, against the advice given by the teachers and professionals (as documented above), autistic children (as well as those with other speech difficulties) could socially and culturally benefit from bilingualism, especially when living in a dual language environment. In fact, bilingualism is reported to enhance flexibility of thinking (often impaired in ASD children, Rubinyi, 2006).

Moreover, some teachers seemed to treat bilinguals as a homogenous group. The most common perception appeared to be that Polish–English bilinguals were sequential bilinguals with Polish as a dominant language. This perception prevailed even when the teacher was in the position of facts, as in Case study 2 (a child born in England, living in a Polish–English family with English being the dominant language) and revealed that teachers assumed that Polish–English bilingual children were mainly immigrants, often born in Poland and raised by two Polish-speaking parents.

Safford and Drury (2013) conclude that, rather than to be viewed as a problem, bilingualism can be seen as a pedagogic resource in the classroom. In the case studies, however, the author saw only shallow engagement of schools with bilingualism (expressed mainly through 'diversity celebrations') and a lack of deeper consideration for bilingual children's needs and talents.

Finally, several Polish parents in this study referred to their perceived lack of personal influence as a result of a lack of sufficient language skills and knowledge and their overall underprivileged position of migrants in the host society, which put them in an inferior position in terms of negotiating support for their children in schools. Even those who, objectively speaking, held a higher socio-economic status in society and spoke English very well, expressed their concerns and a degree of 'powerlessness'. Moreover, some parents expressed their disappointment or even anger with the lack of understanding and support from schools, saying that they did not know what their children were learning at school and felt they had no control over their children's education, which further caused them anxiety. As Sales et al. (2008) note, parents in the Polish education system are much more engaged in their children's learning. Moreover,

> the homework system and centralised curriculum provides parents with detailed knowledge of the curriculum and of their children's progress. Children bring all subject books, exercise books and notebooks home to complete daily revision, homework and show parents their progress. Parents can monitor homework and their children's progress and to help eliminate 'potential gaps in knowledge acquisition'.
>
> *(Lopez Rodriguez, 2005, p. 11)*

This is not possible to the same degree in the English system. Polish migrants expect the same level of 'service' and education as they would receive in Poland (Sales et al., 2008). This developed 'sense of entitlement' and high expectations of education will inevitably exert pressure on the teachers and the system.

## Limitations of the study, tentative recommendations and further directions

This was a small-scale pilot study and generalisation is not possible. However, this study highlighted a few areas of particular tensions or difficulties for teachers, parents and children, which require further investigation and attention.

First, the analysis of the three case studies indicated that some teachers may be unaware of the current research evidence regarding the benefits of bilingualism and most up-to-date advice on how to best support bilingual learners, and there seems to be a lack of appropriate training programmes and information sharing. Therefore, the first recommendation would be to increase the training on offer and perhaps (especially for schools with higher numbers of Polish or bilingual pupils in general) to consider offering a tailored programme, which could highlight some differences in educational systems.

Similarly, Polish parents often do not have sufficient knowledge of the English system of education and this may be a source of misunderstandings, tensions and parents' high expectations (that often cannot be met by schools). Offering detailed information packs, delivering information sessions and generally increasing communication with migrant parents may help lower anxiety and resolve some of the issues. Sales *et al.* (2008) offer some examples of such successful interventions in schools in London. More recently, Lopez-Rodriguez, D'Angelo, Ryan and Sales (2016) updated their toolkit for migrant parents and practitioners titled 'Schooling in England'. This toolkit is free to download and should be recommended by all schools to the new incoming migrant parents.

Finally, this chapter aimed to sensitise the reader to the problems with assessment of bilingual children. These problems are well documented in the literature and are beyond the scope of this chapter to discuss in detail. However, it is important to stress that teachers' subjective perceptions of bilingual children's abilities may have a significant psychological impact on the children's self-esteem, self-image, motivation and their further progress in education. Teachers should be much more careful in forming their opinions, and aware of the risk of bias (especially in terms of judging children by their oral expression) and of the potential educational consequences for the children.

More should be done to understand the experiences and needs of all bilingual pupils in the UK as this is an ever-increasing group of children. In this small sample the author identified some children with very specific needs and psychological risks; pupils whose problems seemed to be 'invisible' to their teachers, as well as those whose talents and high cognitive abilities seemed to be not recognised. In several cases the teachers' opinions did not match the parents' knowledge or their children and, more worryingly, the objective measurements obtained via testing children with OWLS-II. There was hardly any pastoral care available to the children, and few opportunities to voice their needs.

Virtually all parents within this sample felt, to a varied degree, voiceless and frustrated, often lacking agency and unable to successfully share or defend their values, opinions or perspectives. In cases where they were able to challenge the teachers' opinions or negotiate the support they felt was needed for their children, this required a lot of time and energy and the emotional cost was often high (several parents reported exhaustion and frustration with 'fighting the system').

It transpired that, at odds with the 'Listening to and Involving Children and Young People' (DfE, 2014) agenda and the United Nations Convention on the Rights of the Child (UNCRC), the schools (and, more specifically, teachers) retained practically all authority, making crucial decisions for the children, without involving them and their families.

Although there are some data available on Polish pupils in the UK (e.g. Sales et al., 2008), they largely come from teachers or parents. It would be valuable to explore ways of engaging with the opinions and ideas of all children, including multilingual children, and especially those for whom language can be a barrier.

It would also be valuable to conduct a longitudinal study to document these learners' educational journeys in order to identify protective psychological factors and successful interventions.

We also need to draw the policymakers' attention to the evidence base for benefits of bilingualism, emphasising how it can improve the children's long-term educational outcomes and overall well-being.

Finally, there is a need to offer interventions, which can showcase how bi- or multilingualism can be a strength and a source of strong sense of identity, self-esteem and confidence, such as, for instance, a project described in the following chapter.

## References

Alexander, K. L. & Entwisle, D. R. (1996). Schools and children at risk. In A. Booth & J. L. Dunn (Eds.), *Family school links: How do they affect educational outcomes?* (pp. 67–88). Hillsdale, NJ: Erlbaum.
Baker, C. (2007). *A parents' and teachers' guide to bilingualism*. Clevedon, UK: Multilingual Matters.
Bialystok, E. (2001). *Bilingualism in development: Language, literacy and cognition*. Cambridge: Cambridge University Press.
Carrow-Woolfolk, E. (2011). *Oral and Written Language Scales (OWLS-II)*, 2nd edn. Torrance, CA: WPS.
DfE (Department for Education) (2014). Listening to and involving children and young people, London: DfE.
Eccles, J. S. (1999). The development of children ages 6–14. *Future Child*, 9(2), 30–44.
Eversley, J., Mehmedbogovic, D., Sanderson, A., Tinsley, T., Von Ahn, M., & Wiggins, M., (2010). *Language capital: Mapping the languages of London's schoolchildren*. Reading, UK: CILT.
Hamre, B. K. & Pianta, R. C. (2001). Early teacher-child relationships and the trajectory of children's school outcomes through eighth grade. *Child Development*, 72(2), 625–638.

Jankowska, M. (2014). On bilingualism in (monolingual?) English classroom environment: The challenges for Polish-English bilingual children, their parents and schools. *Sustainable Multilingualism*, 5, 99–131.

Krashen, S. & McField, G. (2005). What works? Reviewing the latest evidence on bilingual education. *Language Learner*, 1(2), 7–10, 34.

La Paro, K. M. & Pianta, R. C. (2000). Predicting children's competence in the early school years: A meta-analytic review. *Review of Educational Research*, 70(4), 443–484.

Lauchlan, F. (2014). The nature of bilingualism and implications for educational psychologists. *Educational and Child Psychology*, 31(2), 9–31.

Levine, J. (1990). *Bilingual learners and the mainstream curriculum*. Basingstoke, UK: Falmer Press.

Lopez Rodriguez, M. (2005) 'Capital, identities and strategies for success: Explorations of the perspectives of East European migrant mothers on their children's education in the UK'. Unpublished MA dissertation, London: Institute of Education.

Lopez-Rodriguez, M., D'Angelo, A., Ryan, L., & Sales, R. (2016). Schooling in England – A toolkit for newly arrived migrant parents and practitioners working with migrants. The Social Policy Research Centre (SPRC), Middlesex University. Retrieved from https://mdxmigration.wordpress.com/migrantschools/

McCulloch, A., Wiggins, R. D., Joshi, H. E., & Sachdev, D. (2000). Internalizing and externalizing children's behaviour problems in Britain and the US: Relationships to family resources. *Children and Society*, 14, 368–383.

Morokvasic, M. (2004). Settled in mobility: Engendering post-wall migration in Europe. *Feminist Review*, 77, 7–25.

Office for National Statistics (2018). Population of the UK by country of birth and nationality: 2017. Retrieved from https://www.ons.gov.uk/peoplepopulationandcommunity/populationandmigration/internationalmigration/bulletins/ukpopulationbycountryofbirthandnationality/2017

Portes, A. & Hao, L. E. (1998). Pluribus unum: Bilingualism and loss of language in the second generation. *Sociology of Education*, 71(4), 269–294.

Rawlinson, K. (2013, 30 January). Polish is second most spoken language in England. *The Independent*. Retrieved from http://www.independent.co.uk/news/uk/home-news/polish-is-second-most-spoken-language-in-england-as-census-reveals-140000-residents-cannot-speak-english-at-all-8472447.html

Rubinyi, S. (2006). *Natural genius: The gifts of Asperger's Syndrome*. Philadelphia, PA: Jessica Kingsley.

Rumbaut, R. G. (1994). The crucible within: Ethnic identity, self-esteem and segmented assimilation among children of immigrants. *International Migration Review*, 28(7), 748–794.

Safford, K. & Drury, R. (2013). The 'problem' of bilingual children in educational settings: Policy and research in England. *Language and Education*, 27(1), 70–81.

Saft, E. W. & Pianta, R. C. (2001). Teachers' perceptions of their relationships with students: Effects of child age, gender, and ethnicity of teachers and children. *Journal of School Psychology*, 16(2), 125–141.

Sales, R., Ryan, L., Lopez-Rodriguez, M., & D'Angelo, A. (2008). Polish pupils in London schools: Opportunities and challenges. The Social Policy Research Centre (SPRC), Middlesex University. London: Multiverse.

Sobkow, W. (2014, 5 June). Learning Polish, the UK's second most spoken language, is a plus. *The Guardian*. Retrieved from https://www.theguardian.com/education/2014/jun/05/learning-polish-a-plus-ambassador

Wehby, J. H., Dodge, K. A., & Valente, E. (1993). The conduct disorders prevention research group school behavior of first grade children at risk for development of conduct problems. *Behavioral Disorders*, 19, 67–78.

Winsler, A., Burchinal, M. R., Tien, H., Peisner-Feinberg, E., Espinosa, L., Castro, D. C., & De Feyter, J. (2014). Early development among dual language learners: The roles of language use at home, maternal immigration, country of origin, and socio-demographic variables. *Early Childhood Research Quarterly*, 29(4), 750–764.

# Appendix

**TABLE 3.1** Case study 1: standard scores

| Listening comprehension | Oral expression | Reading comprehension | Written expression |
|---|---|---|---|
| 92 | 79 | 99 | 137 |
| Average | Below average | Average | Very superior (fewer than 2.2% of pupils this age achieve such a score) |

**TABLE 3.2** Case study 1: scale comparisons

| Scale | Scale | Difference | Significant? | % of sample with this difference |
|---|---|---|---|---|
| Listening comprehension | Oral expression | 13 | Y | 25% |
| Listening comprehension | Reading comprehension | 7 | N | |
| Listening comprehension | Written expression | 45 | Y | Less than 1% |
| Oral expression | Reading comprehension | 20 | Y | 10–15% |
| Oral expression | Written expression | 58 | Y | Less than 1% |
| Written expression | Reading comprehension | 38 | N | Less than 1% |

**TABLE 3.3** Case study 1: composite scores

| Composite | Sum of standard scores | Standard score Age | Confidence interval 95% | Percentile rank | Description |
|---|---|---|---|---|---|
| Oral language | 171 | 84 | 79–89 | 14 | Below average (slightly) |
| Written language | 236 | 120 | 116–124 | 91 | Above average |
| Receptive language (LC + RC) | 191 | 94 | 90–98 | 34 | Average |
| Expressive language (OE + WE) | 216 | 109 | 104–114 | 73 | Average |
| Overall language | 407 | 102 | 99–105 | 55 | Average |

**TABLE 3.4** Case study 2: standard scores

| Listening comprehension | Oral expression | Reading comprehension | Written expression |
|---|---|---|---|
| 100 | 118 | 116 | 102 |
| Average | Above average | Above average | Average |

**TABLE 3.5** Case study 2: scale comparisons

| Scale comparisons | | | | |
|---|---|---|---|---|
| Scale | Scale | Difference | Significant? | % of sample with this difference |
| Listening comprehension | Oral expression | 18 | Y | 10% |
| Listening comprehension | Reading comprehension | 16 | Y | 20–25% |
| Listening comprehension | Written expression | 2 | N | |
| Oral expression | Reading comprehension | 2 | N | |
| Oral expression | Written expression | 16 | Y | Over 25% |
| Written expression | Reading comprehension | 14 | Y | 20–25% |

**TABLE 3.6** Case study 2: composite scores

| Composite | Sum of standard scores | Standard score Age | Confidence interval 95% | Percentile rank | Description |
|---|---|---|---|---|---|
| Oral language | 218 | 108 | 103–113 | 70 | Average |
| Written language | 218 | 110 | 106–114 | 75 | Average |
| Receptive language | 216 | 108 | 104–122 | 70 | Average |
| Expressive language | 220 | 111 | 106–116 | 77 | Average |
| Overall language | 436 | 110 | 107–113 | 75 | Average |

**TABLE 3.7** Case study 3: standard scores

| Listening comprehension | Oral expression | Reading comprehension | Written expression |
|---|---|---|---|
| 81 | 84 | 83 | 75 |
| Below average | Below average | Below average | Below average |

**TABLE 3.8** Case study 3: scale comparisons

| Scale comparisons | | | | |
|---|---|---|---|---|
| Scale | Scale | Difference | Significant? | % of sample with this difference |
| Listening comprehension | Oral expression | 3 | N | |
| Listening comprehension | Reading comprehension | 10 | Y | Over 25% |
| Listening comprehension | Written expression | 2 | N | |
| Oral expression | Reading comprehension | 1 | N | |
| Oral expression | Written expression | 9 | Y | Over 25% |
| Written expression | Reading comprehension | 8 | Y | Over 25% |

**TABLE 3.9** Case study 3: composite scores

| Composite | Sum of standard scores | Standard score Age | Confidence interval 95% | Percentile rank | Description |
|---|---|---|---|---|---|
| Oral language | 165 | 81 | 76–86 | 10 | Below average |
| Written language | 158 | 79 | 75–83 | 8 | Below average |
| Receptive language | 116 | 53 | 49–57 | 0.1 | Deficient |
| Expressive language | 123 | 60 | 55–65 | 0.4 | Deficient |
| Overall language | 274 | 64 | 61–67 | 1 | Deficient |

# 4

# BILINGUAL CREATIVE WRITING CLUBS

Giving voice to bi/multilingual children in English schools and bi/multilingual university students and staff

*Dr Maja Jankowska*

## Introduction

The focus of this chapter is a project, Bilingual Creative Writing Clubs, which aimed to provide a platform for bilingual primary school children's voices to be acknowledged, heard and valued. The idea for the project came from the author's perceived need to address a common issue in schools in England, namely that children for whom English is an additional language (EAL) may be perceived as being problematic and at risk of under-achieving, resulting in their linguistic talents being left untapped.

Although children who use a language other than English are not a minority (especially in urban areas in the UK), English classrooms remain largely monolingual and (perhaps to a lesser extent) also monocultural. Monolingualism is perceived as a norm and there seems to be an expectation that children who are not native English speakers should speedily acquire English so that they can be assimilated into the English system of education. Children's native voices are often left outside of the school gates and positioned as separate from schools and curricula. There seems to be little acknowledgement and appreciation of languages other than English and the celebration of diversity is often ad hoc and superficial. The focus tends to be on remedial work (improving their English) and little space is given to the exploration of their voices and potential talents.

In this project, the author attended to children's voices and offered them the opportunity to express themselves in both English and their home language. Both theory and empirical evidence (small but continuously growing) indicate that validating home languages and providing children with opportunities to express themselves in both languages can lead to an increased sense of inclusion, confidence, self-worth and overall well-being.

The data collected within this project indicates that taking part in the Bilingual Creative Writing Clubs project had a statistically significant impact on children's confidence. Becoming a published author of a bilingual story enabled children not only to express themselves, but also to experience an immense sense of achievement and pride. The perception of the children as 'under-achievers' was also successfully challenged within the schools' environment.

## Rationale for the project

The rationale for this project came from the body of literature which shows that educational policy and public opinion (particularly in England) often discourage the use of children's home languages in the classroom (Safford & Drury, 2013), without realising that there is great potential for the transfer of literacy, numeracy and other skills between the languages (Nag et al., 2014). As explained in Chapter 3 of this volume, children for whom English is not their first language are often not a minority (especially in metropolitan areas in the UK). Even so, within the packed curricula of primary and secondary education in England, there is little space for acknowledgement and appreciation of languages other than English and, although schools try to showcase that they 'celebrate' diversity, their efforts can often be seen as ad hoc and superficial.

Moreover, this English language dominance is driven by a high-stakes testing regime. Hence children's other languages are often left outside of the school gates, positioned as separate from school education and the responsibility of parents and the community (Dakin, 2012). Many teachers may also be unaware of the impact of the first language on a child's identity, self-esteem and confidence (Krashen & McField, 2005). A systematic review of intervention research examining English language and literacy development in EAL children conducted for the Educational Endowment Foundation (Murphy, 2015) confirms that most programmes aimed at EAL students concentrate on improving their English language skills (therefore taking a deficit view). No studies listed in the review addressed the issue of the importance of other languages, linguistic transfer or the significance of validation of home languages for the children's sense of identity, self-esteem, confidence or well-being.

Although Murphy's (2015) review did not include any studies that would evidence the effectiveness of interventions which focus on linguistic strengths (rather than deficiencies) and aimed to develop children's literacy through the use of home languages, there is a growing database of studies showcasing that such interventions can be particularly effective. Most of the evidence for effectiveness comes from countries that are much more experienced in the delivery of bilingual programmes (Canada, the United States, South Africa). For instance, Naqvi (2008), from the University of Calgary in Canada, explored the integration of dual language books into the regular school curriculum and engaged students in creating their own dual language books (www.rahatanaqvi.ca). Her website contains a useful database of more than 2,300 published dual language books in over 40 languages.

Cummins and Early (2011) offer an impressive amount of evidence that the pedagogic approach, which focuses on validation of home languages for the children's sense of identity, can be very effective and can make a significant impact on both students' self-image and the quality of their learning. In their book, entitled *Identity Texts: the Collaborative Creation of Power in Multilingual Schools*, they present many case studies of a variety of projects, which included creative bilingual writing. They conclude that these projects:

- encouraged students to connect new information and skills to their background knowledge;
- enabled students to produce accomplished literacy work in the school language;
- increased their awareness of the specialised language of school subject area;
- affirmed students' identities as intelligent, imaginative and linguistically talented;
- increased their awareness of the relationships between their home language (L1) and their school language (L2).

*(Cummins & Early, 2011, p. 4)*

They also claim that such texts represent a powerful pedagogical tool to promote equity for students from marginalised social backgrounds as they 'challenge the devaluation of identity that many linguistically diverse and other marginalised students experience in contexts where their home languages or varieties of language [dialects, accents] are not explicitly acknowledged as intellectual and cultural resources (p. 4)'. These multilingual texts can support 'a "counter-discourse" to the implicit devaluation of students' abilities, languages, cultures, and identities that occurs in classrooms where students' preferred ways of meaning making and home languages are ignored or treated with "benign neglect"' (p. 4). The author of this chapter is particularly interested in designing and delivering projects that support such a 'counter-discourse' in which bilingual children's, students' and staff's voices can be acknowledged, heard and valued and which can help challenge the prevalent discourse of deficiency.

Unfortunately, such approaches are in their infancy in the UK. One small-scale intervention conducted in Bristol (Dakin, 2012) has, however, provided some encouraging insights. Dakin worked with group of year 4, 5 and 6 children who produced dual-language stories. Although these were not published, nonetheless, Dakin observed promising effects such as increased confidence, self-esteem and pride as children could demonstrate their identities and talents that would normally remain hidden beneath a drive for attainment in and through English. Dakin also pointed out that this validation of children's languages increased their sense of inclusion and self-worth. However, the details of the measures used were not provided and it seems that the evidence came mainly from children's evaluation of the project and Dakin's own observations (Dakin, 2012).

Taking into account the above promising evidence and observations, the project discussed in this chapter moved away from the traditional focus on English and instead focused on bilingual children's strengths and abilities, providing a safe forum for showcasing their language skills and validating their home languages, which, in turn, may lead to an increased sense of inclusion and self-worth, as Dakin (2012) suggested in her preliminary, small-scale project. Moreover, the project also aimed to give voice to, and to validate, the languages, cultures and disciplinary backgrounds of the diverse students and staff who were invited to contribute to it from the University of Bedfordshire, where the lead researcher was employed.

An additional rationale for proposing this project came from researching the availability of bilingual resources for children and young people in the local community, within schools, the university library and local libraries in Bedfordshire. The project lead (the author of this chapter) observed that, although there are some (though very limited) bilingual books and resources in the libraries, they are mostly aimed at very young children and usually they are simply translations of well-known stories (such as Little Red Riding Hood) from one language to another. Some contain language errors. Moreover, these stories are also mainly written by adult writers for children. There are virtually no stories written by children for children and limited resources that refer to a particular culture or heritage (for example folk stories or fictional stories that include specific cultural background/context). Therefore, within this project, the author wanted to encourage the children to write their own creative stories for other children of a similar age (7–8 and 9–11 years), which could be based on either folk stories from their own cultures, which would provide the additional possibility of cultural learning, or works of fiction. It was envisaged that the children would be supported by bi/multilingual university students from four different departments, who would work in inter-disciplinary teams of four: one student from each department within a team of four per each school, supported by university and school staff.

In summary, the author of this chapter designed the Bilingual Creative Writing Clubs project in a way that would bring diverse primary pupils, their teachers and parents and diverse university students and staff together and facilitate cross-cultural learning.

## An ecology for cross-cultural learning

The Bilingual Creative Writing Clubs project described here was chosen as one of the cases included in the Cultural Learning, Identity and the European Project (EERA, 2015). It was viewed as an example of an ecology for cross-cultural learning, creativity and community engagement (Jankowska *et al.*, 2016). A metaphor of an organic living ecology, in which all the components interact and from which entirely new products and learning emerge (Jackson, 2016), was utilised to conceptualise the clubs. According to Jackson (2016), ecologies for learning include contexts and spaces (in this project two local primary schools), material resources (or their lack, for example bilingual resources) as well as human resources (teachers, parents, multilingual university students and staff), relationships (between all participants), processes (activities and experiences) as well as attributes of the individuals in the centre of the ecology (his/her will, capability, imagination, creativity, attitudes, and so on) and affordances (in this case Bilingual Creative Writing Club as an opportune space for the creation of bilingual books). The ecology of developing cultural understanding (Jackson, 2016) suggests that people develop their awareness of culture through the ecologies they create to learn, act and achieve in a particular socio-cultural context (such as, for example, a school or a bilingual creative writing club).

## Bilingual Creative Writing Club – a case of cultural learning exchange

This project therefore is a case study for cultural learning exchange (Myers & Grosvenor, 2014) between the schools, in particular bi/multilingual pupils and their teachers, the University of Bedfordshire, UK, in particular students from four departments: Psychology, English Language and Communication, Advertising Design and Teacher Training/Education Studies (working in inter-disciplinary teams) and staff (the School of Psychology and Access and Outreach Team) and the community, in particular bi/multilingual parents and the wider community (libraries, immigrant community groups).

In line with the framework of the Cultural Learning, Identity and the European Project (EERA, 2015), this project emphasised the importance of partnership and public engagement based on the principles of mutual cultural learning exchange. Although the idea for the project initially came from a University of Bedfordshire Psychology lecturer (the current author), the schools, university students, staff and the community engaged in a partnership spirit of action research inquiry. The author drew on the experience of the university's Access and Outreach Team to collaborate in particular with local schools as well as student volunteer recruitment and training, including safeguarding and criminal record checks (DBS).

The project emphasised partnerships and engagement of all participants as a key factor in facilitation of cultural (and inter-cultural) learning as well as cross-disciplinary learning to look at ways in which individuals and groups learn both about and through culture and within and across communities (Macnab, Clay & Grosvenor, 2011) and support bi/multilingual children's voices to be acknowledged, heard and valued.

## An overview of the project

The Bilingual Creative Writing Clubs project took the form of after school clubs in which young, diverse learners (aged 7–10) of different cultural and linguistic backgrounds created bi- or tri-lingual stories. Two local Bedfordshire schools were involved: one lower school and one primary school. They provided spaces and resources for holding the clubs after school on their premises, one hour per week for 11 weeks in the academic year 2015–16, and supported the project, delegating teaching and support staff to contribute to the project and liaise with the author. In the following year, the stories were published and shared with their authors, libraries, schools and community members, and then an official launch was organised.

Overall, 32 children were involved in the clubs. They wrote in many different languages: Arabic, Bengali, Bulgarian, Italian, Latvian, Ndebele, Polish, Russian and Spanish. An attempt was made to replicate this diversity in terms of the university students involved. They worked in two inter-disciplinary and multilingual and multicultural teams, one in each of the schools. They spoke a range of languages: French, Greek, Polish, Romanian, Spanish, Ibo and English. Each team had a student leader, a psychology final year undergraduate student, who co-ordinated the work of the team. Each team reflected after each session and communicated with the project lead and the Access and Outreach team in order to refine the approach. Owing to a variety of practical issues, an exact match between school children and university students' languages was not possible. However, other students' skills and their unique disciplinary backgrounds proved to be invaluable in the implementation of this project.

In the spirit of action research, partnership and engagement, the two teams, the author of this chapter and a member of the Access and Outreach Team, prepared, implemented and refined the weekly sessions in each of the schools. These schools were different in many respects and the working and group dynamics required differentiation of the approach.

Parents were also invited to encourage and support their children at home (writing in the children's home languages) as well as to send their views/comments/requests. One of the parents asked to join the team and supported a small group of Spanish-speaking children in a school where the club lacked a Spanish-speaking university student.

Head teachers gave their permission to run the clubs and were supportive of the project. Some teachers and teaching assistants were also involved, helping within the club as well as motivating and reminding the children to bring their work the following week.

The project culminated in the publication of 26 paperback books (covers of which can be viewed at www.creativebilingual.com/Childrens-Books/), which were offered to the libraries in schools, community (Bedfordshire) and the university as bilingual resources and as the children's 'cultural offerings' to their community. The children are named as authors and the books were launched in 2016 at the university theatre. Representatives from the community, university, the child-authors as well as their teachers and parents were invited to the event.

Although the tangible outcome of the project was the publication of bilingual books, the emphasis was on fostering curiosity about other cultures and languages, learning from each other (cultural learning exchanges), celebrating diversity in an authentic way and having fun. An additional aim was to provide students from four different departments with an opportunity to work together in inter-disciplinary teams and to gain a real-life experience in a real-life setting (a school), hence increasing their employability. It was also hoped that the project would help increase the visibility of bilingual and bicultural learners within the schooling system and showcase their unique talents.

The sessions were highly enjoyable for everyone involved as, apart from the opportunity to write stories, the clubs provided a space to play games (often linguistic or culture-related), and children, as well as the university students, expressed their creativity and linguistic abilities in a multitude of different ways. For example, a group of Polish children in one of the schools spontaneously created a short song, which they called 'a Polish gang song' and which they sang in each of the following sessions as well as during the launch of the books at the university theatre. Children in the other school decided to bring their own cultural food to one of the last sessions and celebrate their work and discuss their home traditions and customs, while sharing a meal.

The project received a multitude of positive comments from children, parents and schools and the clubs' teams also reported working within this project as highly enjoyable and rewarding. The university students commented on the fact that they learned a lot about themselves, working with children, working in a school setting as well as learning about various cultures and disciplines that were represented in this project.

## Layers of learning within the project

An array of different learning occurred within this project, including the learning that was anticipated as a result of the clubs' design but also various types of unintended learning.

### i. Valuing and celebrating a variety of languages and cultures

Within this project the emphasis was on combining pupils' and university students' (and staff's) skills in a variety of languages and English in order to give value and status to their other languages that would not normally be possible. It was clear that children's and students' confidence in using their home languages increased steadily from session to session. Initially the children were shy and unsure how to talk about their home languages. In each group there were some children who had not previously identified others in their year or school as speakers of the same language. The comments such as: 'I had no idea you also spoke Polish' and 'I didn't know your parents came from Italy too' evidenced children's surprise with each other's background and the fact that this was not something that was discussed or paid attention to at school. It became evident that at school children were discouraged from communicating with the children of the same linguistic background in languages other than English and hence they were unsure how to go about it. They were also unsure how to use the home language among the speakers of other languages. They thought it would be impolite and felt that others would not understand them. However, these attitudes quickly changed. Students started sharing information and 'fun facts' (for example, different alphabets, number of letters, letters or sounds different from those in English, words that sound or are spelled the same but mean different things in different languages or words that are similar, etc.), as well as learning words and phrases in other languages very quickly. This was facilitated with the use of linguistic games and role modelling as university students started sharing and using their home languages from the beginning of the project.

The children quickly realised that the club afforded them an opportunity to showcase how good they were at speaking and writing other languages and when they saw the final 'product', their books professionally published on a glossy, shiny paper, listing them as authors, they felt immensely proud (see Figure 4.1).

This was recognised within assemblies and discussed in lessons, and the books are now placed in the library as bilingual resources for speakers of these languages. It was also reported that other children and teachers were not only amazed at the final products (26 books) but they became curious about the cultures and languages, showing deeper interest and engaging in conversations about them with the bilingual children. As one parent explained:

**FIGURE 4.1** Examples of bilingual books

She learned some words of different languages and she has been able to put a small book together so that has been really creative for her and the satisfaction and achievement that she's going to have a book that will go in to libraries. So it's just confidence for her.

*(Parent 1)*

The observations made during the clubs' sessions and the feedback received indicated that the celebration of variety of languages and cultural identifies could be achieved at a deeper level than the traditional, often superficial 'show diversity' activities.

The university students also reported immense joy from being able to use their linguistic and disciplinary skills in practice. One of the psychology team leaders commented on how she was very pleased working with a group of Polish children as this afforded her an opportunity to use her home language, having previously been restricted to talking only with her Polish family. At home she spoke English with her British partner and she realised that her home language had begun gradually to deteriorate. Other students also commented on the fact that participating in the clubs helped them re-connect with their home languages and cultures. Several of them observed, to their surprise and dismay, that they had forgotten certain words, phrases or spellings and generally realised that their home languages had become 'rusty'. This motivated them to utilise and maintain their languages more.

## *ii. Voicing and sharing of identities and cultural heritage*

The initial shyness and tentativeness in sharing home languages and cultural heritage was soon dispelled and the children began opening up and forming new friendships. Children from many different cultural, linguistic, religious and social backgrounds came together and interrogated each other's heritage. For instance, two girls from different year groups, who had not spoken to each other much before, decided to write a trilingual book together. They had no prior knowledge of each other's languages and were surprised to see how different these languages looked in the written form. They felt that the different alphabets would look 'cool' together in their trilingual book and they discovered that co-creation can be both real fun but also challenging as the story line and illustrations had to be negotiated and agreed upon.

Through working with each other and with the university students each week, the children gained confidence in sharing their stories and multiple identities. As one child explained:

I learned how to talk in my language out loud to loads of people. [...] Yes. I am confident to talk to [not only] my Polish friends but to people that are unknown and in front of English people and Polish when they're mixed up. I wasn't completely confident to talk like in a mix of people but now I am.

*(Child 1)*

And another child summed up the clubs' spirit of valuing each individual child's background by stating: 'at bilingual [club] they care about who you are and where you're from. They care about what you write' (Child 7). This was also emphasised by the university students:

> It really advertised the fact that bilingualism is a big issue and it exists in our society and we shouldn't pressurise people to learn just English to integrate. [We] helped children accept who they are and practise their native languages. Some of the children found that they were quite creative, and they wanted to write more which was really good.
>
> *(Student 3)*

Similarly, the teachers realised that valuing the individual children's identity, knowledge and linguistic talents is really important within the classroom:

> Then there's the other script [Cyrillic] and the other children are looking at him thinking 'Oh my gosh, how is he reading that?' And an appreciation for me as well because he often tells me Bulgarian words or a French word and he will say 'we say that in Bulgarian'. It just allows him more of a 'I know I can come in on that, I've got something to say about it and you're going to listen because you're interested' and I think that's definitely come through.
>
> *(Teacher 2)*

See Figure 4.2, 'A trilingual story' and Figure 4.3, 'A bilingual story in Bulgarian'.

Some children, parents and teachers emphasised the importance of meeting children from other years and cultural and linguistic backgrounds as something particularly positive. At the same time, they recognised the importance of having contact with speakers of the same language for friendship and development of positive self-identity:

> It brought different year groups together so maybe these children wouldn't normally on a day to day basis meet each other but within this group they got to know other children and maybe you know build that link with oh you speak that language so do I and work together which was really positive.
>
> *(Parent 11)*

> I think it was quite fun getting to use my other language with other people. [I learned] just that there's a lot more people in my school that speak lots of different languages in my school. I didn't think there would be that many people and languages.
>
> *(Child 1)*

Asked about what difference the club made to the school, children and parents, one of the teachers summarised:

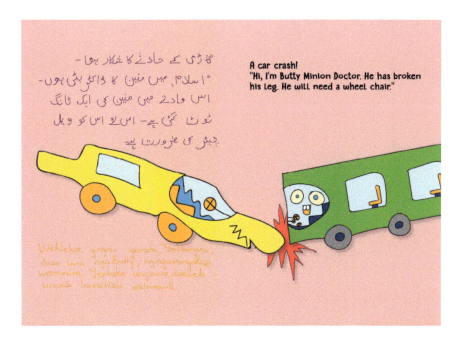

**FIGURE 4.2** A trilingual story

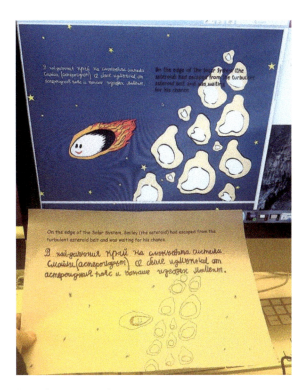

**FIGURE 4.3** A bilingual story in Bulgarian

> I think the children themselves are that much more confident because I think it's almost an appreciation of what they can do that we didn't know that they could do and by us you know highlighting this skill that they have it's really boosted their confidence you know within the class, you know. I teach within each class and to see how they have grown how they have developed and that friendship and that bond and for us to understand them a lot more where they are coming from you know they do not all speak the same language at home than they speak at school you know it's been really, really good, it's a real eye opener to see what they do and how much they can do.
>
> *(Teacher 3)*

### iii. Enhancing a discourse of talent and the 'visibility' of bi/multilingual children

One of the main aims of this project was to challenge the discourse of 'deficiency' of bi/multilingual children, and instead acknowledge their unique talents and linguistic skills as intellectual and cultural resources and therefore increase their visibility within the schools. The achievement of this goal was voiced by all the participants within this project who emphasised a noticeable shift in perception of the children – from underperforming 'underdogs', viewed through the lenses of deficiency, low achievement and low expectations, to appreciated, talented individuals with a multitude of talents that can be tapped into and utilised in order to maximise educational outcomes. As one parent put it vividly:

> I really like it, you hear loads of stories about children who are bilingual who are underperforming so it's helped him and helped us to know that someone appreciates that a child can speak more than one language.
>
> *(Parent 4)*

The parent's voiced concern with the discourse of underperformance/deficiency is echoed in the insightful remark of one of the teachers, who observed the development of the project from its inception:

> From a teacher's perspective as well, I realised we need to be trying to pitch work and not assume the child is SEN until the child can access English, [we need to] know how to approach that, I don't think we do and there's always that danger that you don't really know if it's about their ability or there about the language.
>
> *(Teacher 2)*

As discussed in Chapter 3 of this volume, sometimes teachers assume bilingual children have special educational needs, perhaps because the teachers have little experience, training or measures to thoroughly assess the children and they make a judgement from children's English language expression. This can have particularly damaging effects on children's psychological functioning and educational outcomes and it is good to see teachers reflecting on this issue and changing their focus. One of the teachers realised that focusing on and 'highlighting this skill that they have, it has really boosted their confidence' (Teacher 2) is more beneficial than focusing on remedial work. One of the headteachers took this reflection further by considering whether it was time to reconsider the curriculum:

> I learned that, first of all, we often don't realise the unique talents these children have. We also are able to see different sides of these children and think about what we teach in school, about our curriculum and how we use experiences like this to ensure those children in particular are more engaged with our curriculum. [...] They're now a group who have been recognised especially for their unique achievements and I think that's something that will ensure that they have great confidence going forward.
>
> *(Headteacher 1)*

While this project was positioned outside of the main curriculum, in a format of after-school classes, it is perhaps high time to start considering how elements of this bilingual literacy model can be adapted for mainstream lessons.

The discourse of disadvantage and deficiency was also challenged when teachers realised that bi/multilingual children could work quickly and efficiently, and make rapid progress with some encouragement and appreciation from those supporting them. One of the teachers exclaimed in surprise: 'They achieved so much in that little time, I think. Just to look at the books! It's amazing what they have managed to do in such a short time!' (Teacher 4), while another emphasised how special these 'cultural offerings' (books) are for the schools: 'it allowed the children to recognise that they created for the school a very special resource, so when the books are published that they will be there in the library forever' (Teacher 3).

Both schools held special assemblies and talked about the project and its outcome in and outside of the classrooms, emphasising its benefits to the children and the schools:

> [The project has given] the opportunity for the children to realise that they are very good writers, who tell very good stories in both languages. I also think it's allowed the children to recognise that they created for the school a very special resource, so when the books are published that they will be there in the library forever. They can appreciate they've been a special part of that. What it does, particularly for those children who arrive, as we often have, not in reception but higher up the school with little or no English, it gives them a way in which they can engage quite quickly with the school community.
>
> *(Headteacher 2)*

## iv. Showcasing literacy learning and literacy skills transfer

The project was open to bilingual learners at different stages of their home/ heritage language development. Some children were already confident speakers of their home languages. Some children could speak their home language well but had difficulty writing it. Some children came from mixed background families (and not all families spoke their heritage languages at home) or were born in the UK and their home/heritage was less developed. The clubs were intended to be inclusive and open to all children who wanted to write a bilingual story.

All children learned more words not only in their home/heritage languages but also in English and other children's languages. They learned how to use language dictionaries and online translators while also utilising the strategy of checking words and spellings with peers, university students and their parents. For instance, a parent whose background was Italian but who did not speak much Italian to her children at home commented:

> My child asked loads of questions. Asked about words she didn't understand in Italian, she would look them up to know them. For me it was nice to sit and write something nice with [name of the child] in my own language. I learned that I didn't know as much Italian as I thought I did. [She] learned some words that she didn't know before.
>
> *(Parent 16)*

Many children observed that their written skills and spelling (home language) improved a lot:

> My spelling had improved. I can write better in Polish with my mum's corrections
> *(Child 20)*

> We don't usually do much writing in Polish at home so it's certainly helped us make the link in sentences in English and in Polish
> *(Parent 17)*

But, equally, the project encouraged the children to work on their English literacy skills:

> It's encouraged my child to actually write in English. We understand that he learns English in school each day however exercises like this are not forced and it's allowed him to use his imagination. I think it's been really good.
> *(Parent 12)*

Some children started seeing similarities between languages. 'I was surprised when I saw I could read and understand some Spanish,' said one Italian-speaking child.

Many discussions were held about language 'families' and how words are 'borrowed' as people travel as well as how various meanings, concepts and ides cannot be transferred literally from one language to another and why. These conversations highlighted to the children the complexity of translations and communication with speakers of other languages and fuelled their curiosity.

## v. Learning about book publishing

All children, and also students, parents and teachers, learned more about the process of writing a book for a publication. They learned how to construct a book, from the inception and ideas generation, through a process of writing, translating, illustrating, editing and proofreading to making final decisions on graphic design, aesthetic appeal as well as all extras such as title and end pages. Children understood the importance of editing and grammar, stylistic and spell check as they strove for the best possible quality of their published books.

For the university team, converting the stories into a digital format and preparing them for publication, whilst dealing with so many different languages, scripts, formats and illustrations was the biggest challenge. Students and staff members helped proofread, correct and format the books and they all learned how challenging and stressful it can be, especially when working to a tight deadline.

Although the team had a dedicated Advertising Design student, her job was very difficult. She spent days and nights scrupulously tracing the outline of each word in each heritage language to preserve children's handwriting in their home languages, and transforming them into vector in order to place them one by one into each book in e-format. As the Advertising Design student spoke English and Romanian it was incredibly difficult for her to deal with every complicated letter in different alphabets (see Figure 4.2, for example) and inevitably there were mistakes made as children's handwriting was often difficult to read and trace with a graphic pen, especially in the languages that the team was unfamiliar with. The team nominated the Advertising Design student, Ioana Stoica, for the Bedfordshire Student Union's outstanding contribution to the community award and they were proud when Ioana won this prestigious prize.

## vi. Enhanced creativity and fun

The project emphasised creativity and co-construction from the outset. The children were encouraged to use their imagination and experiment with different forms. The project lead tried to discourage the traditional teaching of how the story should be constructed and how it should evolve as there are different traditions of story writing in different cultures. In one of the clubs, where the teachers tended to be present, it was observed that the English-speaking teacher tried to impose a typical (Western) way of constructing the story, but it was interesting to observe how children were able to resist it.

All children highlighted that for them being in the Bilingual Creative Writing Club was fun. As Child 8 commented, 'The games made it really fun. It was fun thinking of the story and drawing pictures.'

At the evaluation point, many children said that at the beginning of the club they did not think they could be creative, and they were unsure how they would be able to write, illustrate and publish a book. Many children provided comments such as:

> I thought that I had no imagination and my imagination level was, I don't know 1 or 0, nothing, anything, I thought that I had no imagination literally [...]. The top on my list [of what I learned is] that you can be very creative. [...] To me that means I am becoming an author like Roald Dahl [...] I get more imagination and creativity in my brain.
>
> *(Child 19)*

> Oh, I can be a story teller, I do have something to say!
>
> *(Child 24)*

Some university students also found they had a creative talent when they helped children with illustrations. One commented:

> It was fascinating to see them develop novel stories and translate them into their mother tongue. They were welcoming, open to work with us, asking us for help/ advice (if needed) and enjoying themselves in the process. [It is important] to ensure that children are having fun and associating this cultural-linguistic interaction with an activity that is enjoyable and educative.
>
> *(Student 4)*

In fact, several children found the creative process of designing and illustrating books particularly enjoyable. Some children, especially those who felt they were not as good with words, derived their sense of pride, self-esteem and confidence from the creative work they completed (see Figure 4.4 and Figure 4.5).

## vii. Learning with parents, about parents and their heritage and parents' learning and engagement in the project

> Although the project allowed and encouraged parents' participation and engagement, it was difficult to envisage from the outset what contribution and effect this may have on the outcomes for the children. Initially many parents (especially full-time working parents) welcomed an opportunity for their children to attend this club as they saw it as providing a benefit of free of charge after school weekly sessions for their children. Many parents also felt that it afforded their children an opportunity to practise their home language skills (especially writing). As one parent put it: 'I must say he was delighted because he doesn't attend Polish school or anything like this so the opportunity to write in his native language was simply marvellous
>
> *(Parent 21)*

Bilingual Creative Writing Clubs 71

**FIGURE 4.4** Work in progress – a child proudly sharing her illustrations

**FIGURE 4.5** The final product

Although equal participation and engagement were not possible, it was hoped that, as a minimum, the parents would engage with the project by helping their children in their native languages at home. Many parents indeed got involved and observed how their children's curiosity about the home language and the heritage increased. The children started questioning their parents and extended family members more, and exploring their cultural and linguistic heritage themselves, without any prompts, as one parent explains:

They had an opportunity to work together with other bilingual children and also to see the value of that other culture they've got, not just the language but the other culture because what I have noticed now with him, which I haven't seen or never noticed with my other son who is older is that [name of the child] comes from school and he's written a short story in Bulgarian or he comes back in and he's drawn a picture or something to do with Bulgaria, like a flag, the national anthem something to do with, something I have not noticed with my other son or he would want to take a Bulgarian book to school to show to the other children, I don't know whether he does but he's got like more interest if you like in Bulgarian.

*(Parent 7)*

This was also voiced by one of the student leaders:

Some parents and teachers said that the kids would go home after school and they would start writing stories in their own language. One teacher told me that one of the children would go home and write a story based on his day at school but in his language […] It was a really, really positive impact on the children … increased interest in language skills.

*(Psychology Student 1)*

Many parents who observed their children's increased interest in the family heritage became more engaged in the project and expressed their gratitude for providing them and their children with a platform for home discussions and activities.

### *viii. Strong sense of multilingual community (as a resource)*

Another unexpected outcome of the project was the development of a close bond and camaraderie among bi/multilingual children, and, later, also parents. As one of the university students observed: It allowed the small community of bilingual children in the school in to one room and allowed them to realise that they were not the only person who didn't speak English at home(Psychology Student 1)This was also echoed by parents who were pleased with the emergence of multilingual and multicultural community:I think it's helped them feel better and feel like one community. It doesn't matter from which nationality they are or what language they speak, altogether they are all the same(Parent 3)

Children, parents, teachers and university students strongly emphasised the integration of bilingual children in school and the importance of such initiatives in building a more inclusive environment:

The whole project is a step forward allowing to accept and think about immigration in our society. It's great for the children to be able to share their heritage and language skills and culture. It's allowing other people from different backgrounds also to learn things about us as well.

*(Parent 4)*

## *ix. Voicing children's aspirations*

At the backdrop of the dominant focus on remedial work, it was particularly inspirational to see a marked increase in educational aspirations of all the children involved in this project. They voiced their strong feelings of self-pride and increased confidence, explaining that having a book published boosted their self-esteem and showed them what they are capable of. Several thought of writing sequels and taking part in other school activities (which they would not consider previously due to their perceived inability). Some children said they thought they were not 'good enough' to go to the university in the future but the experience of working with bi/multilingual university students and staff increased both their aspirations and self-belief.

## Conclusion and recommendations

This chapter has discussed the Bilingual Creative Writing Clubs project as an example of a practical attempt to disrupt the discourse of deficiency that often surrounds bi/multilingual children. The pedagogical approach used within this project challenged the dominant focus on remedial work and, instead, provided a platform for the children's voices and talents to be acknowledged and valued. As such it provided all participants with affordances and benefits, beyond what had been imagined at the start of the project.

Everyone involved asserted that there are many advantages of being bi/multilingual and that the other languages and cultures should be cherished, celebrated and invited to the school curriculum (rather than kept outside of its gates).

While the author hopes that the project can provide inspiration to others and generate a discussion about how such approaches can be integrated into mainstream education in the UK and other countries, it does not represent a radically new vision of pedagogy. Just like other projects discussed in Cummins and Early's (2011) seminal book, it is aligned with what other progressive educators (such as John Dewey or Paulo Freire) have advocated for decades. According to Cummins and Early (2011) it emphasises the importance of:

- linking curricula and extracurricular content to learners' experiences and identities;
- fostering critical literacy skills along with critical awareness of how language works and how it is used for different purposes and in different contexts;
- enabling learners to become active agents and creators of knowledge;
- enabling learners to explore, express and expand their identities through various forms of cultural production and reproduction;
- promoting a social consciousness that values equity.

The project evidenced that this kind of approach can enable a transfer of skills from one language to another in a way that not only helps with the acquisition of both languages but also fosters children's curiosity about other languages and cultures and their creative expression. It engaged the bi/multilingual children in more meaningful and inclusive learning (both in the clubs and at home) and facilitated the creation of a strong multilingual and multicultural community. It fostered children's and students' independent learning, creative expression and respectful cohabitation, and enabled a deeper and more meaningful celebration of diversity within schools. It brought to light the unique talents and skills of all participants engaged in the project and enhanced their visibility and appreciation. Temporarily, the dominance of English monolingualism and monoculturalism (for discussion, see Chapter 3) was disrupted, showcasing the equal value of other languages and cultures.

Most importantly, it shifted the perceptions (both self-perception and the perceptions imposed by others) of bi/multilingual children as underachievers and as at educational risk, requiring (mainly) remedial work. Children experienced an increase in their confidence, self-esteem and their sense of inclusion.

Unfortunately, these types of pedagogic interventions are still in many contexts positioned outside the mainstream curricula. However, as Cummins and Early (2011) emphasise, individual educators always have agency, even when they work in conditions that are oppressive to them and their students. Although they will never have complete freedom, they can make choices about how to structure interactions in their classrooms. It was with the hope of sparking the discussion and inspiring educators to include home languages and cultures in their classroom environments that this chapter was written.

## Acknowledgements

The author would like to thank all the children, parents, teachers, and university students and staff members involved in this project – their hard work, dedication and commitment culminated in the creation of a strong partnership, sense of community and wonderful bilingual resources.

Special thanks to Ioana Stoica who supported this project as a volunteer student. She not only supported the clubs' sessions in both schools, working with the children on their story creation weekly, but also she was the only Advertising Design student within the project. Without her commitment and fantastic graphic design skills, the books would have never been transformed into electronic format and published in such a professional manner.

## References

Cummins, J. & Early, M. (2011) *Identity texts: The collaborative creation of power in multilingual schools*. Stoke-on Trent: Trentham Books.

Dakin, J. (2012). 'Writing bilingual stories: Developing children's literacy through home languages'. In D. Mallows (Ed.) *Innovations in English teaching for migrants and refugees*. London: British Council. Available at: http://englishagenda.britishcouncil.org/books-resource-packs/innovations-english-language-teaching-migrants-and-refugees

EERA (European Educational Research Association) (2015). Cultural learning, identity and the European project. Available at: http://www.eera-ecer.de/networks/network20/network-activities/workshop-cultural-learning/

Jackson, N. (2016). *Exploring learning ecologies*. Chalk Mountain. Available at: http://www.normanjackson.co.uk/uploads/1/0/8/4/10842717/lulu_print_file.pdf

Jankowska, M., Coleman, S., Rainford, J., Stoica, I., Pac, A., Christian, A., Syngouna, M. Tsoukala, A., Adewuyi, A., & Barker, D. (2016). 'Bilingual Creative Writing Clubs: An ecology for cross-cultural learning'. *Lifewide Magazine*, 17, 86–92.

Krashen, S. & McField, G. (2005). 'What works? Reviewing the latest evidence on bilingual education'. *Language Learner*, 1(2), 7–10, 34.

Macnab, N., Clay, R., & Grosvenor, I. (2011). Cultural learning: From pedagogy to knowledge exchange. Project report. Available at: https://dl.dropboxusercontent.com/u/16522669/Cultural%20Learning%20April%202011.pdf

Murphy, V. (2015). A systematic review of intervention research examining English language and literacy development in children with English as an Additional Language (EAL). Oxford: University of Oxford, Education Endowment Foundation/Bell Foundation.

Myers, K. & Grosvenor, I. (2014). 'Cultural learning and historical memory: A research agenda'. *Encounters on Education*, 15, 3–21. DOI: doi:10.15572/ENCO2014.01

Nag, S., Chiat, S., Torgerson, C., & Snowling, M. J. (2014). Literacy, foundation learning and assessment in developing countries: Final report. London: EPPI-Centre, Social Science Research Unit, University of London.

Naqvi, R. (2008). Opening doors to literacy in Canada's multicultural classrooms: An introduction to dual language books research and the database project. www.rahatnaqvi.ca/files/poster.pdf

Safford, K. & Drury, R. (2013). 'The "problem" of bilingual children in educational settings: Policy and research in England'. *Language and Education*, 27(1), 70–81, DOI: doi:10.1080/09500782.2012.685177

# 5

# LISTENING TO THE VOICES OF INDIGENOUS MĀORI STUDENTS OVER TIME

## What do they tell us about national education policy?

*Professor Mere Berryman and Elizabeth Eley*

### Introduction

In this chapter, we investigate how, over the past decade, indigenous, Māori secondary school learners in *Aotearoa*, New Zealand have begun to experience and understand the central tenet of the Ministry of Education's (MoE's) Māori education policy, 'Māori students enjoying and achieving education success as Māori' (MoE, 2008, 2013). We discuss two studies, the first of which is quantitative, and took place between 2009 and 2013 in 16 secondary schools that were in their fourth year of engagement in Phase 5 of *Te Kotahitanga* (unity of purpose), a government-funded, iterative research and teacher professional development project (Alton-Lee, 2015). A comparison across the country of the results of national examinations shows that, when the conditions are right, Māori students achieve educational success on a par with non-Māori students. Indeed, in pockets, Māori students begin to show the importance of enjoying these educational achievements, *as Māori*. The second study comprises a qualitative look, taken in 2015, at the experiences of senior Māori students (16 to 18 years) describing what 'achieving and enjoying education success as Māori' means to them. These students come from *Kia Eke Panuku* (Building From), a reform initiative that built from *Te Kotahitanga*. These voices tell us what belonging and achieving, while simultaneously being culturally located, can look like from the perspective of the students themselves.

We first set the colonial context for an education system that has continued to perpetuate disparities for Māori, and go on to outline policies that were designed to address them. We then present the two studies described above to understand the sense Māori students were making of these events. These studies move iteratively from schools and classrooms to the education system itself. Through

Māori students' experiences of secondary schooling and their achievement results on national qualifications, we use an iterative process of building on learning from one study to the next. The current authors have been insiders in these studies as Ministry officials, as parents and grandparents, and as researchers.

Study 1 draws from Phase 5 of *Te Kotahitanga*, which ran from 2009 to 2013. This study will be discussed using evidence from both the national examination results of Māori youth and their schooling experiences. The data for Study 2 were gathered in 2015 in collaboration with Māori students under the mantle of their tribal leaders and whānau (families and extended families). These students shared their experiences of schooling, including their success as Māori. This research utilised a relational, that is a relationship-based, and culturally responsive framework (Berryman, SooHoo & Nevin, 2013), a merging of both *kaupapa* Māori (research based, incorporating the knowledge, skills, attitudes and values of Māori society) and critical theories.

Our conclusion attempts to triangulate our iterative learnings from these two studies. By looking at the possibilities and promise for these young people and for our society as a whole, our youth can lose labels that 'minoritise' or 'marginalise', so that they can indeed stand proud and succeed *as Māori*, without education forcing them to fit into the education system through assimilation.

## The New Zealand context

In New Zealand, the prevailing egalitarian rhetoric has long proclaimed our commitment to social justice. Unfortunately, for many people, particularly members of the tribal groups that comprise the Indigenous Māori people, the reality falls far short of the rhetoric. Māori civilisation and culture were well established when the land was 'discovered' by the British in the late 1700s. A deliberate colonisation of the country occurred and, although this was largely peaceful (in comparison with the British colonisation of other nations within the seventeenth and eighteenth centuries), there were disastrous consequences for Māori (Bishop & Glynn, 1999). A key event in the colonising of New Zealand was the signing of the Treaty of Waitangi by Māori tribal leaders and British Government representatives on behalf of the Crown, in 1840. This Treaty mandated a partnership relationship, establishing British governance and full participation by Māori in all the benefits offered by British rule. Māori were also promised ownership and protection of their land interests and *taonga* (cultural treasures), including their language. However, the sovereignty guaranteed to Māori was increasingly ignored, resulting in dire consequences for Māori cultural, social and economic wellbeing, well into the twenty-first century. More recently there has been a greater focus on the original intention of the Treaty. As a result, as Crown policy the Treaty has begun to shape the bi-cultural relationship between Māori and Pākehā (descendants of the colonists) and influence government policy in contemporary New Zealand society today (Tawhai & Gray-Sharp, 2011).

## Impacts of New Zealand Education system on Māori students

In general, Māori students do not remain in schooling as long as other students nor do they achieve as highly (Office of the Auditor-General, 2012, 2013, 2015, 2016a, 2016b). Despite many initiatives to raise Māori student achievement, English-medium schooling continues to return lower achievement rates for Māori than for non-Māori students (Udahemuka, 2016). In 2015, 62 per cent of Māori students left school with NCEA[1] Level 2 or above compared with 83 per cent of Pākehā (students of European descent) students (MoE, 2016). A significant contributing factor to this is the 'culturally subtractive approach' to education policy that lasted into the 1980s (May, Hill, & Tiakiwai, 2004). The purpose of schooling was seen as assimilating Māori students into Western ways of thinking and succeeding; the retention of the Māori language, culture and values was regarded as a threat inhibiting the process of civilising or maintaining influence over Māori (Barrington, 2008).

Most of the learning of our nation's history has come through the curriculum taught within the schools, the same agency and institutions that perpetuated the misinformation and misconceptions about differences between cultures. The positioning of Western (White) culture and values as superior to the 'native' (Brown) culture has continued for many decades. By the beginning of 1960, publicity about social maladjustment in the cities had focused the government's attention on Māori issues, particularly the 'disproportionate numbers in the Court records' and evidenced by 'their educational achievements (but not their capacity) [being] below par' (Hunn, 1961, p. 98).

The response of the state to this problem of 'social maladjustment' was to look for solutions that the New Zealand Ministry of Education came to acknowledge as 'well-intentioned but disadvantageous actions' (MoE, 2015). Many of these actions pathologised Māori by seeking to address and compensate for perceived deficits within the students and their home culture. Teacher actions were influenced by reports such as the Chapple Report (Chapple, Jeffries, & Walker, 1997). This report concluded that the differences in achievement resulted from Māori socio-economic status rather than ethnicity and 'there was therefore nothing significant about "being Māori" that affected education success'. As a result many teachers adopted a 'blaming' attitude and an abdication of responsibility – providing tacit approval for the poor teaching, micro-aggressions and derogatory comments reported by students. Ten years later, a re-analysis of the Chapple Report data demonstrated that ethnicity is a significant factor in achievement over and above socio-economic status (Harker, 2007).

## System-level response

In response to a growing understanding that a system-level response to Māori under-achievement was required, the Ministry of Education embarked on a series of policy initiatives. The first strategy, launched in 1999, recognised that Māori educational success was a Ministry-wide responsibility. The term 'Ka Hikitia', translated as 'to step up' was adopted for the government's policy: a call for the system to 'step- up' to meet the needs and potential of Māori. In 2006, *Ka Hikitia: Setting Priorities for Māori Education* was published as an internal document within the Ministry of Education, setting out the proposed Māori education priorities for the next five years. In 2008, *Ka Hikitia – Managing for Success: The Māori Education Strategy 2008–2012* (MoE, 2008) was released, a four-year strategy document for the public and mandated policy for schools. A subsequent four-year strategy *Ka Hikitia – Accelerating Success 2013–2017* (MoE, 2013) was released with the vision statement being 'Māori students enjoying and achieving education success as Māori'.

These policy developments reflected the political desire, voiced by Māori youth and supported by Māori leaders, both to own the issue of intergenerational underachievement by Māori students and to mandate the need for schools and the education system to 'step-up' to address the issue. However, despite over 20 years of policies and strategies entitled 'The Māori Education Strategy', there is little evidence of changes inside educational settings, including schools. The effectiveness of Ka Hikitia has been evaluated by the Office of the Auditor General (2012, 2013, 2015, 2016a, 2016b). The Auditor General was reasonably positive regarding the *potential* of the policy: 'Overall, I found reason to be optimistic that Ka Hikitia will increasingly enable Māori students to succeed.' However, the report also states:

> The Ministry of Education (the Ministry) introduced Ka Hikitia slowly and unsteadily. Confused communication about who was intended to deliver Ka Hikitia, unclear roles and responsibilities in the Ministry, poor planning, poor programme and project management, and ineffective communication with schools have meant that action to put Ka Hikitia into effect was not given the intended priority. As a result, the Ministry's introduction of Ka Hikitia has not been as effective as it could have been.
>
> *(Office of the Auditor General, 2013, p. 7)*

## Hui Taumata Mātauranga (education summits)

During this period, Māori attempted to engage proactively in the direction education should take for their youth. Māori *kaumātua* (tribal elders) became increasingly strident in voicing their discontent with an education system where, consistently, their youth neither enjoyed nor achieved education success. At the beginning of this century a series of four Hui Taumata Mātauranga were hosted by Ngāti Tūwharetoa, a central North island *iwi* (tribal group). Education officials and politicians attended the *hui* (meetings run along Māori cultural protocols) and listened as kaumātua, Māori parents and grandparents spoke of their aspirations and hopes for their children though the education system. In November 2001, a Hui Taumata was held focusing on leadership in education and the place of Māori in education authority. Another was held in March 2003 that looked at the quality of teacher education and Māori experiences in the tertiary sector.

The final Hui Taumata Mātauranga was held in September 2004 and centred on the views of Māori youth themselves. From the voices of these young people, the following determinants of success were derived:

- relationships for learning;
- enthusiasm for learning;
- balanced outcomes for learning;
- preparing for the future;
- being Māori.

## Listening to Māori students

Unfolding alongside the Hui Taumata Mātauranga was the development of an iterative research and teacher professional development project that became known as Te Kotahitanga. In 2001, principals, teachers, family members and Year 9 and 10 Māori students (12 to 15 years) from five secondary school communities were asked what, in their experience, would engage Māori students in learning. Māori students, identified as either engaged or non-engaged, spoke in depth about the deficit positioning (the ascription of negative stereotypes to Māori students) they endured in schools and mainstream communities, merely for being Māori (Bishop & Berryman, 2006). When the voices of Māori youth from 2001 were first shared with educators in New Zealand and then later published (Bishop & Berryman, 2006), they were considered groundbreaking. For the first time, educators and policy makers could see and read about the impact of their practices on Māori youth. Thus began a drive by many educators to seek solutions by 'gathering student voice'. Immense care had been undertaken in the 2001 research to develop non-dominating power relations with the research participants. Yet, an unanticipated consequence has been the number of educators gathering students' views, using traditional Western research frameworks that, in themselves, potentially, open up acts of societal oppression. These practices will continue to be problematic if educators do not understand how power plays out in these conversations.

There must always be concern about the kind of research that gives 'little regard to participants' rights to initiate, contribute, critique, or evaluate research' (Berryman *et al.* 2013, p. 1). Berryman *et al.* (2013) go on to say that:

> traditionally, the 'right to-be-studied (or not)' and decisions about how the study would be carried out have not been maintained by the researched community, rather they have been sustained by groups of outsiders who have retained the power to research and to define.
>
> *(p. 1)*

The wide acclaim given to the inclusion of 'student voice' in the early research had opened up the need better to understand how to create contexts for students (and others) to be heard through research methodologies in ways that were participatory and empowering for the students and did not inadvertently perpetuate oppression.

This dilemma is a familiar one for those who seek to understand the experiences of young people, especially those of non-Western cultures, in our education system. For example, Tillman (2002, p. 3) refers to research that allows 'opportunities for collaboration, insider perspectives, reciprocity, and voice'. However, despite this positioning, it is still possible for a caring researcher/educator to sit outside of the experiences of the students, to question or to comment on their experiences and not truly and respectfully hear them or even draw on the knowledge, experience and full contribution of the participants.

## *The views of the students*

In 2001, as Te Kotahitanga was being established, the opinions and perceptions of two groups of students were gathered. One group was those Māori students described as 'engaged' (connected to the educational system and learning programmes of the school), the second those described as non-engaged. The major difference between how the two groups (engaged and non-engaged) responded came in their reactions to the overpowering deficit discourses and negative stereotyping being perpetuated by their teachers and non-Māori peers. Engaged Māori students talked about being prepared to compromise their cultural identity and succumbing to the pressures of assimilation in order to succeed at school. They were forced to leave their culture at home. Non-engaged Māori students talked about actively resisting when they felt they had been wrongly treated but being powerless to do anything other than be removed from learning or remove themselves from learning.

To engage in learning, these students explained that educators needed to provide a relational pedagogy (Bishop & Berryman, 2006; Sidorkin, 2002) in which they could also be self-determining (Young, 2004). Both groups of students consistently argued relationships as being essential and foundational to their engagement with learning. They described positive relationships with teachers as those where they were not talked down to, where power was shared and where teachers were committed to their students' success. They believed that, intrinsic to relational pedagogy, was teachers actively rejecting negative stereotyping and raising students' own expectations to realise their power in the learning space.

## *Culturally responsive pedagogy*

In addition to relational pedagogy, students wanted an approach within which they could construct new learning from their own prior knowledge and cultural experiences. Rather than marginalise their prior knowledge and experiences, or try to impose a transmission model of learning, they wanted to bring their own funds of knowledge to their learning (Moll *et al.*, 1992). These views reflect those of Gay (2010) and (Sleeter, 2011): that altering the power relationships and pedagogies within classrooms can enable the emergence of students' cultural values and frames of reference that can enhance cognitive engagement and subsequent achievement.

## Reciprocal dialogic pedagogy

If students are to bring their own experiences to the learning, through active social engagement with others, it requires *determined* opportunities for dialogue to occur throughout the process. Learners need the chance both to seek advice and ask questions of other students without fear of embarrassment or reprimand. Thus, all of the expertise in the class can be activated instead of relying solely upon the expertise of the teacher.

## Influence of students' voices in Te Kotahitanga

What the researchers learned in 2001 from Māori students' views about what would better engage them in their learning was developed into a framework entitled 'The Effective Teaching Profile' that was used as the basis for teacher professional development in the Te Kotahitanga schools. Each school had a team of facilitators to support the work. This initiative was funded by the New Zealand Ministry of Education over five phases of development, between 2001 and 2013. Over the course of these phases, Maori students increasingly spoke of the power of a more dialogic way of working than they had been accustomed to previously. In schools this brought about dramatic shifts in both the quality of the education experience for Māori youth and their achievement.

## The two studies

Evidence for Study 1 has been collated from policy documents and an official report that compared the government's national outcomes data for Māori students in Phase 5 Te Kotahitanga schools with that of Māori students in non Te Kotahitanga schools across the country. It also draws upon the experiences of Māori students on one of these Phase 5 schools.

Data for Study 2 were gathered in 2015 when, as researchers, we sought to deeply respect the pivotal cultural relationships and positionings of Māori students and whānau. We deliberately created a 'research stance where establishing respectful relationships with participants was central to both human dignity and the research' (Berryman & Eley, 2017, p. 1). And, out of respect that all participants identified as Māori, there was an explicit attendance to the notion of 'situated cultural practice' (see, for example, Goodnow, 2002; Lee, 2007; Rogoff, 2003; Rosaldo, 1993). This notion proposes that 'what drives research, its purposes and uses, how meaning is made during the implementation of research practices, and the knowledge and representations that are produced are culturally and socially mediated and negotiated processes' (Arzubiaga, Artiles, King, & Harris-Murri, 2008, p. 310). We wanted to understand how Ka Hikitia was understood and the subsequent implications for Māori students and their teachers.

## Study 1: Māori students in Te Kotahitanga Phase 5

In Te Kotahitanga Phase 5, the final iterative learning from previous phases suggested that the approach in the project should be far more critical and responsive to the schools' leaders and the range of evidence emerging in each one. This was far less of a programme to be implemented across the cohort and more an individual, school-leader by school-leader, evidence-driven, critical response. Rather than each school having a team of facilitators leading the programme, the principal, together with teachers across the multiple levels of the school, formed a Strategic Change Leadership team to operationalise what was understood as most effective from all the previous phases. In Phase 5, leading critically and with moral purpose was central to the implementation (Berryman, Egan & Ford, 2017).

At the end of three years, believing the modifications had resulted in accelerated shifts in Māori student performance in most of the schools, the Chief Education Adviser to the Ministry of Education was asked to undertake an external evaluation of what had been achieved (Alton-Lee, 2015). The group of schools that took part in Te Kotahitanga were largely the schools with either the greatest percentage of Māori students or the greatest number of Māori students, or both.

Alton-Lee's evaluation of the first three years of Te Kotahitanga, Phase 5 (2010 to 2012), compared NCEA results for Māori students in Phase 5 schools (with a mean decile rating of 3) with results for Māori students in a group of national schools that had never participated in Te Kotahitanga. Overall, despite starting at lower levels of achievement on NCEA levels 1 to 3, students in Phase 5 schools improved at three times the rate than those in the comparison schools. By 2012, despite their schools being in the lower decile, Year 12 students' NCEA Level 2 results were on a par with Year 12 Māori students from across all deciles. Furthermore, in Phase 5 schools, retention of students to higher levels was also improved with the proportion of 17-year-olds[2] having increased at twice the rate of Māori students nationally. Māori students in Phase 5 schools, returning or enrolling to year 13, had also increased markedly with year 13 students achieving NCEA Level 3 at almost three times the rate than was achieved in Phase 5 schools at the start of Te Kotahitanga.

Alton-Lee's (2015) report also shows how the voices of Māori students, teachers and school leaders had changed. They showed a greater sense of self efficacy, were positive about being Māori and hopeful for the future. The launch of this report was held at a boys' secondary school. In many respects these institutions in New Zealand maintain many of the appearances and traditions of the colonial heritage. At this gathering were some year 12 and 13 students, family members, teachers, the principal and members of the Board of Trustees, local iwi, Ministry of Education officials, academics and other members of educational initiatives seeking to reform education for Māori. The procedures were formally opened by Māori elders with a Māori cultural welcome that concluded with student-led *waiata* (song). The principal then stood and shared graphs of the year-on-year, NCEA Level 1 to 3 improvements since 2010 for Māori students in this school. His evidence compared the national 2014 NCEA data with the data for Māori students in this decile 4 school. It showed Māori students here were consistently achieving above the national average. The principal then introduced the first of three Māori students, saying that he had asked them to talk about their experiences at this school since year 9. He suggested that his graphs meant little if the students' quality of schooling experiences had not also improved. He explained that the boys had not been coached for their speech and, like us, he would be hearing their experiences for the first time.

The first student shook his principal's hand then moved to the podium to introduce himself confidently and competently in *te reo Māori* (the Māori language). Following this, in English, he located his story in the history of his tribal leaders' migration from Hawaiki to Aotearoa (in legend, Hawaiki is the original home of the Māori people; Aotearoa is the name Māori gave to New Zealand – a name that was changed with colonisation). The student described the voyage as one that was based on aspirations for a better future. He talked about the stars that had guided them and the trials his ancestors had encountered on this journey; how collectively they had overcome much adversity to arrive, settle, and successfully adapt to this new land from which his iwi had flourished and he had grown.

> So, I only find it appropriate to liken this voyage to my journey here at [name of the school]. For the four, soon to be five years, of my high school career, I too have been in search of an island. I have yet to gain insight into what this island holds for me, however it is said to be named 'The Island of Excellence' and floats upon 'The Sea of Mediocrity'. Every lesson learned and every piece of knowledge stored, or skill mastered has blown stronger winds beneath my sails; edging me closer and closer towards my oasis.

Like all compelling story tellers, he then began to make connections, to his own schooling and to his stars, his teachers and family members who had guided him throughout his time in this school to overcome the challenges and to flourish to be the man he is today and will be in the future.

> We are all aiming for that 'Island of Excellence'. Keep an eye out to the horizon, for our voyage has just begun. Let your sails down, believe in yourself, stay persistent, and keep moving forward.

Te Kotahitanga Phase 5 external support finished officially at the end of 2013. However, in 2016 this school won a national Prime Minister's Atakura Award for Excellence in Leading – which is one of the annual Education Excellence Awards that recognises outstanding achievements in government schools in New Zealand. While others are still struggling to adapt to the contemporary fabric of New Zealand society, here is a school that has been weaving new patterns of creative Māori potential (Royal, 2005) and, to judge by its successes to date, will be into the future.

## *Study 2: Māori students enjoying education success as Māori*

In Study 2, we gathered personal perceptions from Māori students from schools participating in 'Kia Eke Panuku: Building on Success' (Berryman & Eley, 2017), a secondary school reform initiative, funded by the New Zealand Ministry of Education that was implemented in 93 secondary schools (approximately one third of all secondary schools[3]). In the context of the Ka Hikitia educational policy, schools are required to ensure that Māori students enjoy and achieve educational success as Māori. We believed by their schools' willingness to participate in Kia Eke Panuku, young people would be attending schools that had demonstrated a commitment to making a difference for Māori students. However, we found a great deal of confusion and uncertainty about how to interpret, let alone implement, the mandated policy.

To gain understandings and provide some guidance for other school communities, we sought input from over 150 senior Māori youth from 58 Kia Eke Panuku secondary schools. We were not aiming for a definitive definition of the phrase 'Māori students enjoying and achieving education success as Māori', but rather wanted to produce a set of ideas as starting points for ongoing reflection and sense-making by school communities[4]. To ensure a respectful, agency-enhancing research stance, set in a cultural context that privileged Māori ways of working, the researchers hosted students in a series of nine *hui* (meeting/s run following Māori cultural procedures) on *marae* (iwi cultural spaces) across New Zealand. We did not directly select the student participants, but asked schools to invite up to three senior Māori students to participate. Prior to the hui, schools received the following questions and identified Māori students who had an opportunity to think and talk about the questions with their peers, their families or other people. The questions were:

- What have been your successes in this school?
- Who has helped you with this success?
- In your experience, what does 'Māori students enjoying and achieving education success as Māori' mean?

At each hui, questions were posed by their accompanying adult (from their school). The responses were often in the form of conversations between the students as they interacted with each other and built on previous responses. They frequently referred to speaking on behalf of others who were not present but speaking with their permission and their blessing. Their accompanying adults did not join in these conversations but listened respectfully.

We observed many school leaders being emotionally moved by the powerful stories told by their young people, who fearlessly took us all to task for injustices and inequities perceived within education and, in equal measure, praised and endorsed the steps taken to redress those injustices. Māori youth frequently reported that across schools, and during the course of Kia Eke Panuku, there had been a repositioning of how their own culture could be more equitably recognised and developed by some of their teachers. Some of the students saw in the actions of these teachers something more than cultural appropriation of knowledge and skills, but rather a response to them as individuals, as culturally located learners.

> We have teachers who have come from England and from other countries who have no te reo Māori (Māori language). They learn te reo Māori and try to understand it. I can help them. That's important for me because it shows that they have motivation, they have a passion to understand students at a deeper level. It shows me that they take into consideration my culture and who I am as a person, as a Māori person. It shows that they appreciate that as well. There's a huge drive on excellence, but there's also a huge drive on keeping your culture, keeping your culture alive … making it known to you and to everybody else that you are Māori and you're proud to be Māori. And yeah, I think that's an important thing you need to have whilst going through education, you need to have that bit of culture just to bring it all back home.

For some, the school environment had become an opportunity to recover what had been taken through generations of colonisation and separation from tribal homelands and family connections. For others there were receptive, non-Māori taking steps to acquire the knowledge, skills and experiences they needed to understand the circumstances and world-view of their students:

> I was fortunate enough to be able to share my culture with the teachers and teach them a little bit of te reo Māori, and it was really cool to see how they were responsive to what I was trying to teach them.
>
> This year has been really good, with teachers stepping up and including Māori culture in what we learn in class. It's been really good. And so, for me, that's what I think is Māori success, being able to have that connection in your subjects to really get the proper understanding that you need.

Students were moved to take direct and collective action where they saw Māori students being under-served:

> My culture's very important to me, so if they're not offering it at our school, if they're not giving students the opportunity then I'm going to fight for that, and I'm not going to let that go away. So, I talked to the principal, talked to teachers and nothing was happening with te reo. I wanted to know why, so I ended up going on to the wider community … and I ended up going on to TV 'cause the community actually were concerned that there wasn't any reo in our school, and so I pushed for that … and now Māori will be offered next year at school, because it's something they deserve to learn, and if it's not being offered, and it's not fair.

Encouragingly, others celebrated their new-found personal agency and defined this in terms of Māori values and practices.

> From a Māori perspective, it's about manaakitanga (building the respect of others), whakawhanaungatanga (making connections as family), tautetanga (supporting others who rely on you), all those things, and āwhina (care). At my school now the teachers tell us, mahi ngā tahi – work as one. And definitely I do ... working in pairs, or in groups. So, the teachers aided me with not working alone ... to put myself out there towards others. And, you know, kaua kei whakamaa: do not be shy. Just work together.

## 'Success as Māori' as described by Māori students

Despite each hui being totally independent of the others, there was remarkably high consistency of experiences across the nine hui. Across all groups, common experiences and understandings were shared. The following ten themes emerged:

- Being able to resist the negative stereotypes about being Māori.
- Having Māori culture and values celebrated at school.
- Being strong in your Māori cultural identity.
- Understanding that success is part of who we are.
- Developing and maintaining emotional and spiritual strength.
- Being able to contribute to the success of others.
- Experiencing the power of *whanaungatanga* (family-like relationships).
- Knowing, accepting and acknowledging the strength of working together.
- Knowing that you can access explicit and timely direction.
- Being able to build on your own experiences and the experiences of others.

These themes were understood as strongly inter-related. For example, the strongest message from these students was that to be successful as Māori within the school system, they had to be able to resist and overcome other people's low expectations and negative stereotypes about them being Māori. Many articulated this as an area where adults and non-Māori could and should be supporting them. Māori students clearly understood that their success required more than their own personal strengths, achievements, values and connections. Some directly attributed their success to the support they had received from a school environment where their own culture and values were explicitly celebrated, modelled and thus valued by others. This was essential to being able to be *strong as Māori*, rather than believing they had to compromise their own cultural identity by trying *to pass* as someone else. Understanding that success was a part of who they were and what other Māori were, or could be, required their being emotionally and spiritually strong. Māori youth understood that at times this had not been the case for them, nor was it the case for many of their peers, friends or whānau, some who had resorted to suicide.

Many talked about being the first of their family to attain success, whether it was cultural success, in the arts, languages, academic and/or sporting success and whether it was at a school, regional, national or international setting. Many talked about their success across a number of these indicators and across the range of these settings. Some talked about not having seen themselves as successful until fairly recently. Across all of the groups, students clearly articulated that their personal success was fully intertwined with their contribution to the success of others. Being able to relate to others in a *whanaungatanga* or familial way meant that they understood and took strength from working together. They understood that by working together, they would be more able to do things on their own in the future. They all talked about benefitting from being provided with timely and explicit guidance and direction, which had helped them to build upon their own experiences but also the experiences of others.

## Bringing the voices together

What Māori students told us in 2001 would engage them with learning, together with what we had learned working iteratively over five phases of Te Kotahitanga, by 2012 in Study 1, had proven sufficiently strong to raise Māori students' achievement levels on national qualifications significantly and make schools places where it was safe to be Māori (Alton-Lee, 2015).

By 2015, the voices of Māori youth in Study 2 agreed, they shared their ongoing need to overcome negative stereotyping around their potential to be strong in their own cultural identity and to be able to access support from the adults in the school who were culturally aware and responsive to their needs. They also identified the need for personal strength and resilience – the need to develop strong conceptions of themselves as successful, to have the emotional and spiritual strength to see them through adverse contexts, and to know and understand the extent of *whanaungatanga* (strong and supportive ties to other Māori in their schools and communities). Our successful Māori students felt that luck had also played a part in their success; there were times when they could have fallen away and abandoned their education due to the weight of the pressures and the negative factors impacting on them. They knew that this had been the case for many of their peers and, in many cases, their family members. While they could celebrate personal successes, they still longed for transformative change within their schools to make a difference for all Māori.

## Conclusion

In 2001, Māori students spoke of the challenges deficit positioning made to their schooling (Bishop & Berryman, 2006). Many Māori students were not only marginalised within their classrooms but often were undermined, put-down and had their potential ignored. At the Hui Taumata in 2004, Māori youth took their messages to the educational decision-makers and policy-setters. By 2012, Phase 5 Te Kotahitanga schools were beginning to be a more positive place for Māori students, and, while the gap between Māori and non-Māori student achievement remained, there were some indications that the gap in these schools was no longer irrefutable. By 2015, now supported by over a decade of research and Māori Education strategies to address disparities and support equitable outcomes for all students, many of the Māori youth in Study 2 had achieved education success without having to compromise their cultural identity. However, they were still challenged by the prevailing rhetoric which suggested that while the problem was 'in hand', many Māori students were still not doing well in the system and were, somehow, personally to blame.

We have learnt of the courage and determination of these young people to influence school experience for future generations, knowing that they may not experience this change themselves but that they could make it better for those who follow them. These young people have become the agents of change, despite all the factors that worked against them, including their youth, their race, and the conditions of oppression under which they have had to operate. With the best of intentions, we perpetuate the status quo when we sit as the lone authority on what is best for students. However, when we draw on the knowledge and experiences of our young people, and honour the self-determination and activism that they bring, the very change we are seeking begins to emerge. When the students' experiences are set within the less-visible framework of government policy – a story of good intentions and lofty rhetoric emerges; sadly, it also tells a story of promise and potential that has languished and still continues to fall short. The young people told us of their own responsibility to support the students following them so that they will feel a sense of belonging in education. They have told us that when education builds from a foundation of relationships that respect them and who they are, when their own cultural experiences, in dialogue with others, are able to contribute to the construction of new knowledge, then we can determine our future together and we will all be in good hands.

If Māori youth truly are to be self-determining then those who hold the power to reform the contexts of education must be prepared to listen and learn from them. Within these contexts a new, ongoing and consistent story of Māori self-determination has emerged, which needs to influence not only teachers and leaders in schools but also the political contexts in which education still continues to marginalise Māori youth. Importantly this also has implications for many other diverse groups of youth across the world. By sharing power with students, by listening to them and seeking to follow their advice, we have learned that educators, researchers and policy makers are more likely to promote contexts through which the voiceless have voice, the powerless have power and from such spaces hope can emerge (Freire, 1994).

## Notes

1 National Certificate of Educational Achievement (NCEA) is the official secondary school qualification in New Zealand. Level 2 examinations are generally taken at age 17.
2 Schooling in New Zealand is compulsory to age 16.
3 The views expressed in this chapter are those of the authors, and not necessarily of the Ministry.
4 Fuller details of the process followed and discussions undertaken can be found on the Poutama Pounamu website: https://poutamapounamu.org.nz/student-voice

## References

Alton-Lee, A. (2015). *Ka Hikitia demonstration report: Effectiveness of Te Kotahitanga Phase 5 2010–12*. Wellington: Ministry of Education.

Arzubiaga, A. E., Artiles, A. J., King, K. A., & Harris-Murri, N. (2008). Beyond research on cultural minorities: Challenges and implications of research as situated cultural practice. *Exceptional Children, 74*(3), 309–327.

Barrington, J. (2008). *Separate but equal? Māori schools and the crown 1867–1969*. Wellington: Victoria University Press.

Berryman, M., & Eley, E. (2017). Succeeding as Māori: Māori students' views on our stepping up to the Ka Hikitia challenge. *New Zealand Journal of Education Studies*, 1–15. doi: doi:10.1007/s40841-017-0076-1

Berryman, M. A. P., Egan, M., & Ford, T.( 2017)Examining the potential of critical and Kaupapa Māori approaches to leading education reform in New Zealand's English-medium secondary schools. *International Journal of Leadership in Education, 20*(5), 525–538.

Berryman, M., SooHoo, S., & Nevin, A. (2013). *Culturally responsive methodologies*. Bingley, UK: Emerald Group Publishing Ltd.

Bishop, R., & Berryman, M. (2006). *Culture speaks: Cultural relationships and classroom learning*. Wellington: Huia Publishers.

Bishop, R., & Glynn, T. (1999). Researching in Māori contexts: An interpretation of participatory consciousness. *Journal of Intercultural Studies, 20*(2), 167–182.

Chapple, S., Jeffries, R., & Walker, R. (1997). *Māori participation and performance in education: A literature review and research programme*. Report for the Ministry of Education. Wellington: NZIER.

Freire, P. (1994). *Pedagogy of hope: Reliving pedagogy of the oppressed*. London: Continuum Publishing.

Gay, G. (2010). *Culturally responsive teaching: Theory, research, and practice*. New York: Teachers College Press.

Goodnow, J. J. (2002). Adding culture to studies of development: Towards changes in theory and practice. *Human Development, 45*, 629–639.

Harker, R. (2007). *Ethnicity and school achievement in New Zealand: Some data to supplement the Biddulph et al. (2003) Best Evidence Synthesis: Secondary analysis of the Progress at School and Smithfield datasets for the iterative Best Evidence Synthesis*. Wellington: Ministry of Education.

Hunn, J. K. (1961). *Report on the Department of Māori Affairs: with statistical supplement*. Public Service Commission. Wellington, New Zealand: Government Printer.

Lee, C. D. (2007). *Culture, literacy and learning: Taking bloom in the midst of the whirlwind*. New York: Teachers College Press.

May, S., Hill, R., & Tiakiwai, S. (2004). *Bilingual/Immersion education: Indicators of good practice*. Final report to the Ministry of Education. Wellington: Ministry of Education.

MoE (Ministry of Education). (2008). Ka Hikitia – Managing for success: The Māori education strategy 2008–2012. Wellington: Crown/Ministry of Education.
MoE (Ministry of Education). (2013). Ka Hikitia – Accelerating success 2013–2017. Wellington: Crown/Ministry of Education.
MoE (Ministry of Education). (2015, 24 August). The Māori Education Strategy Ka Hikitia. Retrieved from Ministry of Education: http://www.education.govt.nz/ministry-of-education/overall-strategies-and-policies/the-Māori-education-strategy-ka-hikitia-accelerating-success-20132017/strategy-overview
MoE (Ministry of Education). (2016). School leaver attainment. Retrieved 16 July 2016, from Education Counts: http://www.educationcounts.govt.nz/statistics/schooling/senior-student-attainment/school-leavers2/ncea-level-2-or-above-numbers
Moll, L.Amanti, C., Neff, D., & Gonzalez, N. (1992) Funds of knowledge for teaching: Using a qualitative approach to connect homes and classrooms. *Theory into Practice*, 21(2), 132–141.
Office of the Auditor-General. (2012). Education for Māori: Context for our proposed audit work until 2017. Wellington: Office of the Auditor General.
Office of the Auditor-General. (2013). Education for Māori: Implementing Ka Hikitia – Managing for Success. Wellington: Office of the Auditor General.
Office of the Auditor-General. (2015). Education for Māori: Relationships between schools and whanau. Wellington: Office of the Auditor General.
Office of the Auditor General. (2016a). Summary of our Education for Māori reports summary. Wellington: Office of the Auditor General.
Office of the Auditor-General. (2016b). Education for Māori: Using information to improve Māori educational success. Wellington: Office of the Auditor General.
Rogoff, B. (2003). *The cultural nature of human development*. New York: Oxford University Press.
Rosaldo, R. (1993). *Culture and truth: The remaking of social analysis*. Boston, MA: Beacon Press.
Royal, C. (2005) 'Exploring Indigenous Knowledge', The Indigenous Knowledges Conference – Reconciling Academic Priorities with Indigenous Realities, Victoria University, Wellington, New Zealand, 25 June 2005.
Sidorkin, A. M. (2002). *Learning relations: Impure education, deschooled schools, and dialogue with evil*. New York: Peter Lang Publishing.
Sleeter, C. E. (2011). The quest for social justice in the education of minoritized students. In C. E. Sleeter, *Professional development for culturally responsive and relationship-based pedagogy* (pp. 1–22). New York: Peter Lang Publishing.
Tawhai, V., & Gray-Sharp, K. (2011). *'Always speaking': The Treaty of Waitangi and public policy*. Wellington: Huia Publishers.
Tillman, L. C. (2002). Culturally sensitive research approaches: An African-american perspective. *Educational Researcher*, 31(9), 3–12.
Udahemuka, M. (2016). *Signal loss: What we know about school performance*. Wellington: The New Zealand Initiative.
Young, I. M. (2004). Two concepts of self-determination. In S. May, T. Moodod, & J. Squires, *Ethnicity, nationalism and minority rights* (pp. 176–197). Cambridge: Cambridge University Press.

# 6

# STUDENTS' AND A TEACHER'S VIEWS OF FACTORS CONTRIBUTING TO POSITIVE LITERACY LEARNING IDENTITIES FOR ALL STUDENTS IN AN INCLUSIVE CLASSROOM

*Professor Janice Wearmouth*

### Introduction

A special quality of the human environment is that it is suffused with the achievements of prior generations in reified form – that is, language, signs, symbols, physical tools, and so on. Among these is writing, which is an important part of the cultural toolkit needed by all students in order to become fully functioning and participating members of their own society in later life (Bruner, 1996). If they fail to learn to write competently at school, they can, potentially, be disadvantaged throughout their lives. Students' identities as writers 'provide the context in which all the learning [about writing] that might be significant actually becomes significant' (Wearmouth & Berryman, 2009). From this view, what students think of themselves as writers, what they think they are good (or, conversely, bad) at, what they think they can (or cannot) do and what they believe others think of their writing abilities (Tatum, 1997; Sarup, 1996) make learning about writing both possible and important for some students but create a barrier to such learning for others.

The current study is conceptualised within a social constructivist view of mind (Vygotsky, 1978), an approach that is pertinent to claims that pedagogies for school literacy learning should be responsive to the strengths and needs of its students and the frames of reference they bring to their school learning. The distinctiveness of this view, sometimes called 'cultural-historical psychology', is that there is an intimate connection between the learning environment and the distinguishing qualities of human psychological processes. This profoundly social explanation of human psychology is underpinned by an assumption that the special mental quality of human beings is their ability to

- mediate their actions through the psychological tools of language, signs, symbols, tools, and so on (Wertsch, 1985) or, as Cole (1996) terms them, 'artefacts', and

- enable rediscovery and appropriation of these forms of mediation by subsequent generations.

As Dewey (1938/63, p. 39), over half a century ago, commented: 'we live from birth to death in a world of persons and things which is in large measure what it is because of what has been done and transmitted from previous human activities'. Dewey's emphasis on 'personal growth' has been hugely influential in the teaching of writing for almost 100 years; his emphasis on the 'experiential' has led to generations of teachers using a growth pedagogy model to facilitate the personal and expressive writing of children as fundamental to their identity formation (Goodwyn, 2016). From this perspective everything in the learning environment in schools is seen as fundamental to learning: materials, interactions between teacher and students, interactions student to student, student interactions with the learning task, the way success and failure is mediated, and so on. The underpinning of pedagogy with a socio-cultural perspective on the learning process therefore has a particular rationale. It enables acknowledgement of the learner's social situatedness in literacy learning in school (Kozulin, 2003), whilst at the same time focusing attention on the social practices that characterise the settings in which young people's literacy learning in schools is acquired. It also forces a focus on the agency of the teacher as a mediator of learning who needs to adopt a responsive approach to young people's literacy learning by recognising and responding to the frameworks for literacy learning brought into the school by students (Glynn, Wearmouth & Berryman, 2006; Wearmouth, 2017), and also have a high degree of relevant literacy specialist and pedagogical knowledge to support students' appropriation of skills and the construction of literacy-related knowledge.

## Learning process

Vygotsky (1978, p. 57) proposed that there are two planes where the learning process takes place:

- the interpersonal, that is the ' between the people' plane, and the
- intrapersonal, within the individual, as s/he thinks about and reflects on new concepts and learning and appropriates psychological tools, skills and knowledge.

A learner 'takes up and makes use of' (Newman, Griffin & Cole, 1989, p. 15) literacy, language and other tools available in society through the process of 'appropriation' (Leont'ev, 1981; Wertsch, 1991). Outward 'interpsychological' relations become the inner, 'intrapsychological' functions, and through this process of appropriation, the learner develops ways of thinking that are the norm in specific cultural practices such as that associated with literacy. Symbolic systems, for example language and literacy that are legitimated within a child's cultures, are remodelled into individual verbal thought. Hence the very well-known quote:

'Each function in the child's cultural development appears twice: first on the social level, and later on the individual level; first between people (interpsychological), and then inside the child (intrapsychological)' (Vygotsky, 1978, p. 57).

From this perspective, personal identity as a literacy learner in the classroom is associated with:

- the kinds of literacy activities that students experience and in which they engage or are prevented from engaging;
- the process of scaffolding of new literacy learning by more expert others such as teachers and peers; and
- the messages that students hear or see about themselves and their literacy achievements, or failures to achieve.

Both cognitive development, in particular language and literacy, and social development are seen as mutually facilitative and inseparable (Glynn et al., 2006) and depend on the presence of mediators during interactions between the individual and the environment. The agents of mediation can be human or symbolic (Kozulin, 2003, pp. 18–19). In schools, teachers-as-mediators can guide, model, and so on the use of symbolic cultural tools, as, for example, language and literacy. Once a student has acquired a measure of competence in literacy, literacy skills themselves mediate cognitive development. Literacy is thus both the product of 'mediated' activity and agent of mediating cognitive development. In schools, students expand their understanding and use of different kinds of text and literacy tools through observing mediators model written language structure and usage, and also by participating in learning conversations on the interpersonal plane, as is illustrated in the discussion of the case study below.

## The current study

The research study discussed in this chapter was carried out in the classroom of a New Zealand primary teacher who had been formally identified by a national body of teachers as having excellent practice in supporting literacy acquisition. The aim of this study was to examine students' identities as literacy learners within the context of her pedagogy and the learning environment of her classroom. In particular the intention was to compare high and low literacy achievers' identities as writers and to identify whether there are any implications for ways in which the overall level of literacy achievement among low achievers might be raised.

## Research design and methods

The research was designed to elicit information about the positioning of literacy learners and how they are 'fixed' into their status as high- or low-achieving writers through:

- the teacher's assumptions about the potential attainment of the different students in the area of literacy, especially writing, and their expressed expectations of success and/or non-achievement;
- models of learning and teaching underpinning literacy pedagogies in the classroom;
- the nature of messages conveyed to students about themselves as writers;
- the kinds of support given to students for active participation in writing activities;
- students' experiences of who they are as writers.

Classroom data were gathered in a primary school classroom in a city on the North Island of New Zealand. (The term 'student' is used as synonymous with 'pupil' in this chapter, as more commonly used in the New Zealand context.)

The research participants comprised the class teacher (female), and her class of 28, mixed gender, 12- to 13-year-olds with a focus on two groups of students. The two groups were identified as high or low literacy achievers by the teacher based on mid-year reporting and literacy assessments. There were four students in the higher achiever and three in the lower achiever group, and both groups were of mixed gender, ability and ethnicity.

Data collection was carried out through:

- an interview with the teacher. There were two strands to this: first, discussion of the current writing curriculum and associated pedagogies; and, second, views about difficulties in writing acquisition, and what the students concerned could or could not do, together with explanations of achievement and non-achievement;
- photographs of the classroom environment to see how different identities as writers were encouraged, or suppressed, in the learning context;
- in-class observations over two days as a context for the literacy curriculum that the students experienced;
- interviews with the students about perceptions of themselves as writers (their 'take' on things), and what helped or hindered their achievement in literacy tasks in the classroom.

The interviews used a method entitled 'Talking Stones', a pedagogic tool that addresses the challenge of engaging with a student's perspective meaningfully. This is a powerful projective technique derived from techniques related to Personal Construct Psychology and developed from Crosby's therapeutic work with adults (Crosby, 1993). In serving as a sensitive device to support student self-advocacy it views learners as active agents in their own learning. During an individual interview, students were given a pile of stones of varying shapes, sizes, colours and textures and encouraged to explore their thoughts and feelings about literacy learning in school and themselves in relation to it by projection onto these stones. The individual chose one from the pile to represent him/herself in school and discussed his/her choice. S/he then selected more stones to represent reading and writing at school and at home, described why the stones had been chosen, and then placed them on a large, rectangular, light-coloured cloth whose edges set a boundary to the positioning of the stones and their distance from each other. Stones, their attributes and their positions in relation to each other were then interpreted by the student as representing his/her individually constructed meanings (see Figure 6.1).

A thematic analysis of all data was undertaken by the researchers who had carried out the fieldwork. Participants' words are quoted verbatim below.

## *Ethical considerations*

Permissions were sought for classroom observations and interviews with students from the parents/families/carers of *all* students in the classes to be observed. Consent was sought from the teacher and the head teacher for the in-class observations, and for all interviews. Students and the teacher were informed of their right to withdraw from the interviews at any stage. No indication was given to any of the students, or to their parents, of the status attributed to them by the teacher as high or low literacy learners. Every attempt was made to ensure that all students in the classroom were treated with similar levels of attention and respect by the researchers. Pseudonyms have been used to refer to individual students in order to maintain anonymity.

**FIGURE 6.1** Examples of the 'Talking Stones'

## Findings

Thematic analyses of the interview with the teacher, of photographs of the classroom environment, of classroom observations and interviews with the students were carried out and the outcomes were combined. The following main themes emerged.

### Teacher interview

Themes from the teacher interview included:

- her personal determination to support all students to become successful writers and sense of the importance of regular opportunities for students to express themselves freely in writing;
- the importance of scaffolding, and mediating new literacy learning from a very informed position.

### Determination that all students should experience success as writers

Right from the very beginning of the year the teacher encouraged her students to see themselves as writers and communicate what they wanted to say freely. She said:

> I say just write for me. Just write, I'll learn to decipher, I'll get you to tell me if I don't understand it. Just write. Because I'd rather I had them all writing, rather than worrying about their spelling, and that getting in the way at the beginning.

The researchers observed activities designed to offer regular opportunities for students to express themselves freely in writing. These included writing very short 50-word stories:

> earlier in the year […] we'd done much more structured writing. We'd looked at report writing and we'd looked at persuasive writing and […] I felt that in preparing the students leading up to our production later this term, we wanted to give the students an opportunity to write a little bit more freely. So we returned to poetic writing and we thought that the 50-word writing offered the students an opportunity to get underway and write without restriction except for the 50 words and it was basically some writing mileage. And we also thought that probably everybody would be successful at doing it. It would be an opportunity, and we'd use it as a lead in to writing about poetry.

Asked how the students had responded to the 50-word writing tasks, she replied:

> I had no bored kids. I had nobody saying that they couldn't manage this, nobody saying this was tough, this was beyond them. I had many trying to negotiate up to 100 words initially and then when I set the 100 word limit I had them renegotiating to go down to 50 which is interesting. I just wanted

them to write and that's what I got, I got writers every day. And sometimes even we'd have writing in the morning, I'd have them asking were we going to get another chance to write again in the afternoon. So I thought that there was real positivity around it, and there were some amazing pieces of writing. And there was some real successes, like I could see where students in the third term had really found some of the persuasive writing a real struggle, those students weren't anxious. They weren't showing any anxiety about writing for the beginning of this term.

She explained her approach to mediating the development of new writing skills so that all her students would experience success:

I look at how I've taught it up until then. I look at where the gaps are. I think about what the genre is and what it requires of them, and I look at what's missing for them in their writing. I break the genre down, so I work out what it is that I need to teach in order for everybody to be successful. And I have specific lessons on that. I try to find either from the writing students have done themselves or from published material, quality examples of that style of writing and I share that with the students, and we unpack what makes it good.

She deliberately encouraged students' active engagement in discussing the structure, content and purpose of writing and then modelled what had been collectively agreed:

We agree success criteria together. If we're looking at introductions, what is it that makes a good introduction? We decide to find that, we agree that that's what we're looking for today, and then we write it, I'll model it.

## Scaffolding, modelling and mediating new literacy learning

The teacher was very aware of her position as both the more expert other and also the mediator of literacy learning. In her view, both constructive formative feedback and modelling examples of good quality writing were fundamental to mediating and scaffolding the learning of new writing skills and she took every opportunity to do so:

If you're going to teach it really, really well, you've got to work out a way of marking formatively their work, giving them the feedback and they've got to have time to read that feedback and then action it. […] I grab children when they arrive in the morning, much to their shock horror, and say, 'Oh I've marked your books and they're here, can I just show you yours?' And I talk to them about it so that when we begin the next writing session they're tuning into that.

Foremost in her view was the importance of examples of effective writing that she could use to model to her students various genres of writing. She linked oral language to writing where appropriate:

> [W]hen we were looking at persuasive writing I was finding pieces of persuasive writing that were published and there are many different types – letters to editors, articles – and I would be sharing that with the students, and I would be asking them their opinions. For some genre of writing you've got to do an awful lot of talking. And that's my experience of doing certainly persuasive writing where you're asking them to formulate an opinion and have a view point. We linked our oral language work to it last term as well and in fact our speech writing was also linked to the persuasive writing where we had children writing speeches and delivering speeches that were based on having a strong and firm opinion about something. So we try to make sure that they're surrounded by that same focus in lots of different places.

Cognisant of the importance of not publicly singling out lower attainers for 'special treatment', all students had writing 'buddies' with whom to discuss their work and broaden their ideas as they wrote. The teacher had guided all her students in the class to behave as writing 'buddies', and they all knew what they were looking for and how to respond constructively and positively. She had modelled this by opening up her own writing to critical scrutiny, and showing students how to evaluate this and how to give, receive and act on feedback.

> Often [...] I'll show them an example, we'll unpack it together and talk about what makes it good, then the students will have a chance to write with a buddy, we'll look at it again and then they'll write individually.

For some students she put in more closely defined scaffolds to concentrate on one aspect of writing only, but in a way that maintained the integrity of the whole writing task. For example, where students found the mechanics of writing problematic she might do the writing herself so that they could concentrate on content:

> There are some students who dictate and I write, for certainly in the transactional writing, that's when it gets hard for some students .... They've got the ideas but actually getting those ideas down on paper or structuring it, it gets in the way for them.

Predominantly, grammar, spelling and text structure were taught within the context of authentic writing. She taught spelling in a number of ways, but mainly as students needed to use the words in their own writing:

> What I do is I have topic related vocabulary that's important depending on what the science or social studies or health topic is and we're looking at that

vocabulary and that's part of the words I want them to learn. I identify spelling errors in their writing – ten to fifteen a week that I want them to be learning.

For those who really struggled there was additional phonic work negotiated with the students so that they could see the purpose of it:

I've got a group of year eights who I've targeted in spelling who really have been struggling with blends and actually hearing the sounds in words ... and in fact they're so keen on that they renegotiated to have two sessions.

### Photographs of the classroom environment

The teacher's and students' voices were very clearly apparent in the classroom displays and resources. These indicated a very clearly integrated approach to supporting student literacy learning by:

- clear valuing of students as writers at whatever level;
- modelling examples of effective use of writing and provision of tools to support the development of student autonomy.

### Evidence of value placed on students

Vibrant and colourful displays of cultural iconography, text, art work, and teaching resources of various kinds filled every available space in the classroom (see Figure 6.2).

On the ceiling was the exhortation 'Shoot for the moon. If you miss you'll land among the stars' (see Figure 6.3).

### Modelling examples of writing and provision of tools to encourage student autonomy

Wall displays showed how the teacher was seeking to encourage the development of writing skills across a whole range of genres: poetry, short stories, flow-charts, static images, and so on. The whiteboard showed work currently underway with a focus on poetry, and included quotes, exemplars and practice examples. The rich complexity of language was modelled and demonstrated, both through the samples of students' work that were chosen for display and in the sophistication of the language sentence structure and vocabulary that were used in the signs attached to these displays. These signs included meta language related to writing that students could use in their own work (see Figure 6.4).

Students were encouraged to share written work within the classroom by 'publishing' completed texts. Booklets of students' prior writing were available for an audience of peers and others to read. The class newspaper display illustrated all stages of writing from draft to publishing and it was clear that the specific content of the newspaper articles included elements of child choice.

**FIGURE 6.2** Wall display referring to Treaty of Waitangi

**FIGURE 6.3** Shoot for the moon

**FIGURE 6.4** Example of a wall display with scaffolding for new writing

There was evidence that the teacher aimed to enable students to revisit prior learning with new understanding and encourage student autonomy. The displays of students' 50-word stories were accompanied by the prompts that had been used to support the writing of the narrative and the proofreading. The students' poetry display was bright and colourful with an outline of the process of poetry-creation. The learning intentions for specific pieces of work were made explicit and connections between the activities with which students had been engaged and specific learning outcomes were clearly outlined in many of the displays.

## Interviews with the students

The transcripts of the student interviews showed far more similarities between the two groups about themselves as writers than differences. It was very difficult in some cases to tell the members of the groups apart. Themes that emerged from the analysis indicated:

- an overwhelming feeling of enjoyment and interest in writing and ability to analyse quality;
- confidence in themselves as developing writers;
- positive reports of writing feedback.

## Enjoyment and interest in writing, and analytical ability

The extent of enjoyment and interest in writing experienced by the students and the developing ability to analyse quality can be exemplified by the comments of 'Hope', a member of the group identified as higher achieving in literacy who talked of herself as a weaver of tales:

> It can really be pretty fun if you've got heaps of ideas and you just write them all down. [...] I quite like just writing stories. It's quite nice also stories about what's happened and like the memories that you can remember the most and stuff. I quite like stories where you know what happens, cos you can write them down quite easily.
>
> I really like it when I've got a good idea and a good kind of like plot, or like story line kind of [...] there are times when I know what I really want to say and it takes a little while to put it all down and get it the right way. Because it's easier to think about it than to actually write it as actually how you want it to be. But, it is quite easy to just write it down, but then there are other days which I just write and I almost like, I don't really know what I'm writing. And then I just read it, and it's like, 'Whoa, I've written that!'.

She explained her choice of the stone that best reflected her as a writer as follows:

> I think sometimes I have some really good ideas and it comes out really easy, so there are parts on it [the stone] that are quite smooth, quite like flowing. But then there are other times which it's quite hard, and so where a bit is jagged, like lines, to get all your ideas down. But I think that after I do it, I think I'm quite like it when it's like colourful – almost kind of like, I really like the stories I write.

Asked to choose a stone to represent what, for her, was writing that is less good, she chose two:

> This one's quite basic ideas, quite just kind of there, they're not very interesting, they're not very … they don't make you really think about it, you just kind of look at it and think, oh that's a normal kind of piece of writing. It's not very like 'wow, I really want to take that one home' [...] and this one, is a bit more interesting, but it's a bit more like jagged and not so kind of like, well put together almost. Not so well shaped. I don't know, it's kind of bitsy almost, like lots of points sticking out and yeah …

She also selected a stone for herself as a reader:

> I'm a pretty basic reader. I read a little bit out of the square, but I don't read that much out of the square. I do think I could do a bit better, but I think it's

almost quite a basic rock, but then it does have a few kind of bits that I do go out in, like I do read some books that people else might not really think that they would really read.

The reason behind her choice of stone to represent poorer readers was:

> Because it's quite flat and not very deep or kind of meaty. It's just kind of by itself and like it doesn't have very many kind of like … it's just almost going round in a circle. Kind of not going out anywhere, almost not going out of the circle kind of. It's just almost like a circle. So they're not really going out to find new books, they're almost just going in circle and reading the kind of books they already know. Or the ones that are quite basic, or quite easy to read, or the ones which are not so many pages. Like small.

(See Figure 6.5, Hope's stones.)

## *Self-confidence as developing writers*

The comments of all four students identified as lower achieving in terms of literacy learning clearly indicated that they recognised themselves as developing writers, albeit at different stages of competence and confidence. To take one example, 'Andrew' had a sophisticated understanding of the power of writing and what he was capable of as a writer. He commented: 'It's quite fun and it lets you express your emotions in a different way. And it's quite a good experience to have in school'. Of poetry writing he said: 'It's a lot of feelings in it and things. And it's one of my strong points as well and I like it, it's really fun as well'. When asked about how he felt towards transactional writing he replied:

**FIGURE 6.5** Hope's stones

Yeah, I loved that as well [...] I might even like that more than poetry [...] That was one of my really strong points as well. It's sort of like poetry in a way because you get to express your feelings, and also it's like you're actually having a conversation with the reader and you're actually like telling them things and stuff. It's quite fun to do.

One topic he felt strongly about was: '[...] hedgehogs having their right, their way on the road'. Asked if he believed they should, he replied: 'No, I believe they shouldn't.' He chose a stone to represent himself as a writer because he saw it as:

Like easy and also hard. Cos, you see how [it's smooth] there's not much detailed patterns and stuff, so it might show that it's not quite complicated or anything [...] Writing for me, [is] like quite easy and things.

For someone who found writing difficult he selected a stone that he described as 'like really detailed and it's got lots of things all over it. And it seems like really complicated sort of ...'. For his own reading he chose a stone that he said was 'reasonably small but it's not completely. So I'm pretty good at reading. Not great. Like I'm good, it's not like my best thing but I'm still really good at it'. He identified this same stone as representing poorer readers: 'It's like complicated, lots of things, hard to understand maybe.' (See Figure 6.6, Andrew's stones.)

**FIGURE 6.6** Andrew's stones

## *Positive reports of writing feedback*

Formative feedback from both the teacher and peers constantly gave them the message that they already were writers and could improve and grow. Many times there were references from all the students to the teacher as the more informed other with the expert knowledge to lead and guide them into new forms of expertise in writing. 'Leroy' for example, a high achiever, said he trusted 'what she says, what she writes'. 'Trent', another high achiever, said:

> and when we're sharing bits, like today, I got told my one was like, really good and like that's quite, it's good to know that your piece is good. You may not be sure whether it's good yourself, think, oh could I have done this a bit better? And then when you hear someone saying that it's good, like … say from [the teacher] if you heard it from her, that would be good cause the teacher really [knows about writing].

'Markus', a lower achiever, said he knew how good he was at writing because: 'Well [the teacher] says and other people say … my friends and people on my table, people that read it [his writing].'

From the students' comments it was clear that the teacher recognised the need to support their developing sense of themselves-as-writers through the way she scaffolded their learning by encouraging them to brainstorm ideas for their writing and offering suggestions herself, and teaching them all what to look for in quality writing and how to offer constructive criticism to peers, so that they could develop and grow. There was clear evidence that all were appropriating her strategies as theirs. Hope, for example, commented:

> It's quite good, before we start writing [the teacher] does it almost like with the class, we get our ideas down and then she like writes, if we're writing a poem, she actually writes one for the class. So that helps because then I know kind of what it's meant to look like, what kind of words you're meant to use. And it's also quite helpful to do brainstorms sometimes to get all your ideas out really quickly so then you can write it. […] I quite liked doing the argument side of it, trying to convince the reader and stuff. And I quite like doing poems. I feel like they don't really have to make sense, they can kind of be almost words put together. And I quite like just writing plays. It's quite easy. You don't have to do all the speech marks and all that kind of thing, you just have to write who's saying it and stuff.

Peer-mediated writing was reported by everyone, in a very positive way. For example, one of the lower-ability writers said he found it helpful when: '[the teacher] picks a table for us with a buddy, at random, and we just go there sometimes. Sometimes I'm near to a friend but sometimes I'm not I have… ideas but it's good to go with smart people'. One of the higher attainers commented:

I really like other people's criticisms ... I like constructive criticism from other people, I don't really think it's finished unless I get some [from] anyone – it makes me just want to get heaps better and makes me want to work harder to get to a point where my writing's good ... Trent, one of my mates in class ... I kind of trust him heaps.

## Discussion

The approach adopted by the teacher in the New Zealand classroom at the focus of this study was clearly that of process writing (Graves, 1983), designed to encourage children to use the processes of adult writers. This can be conceptualised in four stages: prewriting, composing/drafting, revising and editing (Tribble, 1996). The process writing approach in this classroom enabled the teacher to harness the strength of the social and communicative relationships that she had encouraged between peers in the classroom to mediate student learning in a very positive way. Teacher and students could collaborate in constructing the literacy context and developing literacy learning practices in which all could participate.

Crucial to the perspective of understanding literacy learning in the context in which it occurs is the role of the mediator (a teacher, adult, more knowledgeable sibling, or peer) in initiating learners into practices such as writing. The teacher's 'voice' as the expert other in her determination that all her students should becoming writers in authentic situations was clearly articulated in every aspect of the classroom pedagogy. In response the students voiced a genuine respect for her as mediator of their learning, able to inspire them with excitement and pleasure in the art of writing in the approach she was taking. The writing process, the audience for the work and the particular genre were at the centre of almost every activity, with support for new learning carefully planned and structured in ways that included all students in the classroom but also allowed for additional assistance for specific purposes. Everything in the learning environment had been deliberately planned to be constructive, positive and very supportive of all students' identities as developing writers. The teacher used her awareness of their current levels of attainment in writing and her own expert knowledge of literary genres to devise the scaffolds that would support and guide students to new writing achievement.

## Summary and conclusion

The current research study was conceptualised within a socio-cultural understanding of learning and located in a classroom of diverse learners where all were constructively engaged with writing and held a positive sense of themselves as developing writers. Writing in the classroom focused on authenticity and the communicative aspects of the whole text rather than discrete elements of the mechanics. At the same time, however, spelling and grammar were not ignored but were attended to systematically as the need arose for individual students.

Overwhelmingly the impression conveyed by the voices of the teacher and her students was one of positivity, energy, achievement and real sense of focus by everyone, high and low attainers alike. Positive student writing identities were developing in a classroom where the teacher had a very high degree of subject and pedagogical content knowledge, and where her whole approach to supporting writing acquisition of her students was determined rather than random, had an immediacy of its responsiveness in relation to every student's learning and, above all, had a recognition of the importance of positive relationships, teacher to student and peer to peer, in a safe learning environment.

## Acknowledgement

The author would like to acknowledge the support and assistance of Professor Mere Berryman and Mrs Lisa Whittle in data collection and analysis for the study.

## References

Bruner, J. (1996) *The culture of education*, Boston, MA: Harvard University Press.
Cole, M. (1996) *Cultural psychology. A once and future discipline*, Cambridge, MA: Harvard University Press.
Crosby, S. (1993) Crosby's therapeutic work with adults (unpublished report, Centre for Personal Construct Education).
Dewey, J. (1938/1963) *Experience and education*, New York: Collier Books.
Glynn, T., Wearmouth, J., & Berryman, M. (2006) *Supporting students with literacy difficulties: A responsive approach*, Maidenhead: Open University Press/McGraw Hill.
Goodwyn, A. (2016) Still growing after all these years? The Resilience of the 'Personal Growth model of English' in England and also internationally. *English Teaching, Practice and Critique*, 15(2), 7–21.
Graves, D. (1983) *Writing. Teachers and children at work*, New York: Heinemann.
Kozulin, A. (2003). Psychological tools and mediated learning. In A. Kozulin, B. Gindis, V. S. Ageyev & S. M. Miller (Eds.) *Vygotsky's educational theory in cultural context*, pp. 15–38. Cambridge: Cambridge University Press.
Leont'ev, A. N. (1981) *Problems of the development of mind*, Moscow: Progress Publishers.
Newman, D., Griffin, P., & Cole, M. (1989) *The construction zone: Working for cognitive change in school*, New York: Cambridge University Press.
Sarup, M. (1996) *Identity, culture and the postmodern world*, Athens, GA: University of Georgia Press.
Tatum, B. (1997) *Why are all the black kids sitting together in the cafeteria?* New York: Basic Books.
Tribble, C. (1996) *Writing*, Oxford: Oxford University Press.
Vygotsky, L. S. (1978) *Mind in society: The development of higher psychological processes*, Cambridge, MA: Harvard University Press.
Wearmouth, J. (2017) 'Employing culturally responsive pedagogy to foster literacy learning in schools', *Cogent Education*, 4(1), DOI: doi:10.1080/2331186X.2017.1295824
Wearmouth, J. & Berryman, M. (2009) *Inclusion through participation in communities of practice in schools*, Wellington: Dunmore Publishing.
Wertsch, J. V. (1985) *Vygotsky and the social formation of mind*, Cambridge, MA: Harvard University Press.
Wertsch, J. V. (1991) *Voices of the mind: A sociocultural approach to mediated action*, Cambridge, MA: Harvard University Press.

# 7

# THE HIDDEN VOICE OF PRE-SERVICE TEACHERS IN THEIR PRIVATE SOCIAL MEDIA INTERACTIONS

*Dr James Shea*

## Introduction

It is a reasonable supposition that pre-service teachers in contemporary teacher education, for sound reasons, use private social media interactions to network. However, access to data in such hidden online spaces is exceptionally difficult because these data are no longer private and thus trustworthiness becomes suspect (Kontopoulou & Fox, 2015).

The current chapter sets out insights based on a study into the private social media interactions of a large group of pre-service teachers undertaking teacher education in England. The study succeeded in retaining privacy for the participants through careful design of methodology that took account of issues of confidentiality and anonymity, and also was heavily reliant on the trust and positive relationship that developed between the researcher and the participants. Although the study was located in England, it has implications for pre-service teacher student voice in other countries, as will be set out later.

The most significant of these insights is that ideas and knowledge are shared and brokered between pre-service teachers through private social media interactions as part of navigating the challenges of achieving the award of Qualified Teacher Status (QTS) whilst on a postgraduate certificate in education course.

## Current context for teacher education in England

Student voice in teacher education is seen as something relatively new (Enright et al., 2017), although it is used more widely than in other subject areas within Higher Education Institutions (Thomson et al., 2017). Part of the reason for this is that pre-service teachers undertake courses that integrate theory and work-based learning. As an integral part of their course, whilst they are on placement in schools or studying educational theory, they function in educational communities of practice: 'important places of negotiation, learning, meaning and identity' (Wenger, 1998, p. 133). External to the schools, students share the learning space with those who are providing the learning. The learning may be collaborative, as, for example, the study by Rojas, Haya and Susinos (2016), which involved collaboration and co-construction of learning materials, looked at 186 students and worked with them to collaborate in the co-construction (Vygotsky, 1970) of learning materials in order to create more personalised and individualised teaching outcomes (Rojas, Haya & Susinos, 2016). The provider community and that of the student teachers may develop 'idiosyncratic ways of engaging with one and another' (Wenger, 1998, p. 133), which require 'brokers' to broker ideas from one community to another.

Participants operating across these communities are often engaged in a 'boundary encounter' (Wenger, 1998, p. 112) with the broker being able to share practice across the communities.

The core enterprise of the student teachers' community is that of becoming a qualified teacher. The preconception that Higher Education can view its students through a lens that assumes a shared community of practice (Vescio, Ross, & Adams, 2007) has limitations, however. It makes assumptions about the community that pre-service teachers inhabit and about how accessible their thoughts, interactions and practice are in achieving their core enterprise. These assumptions do not take into account two major changes that have occurred in recent years to create boundaries around the learning space inhabited by the pre-service teachers that are impermeable to their tutors and school-based mentors.

The first major change to take into account is technology: the growth in commercially sourced software and technology aimed at new users of broadband connected mobile and fixed technologies. Such technologies were dominated by social media with Facebook (largest social media company since 2008) and the advent of push notifications in 2007. There have been further social media and communications based software companies that have also become very large market players internationally such as Twitter: 310 million users in 2016 (Statista, 2016a), and WhatsApp: one billion users in 2016 (Statista, 2016b). What these technology and social media companies have done is to potentially enable the building of communities of practice with speed and privacy built in. Students in higher education (HE) who disliked working in 'public view' could now remove the view of the public and select their audience (Carmichael et al., 2006).

This creates an issue with research into how ICT is used in UK higher education institute (HEI) based teacher education to facilitate online learning communities. Much of the research that looked at how pre-service teachers in UK HEIs interacted was limited to provision of ICT and virtual learning environments (VLEs) by the HEIs themselves (Hramiak, 2010). One possible solution would be to enable social media provision and offer this alongside the course and its VLE (Neier & Zayer, 2015). However, this does not remove the 'public view' highlighted as an issue by Carmichael et al. (2006) – privacy is not absolutely within the choice of the student. A higher education student can currently choose to interact with social media based communities of practice where the level of privacy is a choice and they can prevent the HEI tutor or other specific peers from viewing those interactions. With the nature of private social media interactions being unsearchable or available it is no longer possible to review the way students in HE or, in particular, pre-service teachers have taken the speed from push notifications and the privacy of social media and technology enhancements to establish and use private communities of practice as part of their learning.

As smartphones have become popular with students in UK HEIs, so it has had an impact on the HEIs' ability to draw student web 2.0 traffic to their VLEs. It is evident in pre-service teacher education that pre-service teachers are eschewing visible (i.e., non-private) interactions and opting instead for private interactions hosted and facilitated by the converged push notifications with social media (Bruneel et al., 2013).

To summarise, pre-service teachers can and do use their tablets, laptops, smartphones and social media software to communicate through private social media interactions that are inaccessible to those who share responsibility for supporting their learning, such as the higher education tutors or school based mentors.

The second major change to take into account is the way pre-service teacher education has developed in recent years for the cohort that formed part of the study this chapter is based on. There has been a shift in the way education has been organised by successive recent governments in England that reflect ideological and political positioning that can be seen in other countries worldwide such as the United States (Hursh, 2004). Instead of the post-war consensus that there is direct state responsibility for the delivery of education services such as teacher education, Ball (2013) says that from the 1979 Conservative government onwards, the introduction of a 'neo-liberal marketisation' of education has outsourced the accountability from the state to individual providers. Instead of the state directly providing an accountable service to the public, it is now only indirectly accountable as it outsources the provision to multiple and competing providers. By having multiple providers of the same service and by quantifying aspects of education it is possible to create an 'economy' in which different providers compete to provide this education (for example, in the way of school league tables) and in doing so accept direct accountability in lieu of the state. However, rather than having an even and fairly distributed 'comprehensive' system, in this marketised educational context there are different providers who vie to be as selective as possible in order to achieve the 'economy of student worth' (Ball, 2013, p. 3).

In terms of teacher education and teacher provision, the UK coalition government of 2010–15 introduced mainstream changes to teacher training in England through an openly declared shift in marketisation of teacher education provision through the School Direct initiative. This initiative enabled schools to band together with a partner HEI and 'bid' for teacher training provider places. School Direct is a UK teacher training programme in which the places are allocated to schools who can then select their preferred provider-partner university as part of the pre-service teacher education provision. School Direct was introduced in 2012 (DfE, 2012) with the aim of encouraging schools to offer teacher education provision in addition to local HEI, Teach First and SCITT schemes. School Direct pre-service teachers are recruited by 'named' school partners (in the application process, pre-service teachers apply to a named school). By 2014, the number of School Direct schools acting as providers either alone or in groups had risen rapidly to 9,786 schools (NCTL, 2014). In order to monitor standards there has to be a line of accountability and the UK government allocates this accountability to a quasi-autonomous non-governmental organisation, the Office for Standards in Education, Children's Services and Skills (Ofsted) who undertake inspections on the UK government's behalf, which it has done since The Education Act 1994. Changes to the inspection framework have meant that this inspection reduces the quality of provision to that of a single grade overall: 1, 2, 3, or 4. Achievement of the inspection grade affects the ability of the provider to bid for teacher training places as set out by the National College of Teaching and Leadership (NCTL), 'We will only allocate provider-led places to ITT providers graded "good" or "outstanding" for overall effectiveness by Ofsted' (NCTL, 2014, para. 17). This arrangement thus enables the provider to claim their accountability in the 'economy of student worth' and enter the market of pre-service teacher education.

These two changes have had a profound impact on the way that pre-service teachers operate during their one-year postgraduate teacher education course in England. The first change, that of technology, has had an impact on the habitus that pre-service teachers bring with them to the course and the way they build on this habitus to help prepare themselves for entrance into the teaching job market. Developing habitus as defined by Bourdieu (1977) is recognised by Wenger (Lave & Wenger, 1991) as an influence on their understanding of how communities of practice construct learning and affect the participants. In Bourdieu's words, habitus is 'acquired, socially constituted dispositions' (Bourdieu, 1990, p. 13) with Bourdieu firmly focused on the notion of owning and reproducing cultural capital, whereas Wenger focused more on access to and reproduction of more than simply capital. Instead, Wenger looked specifically at the generation of new knowledge and the reproduction of learning and new knowledge.

The term habitus itself is Aristotelian and Bourdieu appropriates it to describe a specific set of dispositions. Dispositions are both inculcated and structured according to Bourdieu (1977); in other words, they are learned through repeated mundane processes of training, but also reflect the context through which they were learned. It is clear to see just how this notion of habitus works alongside the notion of communities of practice as participants also participate in repeated low-level interactions, 'legitimate peripheral participation' (Lave & Wenger, 1991) within a situated context of boundaries that frame the community of practice.

The key notion for the study under discussion in this chapter is that Bourdieu sees habitus as transposable knowledge. Bourdieu saw that an academic qualification alone is not the sum total of one's knowledge: 'Academic qualifications are a weak currency and possess all their value only within the limits of the academic market' (Bourdieu, 1977, p. 505). This separation of that which is learned through the academic course and then additional knowledge or skill over and above the course is what emerged from the study of the private social media interactions in this study. Identifying exactly what that additional knowledge or skill *is* can be challenging. By removing the emphasis of Bourdieu's on cultural capital and exploration of class divisions from the concept of habitus, one can then reapply the notion to pre-service teachers who are not just accessing a credential, but further unquantified knowledge or practice, which may or may not form part of that credential or have a relationship with that credential through the existence of a community that relies upon the credential for existence. This is 'the core enterprise' of the community of practice (Wenger, 1998).

For the pre-service teacher operating within a community of practice, this notion of habitus has two applications. The first is that the habitus they have built up through using private social networking prior to entering teacher education can be seen as the repeated low-level interactions, and thus pre-service teachers without notion or 'conscious strategy' will seek to continue to use private social media interactions in the same way that they always have to help them access the 'market' of teaching (Hall & McGinity, 2015). The second notion is that with habitus being transposable, such private social media interactions may reveal themselves to be, consciously or otherwise, contributing to the ability of a pre-service teacher to enter the market of teaching and to move from school to school. The introduction to Bourdieu's collection of essays, *Language and Symbolic Power*, captures this effectively.

> The habitus also provides individuals with a sense of how to act and respond in the course of their daily lives. It 'orients' their actions and inclinations without strictly determining them. It gives them a 'feel for the game', a sense of what is appropriate in the circumstances and what is not.
> *(Bourdieu & Thompson, 1991, p. 13)*

Looking at pre-service teachers through this lens of Bourdieu's work highlights how their 'actions are shaped by the values and expectation of the fields in which they work' (Dwyer, 2015, p. 95). Through this process, the pre-service teachers can begin building a teacher identity or concept of self that contains the habitus needed to move from school placement to school placement both during their pre-service teacher education course and during their career. While the pre-service teachers may not know exactly what it is they are building and what future challenges they are building this habitus for, their efforts can still contribute to a transposable habitus and enable them as a community of practice to work towards this habitus as part of the core enterprise of becoming qualified teachers.

The impact of the second change, that of the splintering of teacher education into large numbers of small providers with very small groups of subject-related pre-service teachers, is to affect the physical creation of communities of pre-service teachers. Private social media interactions rely upon the creation of physical groups of subject-related pre-service teachers. Without these sizeable groups of pre-service teachers being established there can be no community of practice and no private social media interactions in existence. If, as this study found, pre-service teachers are aided in the growth and development of their transposable habitus through collaboration as a community of practice facilitated by private social media interactions, then the competition brought in under the guise of neo-liberal marketisation could have the opposite effect to that intended. It could reduce the support and learning that a pre-service teacher has access to as part of being a community of practice facilitated by private social media interactions and limit their ability to develop a transposable habitus for their future career.

To summarise, then, pre-service teachers are entering markets where knowledge that is not part of their qualification could be just as important in terms of their future success as knowledge that is. They have to both compete with each other and collaborate with each other at the same time as achieving their pre-service teacher qualification.

These two major changes have affected the way student voice in HE can be viewed and in particular the voice of pre-service teachers who are carefully navigating marketised provision of teacher education in order to access a marketised education school network for employment.

## Outline of the study

The rationale behind this study was the observance of the two contextual changes outlined above having an impact on the pre-service teacher communities in terms of how they operated on the course that featured in this study. While anecdotal evidence of private social media interactions was present to the university tutors, no real insight into these interactions and the way they worked with the pre-service teachers could be possible without a formal research project designed to circumnavigate the thorny issue of privacy. How could the tutors on the course interact with a community whose interactions were hidden and private? If good practice was happening, were there ways in which the course tutors could use this good practice to educate future pre-service teachers?

The study set out some key research questions:

- What interactions sustain the social networking community of pre-service teachers?
- What ideas do the pre-service teachers explore and broker about what it means to be professional from the group discussions in the social networking community?
- What ideas, if any, do the pre-service teachers discuss about teaching, which are different or similar from those seen in their placement schools?
- What issues do the pre-service teachers discuss that are related to their school experience or government policies through social networking?

The participants in the study were pre-service teachers in England on a one-year postgraduate certificate in education. They were on the course for one year and would undertake two school placements and attend taught university sessions as part of the course. On the course, they were grouped for their taught sessions. Mainly the groupings were by the subject that they taught: mathematics, science, English, physical education, computer science or modern languages. There were some other groupings, which were for professional study type activities. For these sessions the pre-service teachers were grouped by geography of school placements.

The design of the study had to provide insight into the different communities that emerged over the course of the PGCE course and how private social media interactions were part of those communities; in particular through the use of push notifications and through private or closed communications. Thus, the design of this study related to the focus of the research with the nature of the community of practice at its centre, and the kind of data required to address the main research questions.

The data to be collected was the nature and content of those private interactions on private social media: closed Facebook pages, messenger groups, texts, WhatsApp group and email were all used by the pre-service teachers to interact privately with each other whilst on the course. Access to this data was through the transcripts of recorded group interviews at regular points in the course. At no point did the researcher have access to the physical data of the private social media interactions. Such anonymity measures and by not being an insider researcher such as in Kontopoulou and Fox's (2015) research meant researcher influence was reduced as much as possible. By having the participants in the study undertake group reflective interviews on a regular basis in which they reflected using their first-hand knowledge of the community's interactions, the precise content of those interactions could remain private while the nature and themes of the community's interactions could be revealed.

The participants were interviewed at four key stages of their course: at the start and end of their two placements. It was important to allow the pre-service teachers to begin on their placement before interviewing them so that enough time was allowed for the pre-service teachers to set up social media structures and to interact privately through social media and thus be in a position to reflect on their interactions within private social media through the opening phase of the placement. The first and third interviews, then, were sequenced to be just after the start of each of the two placements.

Following the interviews, a transcriber produced transcripts of the interviews and in doing so removed any inadvertent references that could identify people or schools. It was these transcripts that were analysed through annotation and the generation of themes for further analysis. From there, memoed logs were created (Lempert, 2007) to show how the research questions and literature review interacted with the outcomes from the transcripts.

## Findings and discussion

The findings of the study were that private social media interactions did, viewed through the lens of Wenger's (1998) communities of practice, resemble legitimate peripheral interactions (Lave & Wenger, 1991). The pre-service teachers were operating much as Wenger set out in his theory about communities of practice with brokerage, sharing of practice and being supportive of each other all in existence. The key themes that emerged from the annotation of the transcripts were:

- Establishment of a community of practice.
- Achieving the core enterprise of the community.
- Brokerage within the community.
- More knowledgeable others as brokers.
- Issues and challenges in relation to achieving the core enterprise.
- Shared practices.
- Behaviour management.

The full findings of the study reflect on each of the different subject-based communities of practice against these themes. However, the word length of this chapter precludes discussion of each, hence the section below draws on findings that have a particular salience for student voice:

- How and why behaviour management issues could not be articulated outside of private social media interactions.
- The difference between private social media student voice and physical student voice.
- The way student voice in private social media interactions can affect the assessment of a pre-service teacher.

## Behaviour management

Behaviour management stood out in all of the pre-service teachers' communities of practice as one of the issues of professionalism that was discussed. Sometimes it centred on a school policy such as a 'no contact' policy and whether this was industry wide or school specific – pre-service teacher private social media based exploration of this topic revealed it to be the latter.

The interviews with the pre-service English teachers revealed that members of their community managed this challenge by hand picking a select group from the private social media based community of pre-service English teachers and by using private interactions within Messenger to help develop their skills and strategies in behaviour management. By selecting the key people to reveal their challenges around behaviour management to, they limit the issues in sharing this information and gather support and different ideas about how to overcome these challenges. The privacy and use of the Messenger tool could be a key difference here between socially networked pre-service teachers and pre-service teachers who have a high degree of isolation and lack of opportunities to raise such challenges around behaviour management with peers – especially if they were having short-term issues, e.g., teaching the same class or difficult to manage individuals repeatedly before they would next meet their peer pre-service teachers face to face who might be able to offer support, shared practice or brokerage of ideas from other communities in the role of more knowledgeable others.

This finding has clear implications for anyone working with students in HE. A notion that there are occasions, particularly in assessment of 'performance' where to declare an insecurity in knowledge, understanding or ability to meet the assessment of the performance is not standard practice. It goes further, because it demonstrates that assessment could be flawed. What then emerged through this case study of private social media interactions by pre-service teachers, is an issue of acknowledging the role of private social media interactions when assessing the standards of pre-service teachers. As outlined in Hall and McGinity's (2015) report on the neo-liberal marketisation of provision, and changes to education (Ball, 2013; Ward, 2014), the allocation of teacher training places (DfE, 2014) has led to an increase in school-centred teacher educations courses that have smaller cohorts who could lack online and physical interactions within a pre-service teacher community. Not having that combination of private social media and successful face-to-face interaction would mean that they would have less access to opportunities for shared practice, support and access to brokerage of ideas from other communities that the pre-service teachers in this study seemed to value so much. This is the place of student voice in HEI based teacher education. Student voice does not necessarily mean student voice that is heard by the HEI provider. Student voice stands as a source of knowledge and development as well as an influence on assessment due to the way communities of practice operate: in particular, this modern notion of private social media interactions and how they facilitate the community to interface with the context that the community must achieve the core enterprise within.

## Difference between private social media student voice and physical student voice

At this point it is worth considering a limitation of the student voice as facilitated by private social media interactions. One of the key observations of the case study that this chapter is drawing from is that some pre-service teachers were less comfortable with accessing private social media. Access to the private social media interactions as part of a community of practice of pre-service teachers is thus related to an individual pre-service teacher's notions around privacy. For example, WhatsApp requires the sharing of telephone numbers and thus some of the pre-service teachers were not comfortable sharing their telephone number with others. This means there could be varying levels of support and access to shared practice, knowledge and approaches and thus variable levels of the presented identity of a professional teacher. One of the suppositions of the case study is that pre-service teachers' professional identities, enhanced by access to private social media interactions, could be affecting the expectation by schools and mentors of the standards to be demonstrated by all pre-service teachers. If it is assumed that the 'expected' level of professionalism is being modified by the private social networking, then what could be perceived as a lower level of presented professionalism could actually be an aversion to using private social media and thus a lack of access to the support and enhancement accessed through private social networking interactions of communities of pre-service teachers rather than a lower level of professionalism. HEIs see organisation as an important part of a HE student's ability to progress during their time on the course. Yet, private social media interactions are affecting this considerably. Particularly so for pre-service teachers.

PRE-SERVICE MODERN LANGUAGES TEACHER B: We haven't really been speaking very much since last December. Over Christmas we did not have any contact and after that we have been talking about the RT [Reflective Teacher Masters Level Assessment] and when it was due in. In the primary week we did contact each other more, such as how was everything going since Christmas and when did we need to submit the RT work? Then we had a break and we didn't speak in a while but we have a Cluster WhatsApp group and we text each other a lot reminding people where they are and what to bring such as PRP2 (formal assessment against teachers' standards).
INTERVIEWER: So it is organisational things?

## Private social media interactions and pre-service teacher assessment

In this extract from the third interview, it is clear that the pre-service teachers interacted together at specific times. These legitimate peripheral participations (Lave & Wenger, 1991) were focused on ensuring the pre-service teachers performed well during times when assessments were due. This is a student voice that the HEI does not hear. There are questions around the assessments for a pre-service teacher that need answering and indeed are answered for those participating in the communities. These interactions remain hidden behind a layer of privacy. In respecting the privacy whilst accepting that private student voice is a desirable outcome, HEIs can better perceive how students are navigating the course that they are on – in this case pre-service teachers. The key word that pre-service teachers used was reassurance – they used private social media to contextualise their efforts and to ensure that they were managing their personal levels of risk proportionately to the rest of the group and could access support and (as termed by Wenger) brokerage when required. In the interviews within the case study that this chapter draws from, the pre-service mathematics teachers were asked to explore exactly what is was that drove the group to use the social media based pre-service teacher community of practice – what were the things that they perceived to be useful from networking online through social media?

PRE-SERVICE MATHEMATICS TEACHER C: So it was good for support when we had a query about university work.
INTERVIEWER: So not just school-based stuff but university based stuff, so as a problem-solving tool?
PRE-SERVICE MATHEMATICS TEACHER A: We ran things past each other as some assignments were due in terms of referencing or how many things you linked to.

INTERVIEWER: To increase your ability to pass the assessment to a good standard that was something you worked towards?
PRE-SERVICE MATHEMATICS TEACHER A: Just for reassurance that everyone is doing it in the same way that you are or understood it in the same way you have.

Quite quickly, the notion that private social media interactions as a driver of reassurance in terms of standards, comprehension of tasks and organisation of university based assessments can be seen. Students who interact through private social media were using student voice to attain the core enterprise of their community of practice. In this case, to become a pre-service teacher in terms of both completing the university assessment and the school placement. However, this version of student voice is private and deliberately excludes those in positions of power. Cook-Sather's (2017) research shows that educational institutions are beginning to harness the power of digital media in their interactions with student bodies, but this still makes the assumption that Wenger does – that public interfacing of student voice is the way to achieve positive outcomes (Wenger, Smith & White, 2009). What HEIs need to see is that trust and privacy issues affect the way HEIs speak with students (Kontopoulou & Fox, 2015). Just because a HEI does not 'hear' the student voice, it does not mean that the voice is not active and making a difference to student outcomes or that HEIs are not aware of the student voice. It is possible for hidden student voice to co-exist with traditional open student voice and influence HEI courses.

The pre-service PE teacher in the case study this chapter is based on, for example, raised the need for private social networking that does not involve the university tutor and there is a sense that, collectively, the group of pre-service teachers can resolve problems without alerting the tutor to the fact that these problems exist.

PRE-SERVICE PE TEACHER A: We have Glassboard as well but that is open to our tutor but the Facebook is closed.
INTERVIEWER: Is that something that appealed to you, having a closed space whether neither school or university staff are participating but only you as students?
PRE-SERVICE PE TEACHER A: If anyone has a concern that does not need to go the tutor then you can deal with it in your group rather than get anyone else involved, usually it's small issues.

## Summary

Private social media interactions are not only a valid form of student voice, but also this voice has changed because of private social media interactions. When those interactions were within the purview of ITE providers (Hramiak, 2010; Neier & Zayer, 2015) it was possible to observe and influence good behaviour for online learning (Shea & Stockford, 2015) within the community of practice, but now they are behind a wall of privacy, HEI tutors have to consider this new hidden voice.

Even though the pre-service teachers' communities of practice operate through private social media, this chapter has established that *how* they use private social media to enhance the core enterprise of becoming a qualified teacher should be enhanced through intervention from the HEIs. Although the selection of the appropriate social media of private interactions will always be up to the pre-service teachers, outlining to them at the start of the course about how the different features are used could lead to pre-service teacher communities selecting social media that offers opportunities for rapid asynchronous communication through push notifications, selection of small sub-groups within the community and multiple layers of privacy – features that were not available to software such as Glassboard. This would enable the pre-service teachers to better evaluate the competing commercial software providers and their ability to successfully host the pre-service teachers' private interactions in a way that enhances the core enterprise of the community – becoming a qualified teacher.

In addition to advising about features of social media, it is also possible to instruct pre-service teachers on the notions of private social media based communities of practice and how to recognise features that accentuate the core enterprise of becoming a qualified teacher. These could include encouraging certain key practices: inclusivity of membership, allowing 'lurkers' to interact, use of speed and privacy to handle challenges and issues, and the notion that ideas can be brokered from one community to another. This instruction needs to happen during the induction phase so that pre-service teachers understand some of the notions of how communities of practice work as well as the balance between power and privacy that is delivered by private social networking interactions.

## Conclusion

Within the different communities of pre-service teachers there were consistencies in the way that many of the private social media interactions were related to face-to-face social interactions. As identified by the pre-service English teachers, such face-to-face social interactions were also opportunities to discuss educational matters. Some of the communities of practice of pre-service teachers in this study, such as those for the pre-service modern foreign language (MFL) and PE teachers, were very active in terms of the level of private social media interactions. HEI staff do not always recognise just how much interaction takes place on social media to verify formal information and there is a noted gap between how much HEI staff value this interaction and how much university students value such interactions (Kim & Sin, 2016).

There is a hidden student voice within pre-service teacher education courses. This hidden voice is generated because the students arrive with the habit of using private social media interactions to generate knowledge that is not found as part of the course and they immediately set about establishing the infrastructure and habits of this approach within the pre-service teacher course. Not all students have access to this voice and none of the tutors will. Yet this hidden voice remains a powerful and influential force due to the way it operates as a community of practice for those who do participate. Encouraging membership, inclusive practice and highlighting the strengths of this hidden student voice to those who begin any pre-service teacher education course is vital to ensure that any reproduction of power or knowledge is accessible to as many on the course as possible – their personal objections to using modern social media notwithstanding.

This type of student voice is thus new and will be met more regularly by those university tutors working in societies where private social media interactions are part of the habitus of students who enter their courses. However, despite the hidden nature of these interactions, the student voice needs to be acknowledged in terms of its positive impact and the fact that university tutors can still engage with the hidden student voice: both to encourage and validate it as well as to communicate with it.

## References

Ball, S. (2013) *Education, justice and democracy: The struggle over ignorance and opportunity*. Available at: http://classonline.org.uk/docs/2013_Policy_Paper_-_Education,_justice_and_democracy_(Stephen_Ball).pdf (accessed: 23 April 2016).

Bourdieu, P. (1977) *Outline of a theory of practice*. Cambridge: Cambridge University Press.

Bourdieu, P. (1990) *In other words: Essays towards a reflexive sociology*; translation by Matthew Adamson. Cambridge: Polity Press.

Bourdieu, P. & Thompson, J. B. (1991) *Language and symbolic power. English translation*. Cambridge: Polity in association with Basil Blackwell.

Bruneel, S., De Wit, K., Verhoeven, J. C. & Elen, J. (2013) 'Facebook: When education meets privacy', *Interdisciplinary Journal of E-Learning & Learning Objects*, 9, 125–148.

Carmichael, P., Procter, R., Laterza, V. & Rimpiläinen, S. (2006) 'Sakai: A virtual research environment for educational research', *Research Intelligence*, 96, 18–19.

Cook-Sather, A. (2017) 'Virtual forms, actual effects: How amplifying student voice through digital media promotes reflective practice and positions students as pedagogical partners to prospective high school and practicing college teachers', *British Journal of Educational Technology*, 48(5), 1143–1152.

DfE (2012) Press release: New schools direct programme opens. Available at: https://www.gov.uk/government/news/new-school-direct-programme-opens-28-september-2012 (accessed: 4 February 2014).

DfE (2014) Initial teacher training allocations 2014–15. Available at: https://www.gov.uk/government/publications/initial-teacher-training-allocations-for-academic-year-2015-to-2016 (accessed: 4 February 2015).

Dwyer, R. (2015) 'Unpacking the habitus: Exploring a music teacher's values, beliefs and practices', *Research Studies in Music Education*, 37(1), 93–106.

Enright, E., Coll, L., Ni Chroinin, D., & Fitzpatrick, M. (2017) 'Student voice as risky praxis: democratising physical teacher education', *Physical Education and Sport Pedagogy*, 22(5), 459–472.

Hall, D. & McGinity, R. (2015) 'Conceptualizing teacher professional identity in neoliberal times: Resistance, compliance and reform', *Education Policy Analysis Archives*, 23(88), 1–21.

Hramiak, A. (2010) 'Online learning community development with teachers as a means of enhancing initial teacher training', *Technology, Pedagogy & Education*, 19(1), 47–62.

Hursh, D. (2004) 'Undermining democratic education in the USA: The consequences of global capitalism and neo-liberal policies for education policies at the local, state and federal levels', *Policy Futures in Education*, 2(3–4), 607–620.

Kim, K. & Sin, S. J. (2016) 'Use and evaluation of information from social media in the academic context: Analysis of gap between students and librarians', *The Journal of Academic Librarianship*, 42, 74–82.

Kontopoulou, K. & Fox, A. (2015) 'Designing a consequentially based study into the online support of pre-service teachers in the UK', *Educational Research and Evaluation*, 21(2), 122–138.

Lave, J. & Wenger, E. (1991) *Situated learning: Legitimate peripheral participation*. New York: Cambridge University Press.

Lempert, L. B. (2007) 'Asking questions of the data: Memo writing in the grounded theory tradition'. In A. Bryant and K. Charmaz (eds.) *The SAGE handbook of grounded theory*. London: Sage, pp. 214–228.

NCTL (2014) NCTL Allocations data 2013–14. Available at: https://www.gov.uk/governm ent/publications/initial-teacher-training-allocations-for-academic-year-2015-to-2016 (accessed: 12 April 2016).

Neier, S. & Zayer, L. T. (2015) 'Students' perceptions and experiences of social media in higher education', *Journal of Marketing Education*, 37(3), 133–143.

Rojas, S., Haya, I., & Susinos, T. (2016) 'Growing student voice in curriculum decisions at the university', *Journal of Research in Special Educational Needs*, 16(1), 563–567.

Shea, J. & Stockford, A. (2015) *Inspiring the secondary curriculum with technology: Let the students do the work!* London: Routledge.

Statista (2016a) Number of monthly active Twitter users worldwide from 1st quarter 2010 to 1st quarter 2016 (in millions). Available at http://www.statista.com/statistics/282087/ number-of-monthly-active-twitter-users/ (accessed: 7 January 2016).

Statista (2016b) Number of monthly active WhatsApp users worldwide from April 2013 to February 2016 (in millions). Available at: http://www.statista.com/statistics/260819/num ber-of-monthly-active-whatsapp-users/ (accessed: 3 June 2016).

Thomson, K. E., Da Silva, R., Draper, P., Gilmore, A., Majury, N., O'Connor, K., Vaquez, A. & Waite, J. (2017) 'Student voice in work integrated learning scholarship: A review of teacher education and geographical sciences', *Teaching & Learning Inquiry: The ISSOTL Journal*, 5(1), 1–13.

Vescio, V., Ross, D. & Adams, A. (2008) 'A review of research on the impact of professional learning communities on teaching practice and student learning', *Teaching and Teacher Education*, 24(1), 80–91.

Vygotsky, L. (1970) *Thought and language*. Cambridge, MA: MIT Press.

Ward, H. (2014) School Direct to train more teachers than PGCE. Available at: https:// www.tes.com/news/school-news/breaking-news/school-direct-train-more-teachers-uni versity-pgces-2015 (accessed: 4 February 2017).

Wenger, E. (1998) *Communities of practice: Learning, meaning, and identity*. Cambridge: Cambridge University Press.

Wenger, E., McDermott, R. & Snyder, W. (2007) *Cultivating communities of practice: a guide to managing knowledge*. Boston, MA: Harvard Business School Press.

Wenger, E., Smith, J. D. & White, N. (2009) *Digital habitats: Stewarding technology for communities*, 1st edn. Portland, OR: CPsquare.

# 8

# A VOICE FOR ADVANCING THE PROFESSION OF TEACHING?

*Professor Andrew Goodwyn*

## Introduction

It is now a global phenomenon that most education systems have recognised a significant problem in seeking to keep the best teachers in the classroom where they make the biggest difference to students' lives. There are two major issues. Many very good teachers either simply leave the profession, becoming worn down by constant externally imposed changes, or move out of the classroom to take on management roles. A range of countries are trying to tackle this challenge by creating an alternative career structure (Goodwyn, 2016) that provides recognition, status and reward and keeps the teachers working in their own classrooms but also helping to develop other teachers. These authorised teachers can be seen as special representatives of the profession, providing at least one strong voice based on being teachers with true expertise.

In England, The Advanced Skills Teacher scheme that was initiated in 1997 was summarily abolished in 2013 with no consultation and with the vague suggestion of a 'Master Teacher' model instead to replace it. Nothing has come of this proposal (Goodwyn, 2016). Of course, there is nothing unusual about such peremptory and undemocratic political decisions affecting teachers. The General Teaching Council (GTC), meant to become the equivalent of the General Medical Council and other similar independent professional bodies, was set up in 2000 and abolished in 2012. The GTC was not popular with teachers (Goodwyn, 2010) and has not been 'missed' but the reason for this unpopularity was principally that teachers felt it had no voice of any significance and was merely a regulatory body not an advocate for the profession that might, when necessary, challenge and resist political impositions. What its demise illustrates is that teaching needs 'voices', perhaps representing different strengths and perspectives. The teacher unions (another global phenomenon) certainly have a key role to play in ensuring that the working conditions of teachers are protected and improved, but their voices are limited and they therefore cannot be the sole representation.

This chapter tells the story of the Advanced Skills Teachers (ASTs), drawing on extensive research data with ASTs themselves (see Fuller, Goodwyn, Francis-Brophy & Harding, 2010, and Fuller, Goodwyn & Francis-Brophy, 2012), Local Authority AST coordinators and a range of Senior School Leaders. It gives voice to the experience of ASTs, their passion for teaching and learning, and their anger and disappointment at the summary abolition of their hard-earned status. It also airs the views of Head Teachers and others who were equally concerned about this peremptory policy change. The AST model was not perfect and some of these voices also articulate criticisms of the role and put forward ideas for improvements, should there be a new national model.

The chapter concludes by putting forward a new conceptual framework – drawn from the research and examples from other systems – emphasising the nature of the 'voice' that leading teachers can offer the profession as a whole. It also examines the need to overcome the empty rhetoric of politicians who make much noise about 'world class teachers' but do nothing to develop the profession to achieve such a level. In addition, it addresses the narrow prejudice of the media who often deride these models as 'Super Teachers' (Goodwyn, 2001a). What society needs to be able to hear is the voice of its leading teachers who can be the best advocates for the importance of the teaching profession.

## Background and context

It was a slogan of the 1990s that 'Every Child Matters' and of course that is both true and at the heart of what a decent education system strives to achieve. It is not a contradiction to say, however, that 'Every teacher matters', but that is currently not the experience of the profession in England, where this case study of The Advanced Skills Teacher (AST) is set. Schools in England face a very serious recruitment and retention crisis with many teachers leaving before they complete five years in the classroom and many experienced teachers either retiring early or changing careers. There are many suggested solutions to this problem but they tend to be very short term (teacher training bursaries, for example). What is really needed is a politically neutral, long-term strategy focused on raising the status of the profession and making it much more attractive for bright graduates to sign up and, even more important, to keep them becoming increasingly expert practitioners, developing years of cumulatively valuable experience. It will be argued, without any notions of elitism, that certain teachers do matter more to some students and that some teachers can matter more in terms of how they can support and develop other teachers (see the meta-analysis by Hattie, 2003). All teachers matter and some, those that take on an extra level of challenge, may be given a form of recognition that makes them leading voices for all teachers.

England faces a particular crisis but the nature of the issue is global, as is established below. One scheme – not a panacea – but certainly a longer term strategy, was the creation of The Advanced Skills Teacher (AST), a project that had great potential to raise teachers' status in comparisons to other top tier professions and to keep the best teachers in the classroom, with better salaries and a career structure that would provide recognition and reward, both intrinsic and extrinsic. The AST was thus a particular voice for the profession, a high-level status to recognise and celebrate the best teachers. What can we learn from this story and the fact that the role was summarily abolished in 2013? As the relatively new Chartered College (established in 2015) for teaching begins its work to create 'Chartered Teacher Status' (for the decision to use the term 'Chartered' see Goodwyn & Cordingley, 2016), what are the signs of a new voice developing for the profession?

## A global phenomenon

That teachers are generally valued is a global phenomenon. However, it is perhaps ironic, that in what have been called 'high performing jurisdictions' (Barber & Mourshed, 2007), teaching is regarded as very much a second tier profession. Certainly this is true of England (Goodwyn, 2001b) but also, for example, the United States and Australia. The other increasingly global phenomenon is the establishment of a variety of models of 'expert teaching' in different systems; these systems are increasingly borrowing and adapting models from other systems. This can be briefly illustrated here to set the AST into an international context (for a very detailed characterisation see Goodwyn, 2016).

The first creation of a descriptor for these specially recognised teachers was probably the Advanced Skills Teacher in Australia in the 1970s (Ingvarson & Chadbourne, 1997). This was a very modest scheme, chiefly involving a minor pay increase and the award of this title to very experienced teachers whom the senior management wished to retain in the classroom (Goodwyn, 2010). A much more substantial scheme was created in the United States in 1988. The National Board for Professional Teaching Standards (NBPTS) was set up to recognise Highly Accomplished Teachers (HAT) (for an evaluation of its impact see National Research Council, 2008) and its remit was to develop subject specific standards for teachers and then design a *credentialising* programme. To be awarded this status a teacher has to go through an elaborate process of providing evidence; in summary they have to spend a year developing a substantial portfolio of evidence, which includes a video diary and commentary, and also to attend an assessment centre; it is a pass/fail model and the HAT status is for an initial five years. The fee is about $3,000 and most teachers pay for themselves, typically getting the money reimbursed by their school or their state if they pass. The NBPTS is entirely independent and self-funded (for details see its website: https://www.nbpts.org/).

Given that the proposed new scheme in England is designed to give Chartered Teacher status, it is important to mention the Scottish Chartered Teacher Scheme. This began with much consensual optimism as the Ministry, the teacher unions and the universities providing Teacher Education all backed the scheme. However, after five years it was abolished in the same summary way that the AST was abolished in England (for details, see Goodwyn, 2016). Interestingly, Australia has now moved on from its AST model and has a relatively new organisation, The Australian Institute for Teaching and School Leadership (established in 2010: https://www.aitsl.edu.au/), which is working with a new scheme with four levels of recognition of teachers: The Graduate, The Proficient, The Highly Accomplished and The Lead Teacher. The global phenomenon is also a phenomenon of borrowing and adapting with the importing of the term Highly Accomplished Teachers from the United States to Australia. In 1997 the Department for Education and Employment (DfEE) in England imported the term Advanced Skills Teacher (AST) from Australia, and the grade was formally introduced in September, 1998. The Chartered College in England, if it is to become a voice for the profession, needs to learn from and adapt ideas from these previous and extant models and schemes.

## The Advanced Skills Teacher in England

Teaching is a modest profession and teachers do not like the term 'expert'. AST generally was a more acceptable term although there was no consultation about its rather sudden introduction. Other terms have been used in England with the government's inspection agency, the Office for Standards in Education (Ofsted), for many years identifying 'outstanding teachers' and there was a scheme meant to run alongside the AST, The Excellent Teacher, but only 57 teachers applied for it and so it never got off the ground (Goodwyn, 2010). It is notable that the Further Education sector in 2017 launched 'Advanced Teacher Status', arguing that:

> Advanced Teacher Status (ATS) is the badge of advanced professionalism and mastery in further education and training. It is an advanced professional status that is conferred by the Education and Training Foundation (ETF) through the Society for Education and Training (SET).

This status recognises experienced education professionals who can demonstrate:

- mastery in teaching and/or training;
- an exemplary degree of subject knowledge in their area of professional expertise;
- effectiveness in working collaboratively to improve teaching standards amongst their peers and within their organisation or network.*(ETF & SET, 2018, p. 1)*

Finally, only three years ago, the government announced the creation of a National Teaching Service, which would 'parachute' 3,000 excellent teachers into the most underachieving schools; this was so unappealing and so unfeasible that it was dropped within a few months.

The genesis of the AST in England was never explained. It was first announced as part of a White paper in 1997 (DfE, 1997) and then the scheme was suddenly launched as a way to recognise and retain the best teachers in the classroom and to pay them on the equivalent to the Leadership scale for undertaking specialist duties.

By 2009, when the scheme had matured, a substantial document, 'Advanced Skills Teachers: Promoting Excellence', was produced by the DCSF (Department for Children, Schools and Families [one of the more bizarre descriptors of the Ministry for Education]), which summarises the main purpose of the AST as: 'The distinctive function of the AST grade is to provide pedagogic leadership within their own and in other schools driving forward improvements and raising standards in teaching and learning' (DCSF, 2009, p. 9).

In answer to the question 'What is an Advanced Skills Teacher?' the document states:

> An Advanced Skills Teacher (AST) is an excellent teacher who achieves the very highest standards of classroom practice and who is paid to share his or her skills and experience with other teachers. AST posts can be based in all types and phases of maintained schools and normally involve some outreach work. In order to take up an AST post a teacher must first have been assessed as meeting the applicable standards – those standards that are between a teacher's current career stage and AST status.
> 
> *(DCSF, 2009, p. 4)*

The document states very clearly the rationale for having this model:

> We need to recognise and retain the best teachers. Until the introduction of ASTs, promotion into management was the typical career route for most excellent teachers. The AST pathway offers teachers who want to stay in the classroom an alternative career route with the potential to earn a salary equivalent to that of many leadership posts. Together with the performance threshold, the Fast Track programme and Excellent Teacher status it is widening career progression opportunities and rewards for the best teachers. AST posts concentrate on good teaching and learning and benefit the profession by helping to raise achievements and spread excellent practice both within and beyond the teacher's school. The creation of an AST post can provide a focus for and leadership in the development of teaching and learning across the school as well as the contribution they make to the development of individual colleagues. The AST outreach role also supports networking between schools and encourages collaboration.
> 
> *(DCSF, 2009, p. 4)*

This rationale was extended by itemising the impact of the role:

> The AST role benefits:
> - their own school by retaining their services as a classroom teacher, spreading their excellent practice through the school and building on the good ideas they bring back from other schools;
> - other schools through the outreach contribution the AST is able to make and the potential for building collaborative links;

- the Local Authority (LA) by sharing good practice across schools and raising standards overall;
- the AST by broadening experience and providing new challenges;
- the profession by providing another career option;
- pupils and students through the AST's special contribution to raising teaching and learning standards.

(DCSF, 2009, p. 4)

At this time there were Standards for Teachers at a number of levels, beginning with initial teacher training (ITT) and Qualified Teacher Status (NQT), but what concerns us here are the Standards for ASTs, which, as summarised by the Training and Development Agency for Schools (TDA, 2007, p. 7) were:

> Professional attributes.
> Advanced Skills Teachers should:
> Frameworks
> A1 Be willing to take on a strategic leadership role in developing workplace policies and practice and in promoting collective responsibility for their implementation in their own and other workplaces.
> Professional skills.
> Advanced teachers should:
> Teamworking and collaboration
> A2 Be part of or work closely with leadership teams, taking a leadership role in developing, implementing and evaluating policies and practice in their own and other workplaces that contribute to school improvement.
> A3 Possess the analytical, interpersonal and organisational skills necessary to work effectively with staff and leadership teams beyond their own school.
> (TDA, 2007)

However, these specific Standards were not sufficient. A later document (DCSF, 2009, available at http://dera.ioe.ac.uk/12009/7/ast%20guidance%20eng%20web_Redacted.pdf) outlines all the other standards of which there were a total of 28, falling under three main categories:

- Professional attributes.
- Professional knowledge and understanding.
- Professional skills.

This illustrates just how demanding was the nature of the role. This high demand gave the role authentic credibility to such teachers having a special voice within and for the profession, although that aspect of the AST was never fully developed.

In order to become an AST, teachers had to prepare a portfolio of evidence and then pass a two-day assessment by an external consultant who observed the teachers and also interviewed senior management, students and parents in order to satisfy the criteria. Any teacher of any age could apply to become one with their Head Teacher's backing. Local Authorities (LAs) were also involved in the recruitment (and later deployment) of ASTs. Initially the funding came from Central Government, so there was nothing to stop a school or a Local Authority having a number of ASTs. Later funding became much more complex and central funding was reduced so some LAs provided it and also some schools.

The scheme was by no means universally approved. The teacher unions were very negative about the role, seeing it as divisive, and some LAs refused to work with it (see Goodwyn & Fidler, 2002). More strikingly, the media reacted by characterising the AST as 'Super Teachers' with cartoons of them flying in the classroom window. Coincidentally, but revealingly, a new scheme, launched in Norway in 2017, with which the current author is working, has had exactly the same representation in the media. This media reaction raises an important question about how the public sees teachers. When teachers appear in the national media it is generally for negative reasons, especially sexual scandals and the like. Good stories about teachers will appear in local news but rarely nationally. Unusually, the award of the Global Teacher prize to a teacher from England in 2018 has had significant media coverage, but that is hardly representative of the profession (Goodwyn, 2016). Equally, the national awards of various categories of recognition receive brief media attention. What is suggested here is that role models such as ASTs might form a very powerful voice for what is the best in the profession.

After this unpromising start, and over time, the AST role became credible with LAs, with other teachers and with the Senior Leaders in schools, as the research cited below demonstrates. Although it was never significant proportionally, and there are no official figures, research in 2011 suggested that there were typically about 5,000 ASTs in post in the period 2000–2013; that was about 1 per cent of the teacher workforce. The HAT model in the United States is proportionally about the same (Goodwyn, 2016, National Research Council 2008).

## Research in the AST role and the views from within the profession

Given the limitations of space, the reporting of this research is necessarily limited but it provides much insight into the role and gives some space to the voices of ASTs themselves. There were three small-scale investigations into the work of ASTs, two by Ofsted (Ofsted, 2001, 2003) and one by The Centre for British Teachers (CfBT, 2004). The three initial studies were all positive about the value of the, then, new role. The scheme gradually became truly national, although again the DfE never provided a clear overview of how many teachers were ASTs, how many had specialisms in which subject or expertise areas, and not even how many were secondary or primary focused. As most ASTs were both phase specific and typically had two specialisms, for example Secondary Maths and also NQTs or Primary Literacy and Initial Teacher Training, these figures would have given a very interesting data about the range and depth of the AST workforce. This inattention to the AST scheme as a potentially systems changing agency was part of the long-term instability of the model. The only large-scale work was undertaken by this author and colleagues over a five-year period, including a major survey of ASTs in 2010, a follow up of survey with LA coordinators and then qualitative interviews with school senior leaders in 2013 and 2015.

## The surveys

Data were collected using a mixed method research design, through online survey and in-depth interviews with ASTs in England. Using a national database of 1,400 ASTs as the sampling frame, ASTs were invited to participate in the study via email. In total, 829 ASTs from across England participated in the online survey, giving an extremely high response rate of 69 per cent. The national survey gave a detailed and authoritative picture of ASTs. A further 40 follow up in-depth telephone interviews were then carried out.

Of those included in the survey: 75 per cent were female and 25 per cent male; 40 per cent worked in secondary schools; 33 per cent in primary schools; and 7 per cent in special and 'other' schools, for example Sixth Form, Pupil Referral Unit, and so on. All curriculum subject areas were captured in the survey, with science (12 per cent), English (9.5 per cent) and maths (9 per cent) most frequently represented – this replicates the main subject areas for ASTs in the English secondary sector. Significantly 85 per cent of AST posts were funded by their Local Authority (LA), with the remaining 15 per cent being funded by their employing school.

The online survey included closed and open-ended questions. Forty ASTs were interviewed using a semi-structured interview schedule that was devised following an analysis of the survey results. Questions addressed the main topics of the survey, focusing on particular examples of support, impact, changes to their status and views on the policy instrument overall. Some chi-square tests of the association between certain key variables, for example whether training was provided between assessment and starting the role and since becoming an AST, were included in the findings. Direct interviewee quotes are used here to highlight key themes in the complex working lives of ASTs.

## Survey results

### Assessment and preparation

Of the participating ASTs, 60 per cent found the assessment process time consuming and, at worst, a frustrating process for a small minority (7 per cent). More than half of the surveyed ASTs, however, felt that the level of assessment 'was about right'. Only a quarter of ASTs received any training before starting their role, meaning that most felt ill-prepared. Of this group of ASTs who had training between assessment and starting the role, 91.5 per cent had received additional training since becoming an AST. Even though a small proportion had training early on, they were nevertheless highly significantly more likely than those who did not receive prior training to also go on to additional training ($X^2$ (1df) = 31.482, p <0.000). How well prepared teachers considered themselves to be is very significantly associated with training and support ($X^2$ (4df) = 34.530, p <0.001).

> I seem to remember having an hour's chat with the co-ordinator and that was my introduction ... I tried to take it as a positive challenge but, in all honesty, it would have been good to have had some training.
> 
> *(Male, Secondary)*

Twenty per cent of teachers found out about the AST role for themselves. The 80 per cent who were directed towards the post were primarily encouraged by their heads, school leadership team (SLT), Ofsted or LA advisors. Proportionally, teachers whose headteacher suggested they become an AST felt the most prepared.

## 'Being' an AST

Of the respondents, 85 per cent enjoyed being an AST 'most of the time', with more than two fifths stating that the role was what they expected it to be. However, almost all ASTs found the role demanding, primarily because of large workloads (24 per cent) and the amount of time it required (33 per cent). Levels and perceptions of support varied but primarily centred on practical issues that related to the facilitation of out-reach work and appropriate preparation time. A key focus for the work of an AST was the 20 per cent of teaching time spent on out-reach. However, issues around timetabling, lesson cover, as well as attitudes of the head and the SLT to the role, had an important impact on how well this requirement was facilitated.

> [S]ometimes I only have one period for outreach and so for me to travel there and then get back for my next lesson means it's just not possible for me to go and do it.
> 
> *(Female, Primary)*

> [H]ow well you are supported in your own school and how your colleagues see you will be very much dependant on the head's attitudes ... the first head I had was completely opposed to out-reach so was not supportive. She wanted my focus to be on my own school. My new head is much more behind out-reach and so it is easier.
> 
> *(Male, Primary)*

A chi-square test indicated a highly significant association between how much an AST enjoyed the role and these levels of support ($X^2$ (4df) = 53.928, p <0.001). Staff who enjoyed the role least were more likely to consider giving up the post or leaving teaching altogether. In addition, while most ASTs reported feeling that their work and skills were appreciated and respected in school, 13 per cent did not, experiencing either direct negativity from colleagues (15 per cent) or simple ignorance about the nature of the role (15 per cent). One commented, for example, 'despite explaining to colleagues, some feel I get paid a high, full time wage for doing less teaching than they do'.

## Deployment and impact

It was difficult definitively to outline an AST's role as much of their work was dependent on Local Authority and school priorities. Its focus could range from 1:1 mentoring support for a struggling teacher, INSET training provision to departments or whole school intervention strategies. Interestingly, just over half of ASTs believed their schools were currently allowing them to make the best use of their skills. In addition, a shift in emphasis over a period of years saw far greater focus on schools in special measures. An example of the kind of comment that was made was:

> [T]he job isn't what it was when I first started as an AST, it's a lot harder now. I used to go into any school that asked for my support but now it's just the schools on Special Measures ... and it's about dealing with either poor teaching or poor leadership ... it makes it harder because often they don't want you there, well not at first. It's just a really challenging environment and I guess it's that which makes the role harder than it was.

A fifth of ASTs did not feel they were doing enough out-reach; with 41 per cent stating they wanted more than they were actually doing. However, based on feedback, teachers were clear they were having an impact, with support of teachers (38 per cent) and the training provision (31 per cent) being their biggest contribution as an AST:

> [M]y greatest impact is with NQTs, because they've been successful ... from the feedback ... they stay in the school.
>
> *(Female, Secondary)*

> [W]ell, results have gone up, department wise and (when I work with individuals) teaching quality has gone up ... from the informal feedback (I get) from teachers.
>
> *(Female, Secondary)*

> I think I've had a huge impact, not just in the county but nationally. I'm invited to give workshops in schools all over the country and I've had a lot of people come and observe me and I do training with them: deputy heads, new advisors.
>
> *(Male, Secondary)*

> [W]hen you get asked to do things more than once, that feels like they value what I do and get a lot out of it. Some of my work comes as a request from people who have spoken to other people so, it's sort of 'word of mouth'. That feels like a way of measuring impact. The things I organise outside of school time; that are voluntary in terms of attendance, they are repeatedly well attended and people are keen to take part. This is informal evidence to show my role as an AST is effective.
> *(Male, Secondary)*

Quantifying this 'impact' however, is clearly problematic, given the diverse ways that ASTs are deployed and utilised:

> I can't generalise on my impact because the role is so varied ... and it would depend on how you measure these things.
> *(Female, Secondary)*

In terms of the government's policy initiative and the key aims behind the introduction of the grade of AST, almost all teachers agreed that the role was achieving what the government intended it to in terms of raising standards and retaining teachers. As one commented: 'all I can say is that I do really think that ASTs are shaping educational policy in the classroom'.

## *Feedback*

Feedback to ASTs was not systematic and varied from performance management, evaluation sheets and self-evaluation, to informal feedback based on conversations. The research demonstrated that 70 per cent of ASTs received some form of feedback while 30 per cent received none. Headteachers were responsible for 25 per cent of the feedback received, SLT and Heads of departments accounted for 22.5 per cent and LA coordinators 39 per cent of feedback to ASTs. Of those ASTs who received no feedback, 87 per cent stated they would find it helpful to have some.

> I do get feedback ... from my line manager and outreach schools and from the performance management of my role.
> *(Male, Secondary)*

> Well I suppose I do ... by what teachers and students say.
> *(Male, Primary)*

It is interesting that while 61 per cent of headteachers suggested the AST role to teachers, only a quarter were a source of feedback for ASTs.

In terms of Advanced Skills Teachers planning to leave the role, only a small minority, some 7 per cent of teachers surveyed, planned to cease being an AST or leave teaching altogether, largely because they felt unsupported, stressed or disillusioned.

## Having Advanced Skills Teacher status

Alternatives to the title of 'Advanced Skills Teacher', for example, 'highly accomplished teacher', 'experienced teacher' or 'expert teacher' were preferable to almost 75 per cent of ASTs. However, over half the teachers agreed that the title summed up well their level of expertise. From interviews it was apparent that the award of Advanced Skills Teacher status confers a sense of professional recognition that is important to teachers, contributing significantly to their sense of professional self-esteem and well-being:

> I got through the assessment process so, I do feel recognised as male and primary ... you feel you have status, you've got it on paper and they can't take that away from you. There is some pressure that comes with it but, in the end, you've earned it.
> 
> *(Male, Primary)*

> I feel more respected, because of my role.
> 
> *(Female, Secondary)*

> [Y]ou are not in the same position as a deputy or assistant head but you have a range of knowledge and expertise so, yeah, your colleagues hold you with a certain amount of esteem.
> 
> *(Male, Secondary)*

> It's nice to be recognised, that I take my job seriously.
> 
> *(Female, Primary)*

> I feel recognised and rewarded. Outside of my school I get quite a bit of kudos before I meet anyone. It gives you a head start, which is good. I don't feel I have to prove myself and people trust my word a little bit more.
> 
> *(Female, Secondary)*

> [M]y status has grown and I feel good for it 'female, secondary', I know that the parents of my kids like the fact I am an AST, they feel that their children are being taught by an expert and they seem to respect me for it.
> 
> *(Female, Secondary)*

According to the ASTs, the route was achieving one of the government's key aims in that these highly skilled teachers remained in the classroom and benefited other teachers and schools through outreach work. The ASTs in this research were adamant about the need for career challenges and for professional development. It remains highly probable therefore, that without this viable alternative to leadership and management those accomplished teachers might well have been lost from the classroom. As already mentioned, what the whole scheme lacked was evidence of its value from independent research.

## Senior Leader Research study

Partly to address this issue of a lack of perspective on the importance of the AST role, the Senior Leaders in Education (SLE) study consisted of 2 rounds of 25 semi-structured interviews with SLEs, 13 in secondary schools and 12 in primary schools. The participants in phases 1 and 2 all came from the same schools but five participants changed between the two phases. Phase 1 was summer 2013 and phase 2, summer 2015. All interviews were transcribed and extensive field notes were made. The transcripts were analysed to identity significant and generative themes. This was the first qualitative study of the views of SLEs investigating their concerns about the role of their leading teachers. The findings revealed the need for some changes to UK policy and, by implication, the importance of evaluating the current policies of other high performing jurisdictions that operate leading teacher models. It was clear that SLEs remain adamant that a proper national scheme, like the previous Advanced Skills Teacher model, is vital for retaining the best teachers in the classroom and so, ultimately, to raising the standards of student outcomes. What follows is a selection of key findings.

Senior leaders in the study viewed the status of the profession as low, especially compared with 'top' professions (Law, Medicine) and felt that teaching was now an unattractive career for the best graduates, partly because of relatively low pay and very high living costs, especially accommodation in the South. They all had low retention rates in years 2–5 of teacher careers. They felt there was a constant negative attention from politicians and the media, which did not recognise the chronic teacher shortages or the fact of an ageing profession with significant numbers of early retirement.

SLEs considered that some form of 'expert teacher' status remained important to the profession. They agreed that, in the terms of 'impact', ASTs offered value and made a real and significant contribution to teaching and learning, particularly with supporting struggling teachers and broader teaching leadership developments within school. In addition, some felt there was an important element of professional status to employing ASTs and this was something that was valued by parents and the local community. They especially valued the fact that this had been a national scheme, that ASTs were externally assessed and accredited (no SLE favouritism) and that this scheme provided an alternative to a management style career. There was strong agreement that recognising teacher expertise was an important mechanism for teachers who were aspirational and for teacher development. In some schools they had replaced the AST model with their own schemes using a variety of terms with 'Leading Practitioner' or 'Leading Teacher' being the most common. They had not approved the term Master Teacher. However they had deep anxieties about the future health of the profession and its increasingly negative image. They unanimously felt that a combination of negative political and media rhetoric, a recovering economy and the profession's recognition of its increasing performativity and draconian accountability meant that the future best teachers were leaving after a few years and existing ones were leaving early.

In 2015 they were asked about the possible College of Teachers being introduced and whether they welcomed that idea? There were mixed views about a college for teachers, a third were openly dismissive and cynical, a third liked the idea but doubted it could avoid political interference and a third were profoundly aspirational that this was potentially a huge opportunity to establish a real voice for the profession that might help to make teaching an attractive and respected profession, both the latter groups felt an expert teacher recognition should be part of the remit of the College.

## Conclusions and some future prospects: developing a special advocacy voice for the status of teachers

It is important to reiterate that there was never a proper national evaluation of the scheme or its impact. Given that this was an expensive scheme funded by the tax payer, this was poor government work. The AST scheme also lacked a leadership model to manage it – for example an executive committee or some form of trustees etc. In that sense the AST itself lacked a proper voice. Ultimately it meant it could be summarily abolished as there was no substantial evidence that the scheme was fulfilling its potential or benefiting other teachers and students. There is strong message here for the Chartered College of Teaching, or any similar nascent body, to ensure that it collects evidence that its Chartered Scheme is working and that this is independently verified. What that evidence should consist of is a complex question.

A model like the AST could not be 'measured' by a crude relationship to the test results of the teachers themselves or those they worked with during *inreach* or *outreach*. What is suggested here is a different conceptual framework aimed at giving teaching higher status and a clearer voice about the value of the profession.

The model must have conceptual internal and external coherence and comprise at least some of these elements:

- It must be administered and controlled by a completely independent – politically neutral – professional body comparable to other successful such organisations in other jurisdictions.
- Its rationale must be premised on retaining the best teachers in the classroom and it must provide an alternative career structure to management.
- There must be a quantitative and qualitative, externally validated assessment and selection model which has credibility with the profession not subject to any political interference.
- It must have a set of descriptors (standards is too uniform a notion) that captures the qualitative nature of the role. These descriptors should be subject to regular (perhaps every three years) review by a body made up of leading teacher peers, senior leaders, researchers and some international perspectives – no politicians or civil servants will be included.
- It needs a strong support network (local, regional, national, virtual) that provides sustaining camaraderie for the teachers.

- It needs a model of leadership from amongst the teachers themselves with additional support from other experienced professionals.
- Over time it needs to create procedures to generate substantive evidence of the value (not 'impact') of the role. This aspect requires further research.

## External coherence

There are a number of additional factors that relate to the external coherence and credibility of the proposed model:

- The role must be 'visibly' controlled by an independent, politically neutral organisation. This body itself must have a strong advocacy voice.
- The organisation must be public facing and create an understanding amongst parents and communities of the value of the role; engaging with this work should be part of the remit of all the teachers.
- The body and its selected and accredited 'special' teachers must see 'out reach' as a public facing role, engaging with all forms of media, speaking to young people about becoming teachers, developing stories about helping individual students and families that are meaningful to the public, demonstrating the highest standards of professionalism and ethical caring.
- These teachers need to 'voice' the deep aspirations of the profession and aid its recognition as a top tier profession.

## References

Barber, M. & Mourshed, M. (2007) The McKinsey Report: How the world's best performing education systems come out on top, New York: McKinsey.
CfBT (2004) The work of advanced skills teachers, report, Reading: CfBT.
DCSF (2009) Advanced Skills Teachers. Promoting excellence, London: DCFS.
DfE (1997) White paper: Excellence in schools, London: HMSO, pp. 48–49.
ETF & SET (2018) ATS: Advanced Teacher Status, London: ETF & SET.
Fuller, C., Goodwyn, A., Francis-Brophy, E. & Harding, R. (2010) Advanced Skills Teachers: Summary report, Reading: University of Reading.
Fuller, C., Goodwyn, A. & Francis-Brophy, E. (2012) 'Being an advanced skills teacher: professional identity and status'. *Teachers and Teaching: Theory and Practice*, 19 (4), 463–474.
Goodwyn, A. (2001a) 'Who wants to be a super teacher? The perils and pleasures of recognising expertise in English teaching'. *English in Australia*, 129–130, 39–50.
Goodwyn, A. (2001b) 'Second Tier professionals: English teachers in England'. *L1-Educational Studies in Language and Literature*, 1(2), 149–161.
Goodwyn, A. (2010) *The expert teacher of English*, London: Routledge.
Goodwyn, A. (2016) *Expert teachers: An international perspective*, London: Routledge.
Goodwyn, A. & Cordingley, P. (2016) 'The potential of Chartered Teacher Status'. *Education Today*, 66(2), 21–44.
Goodwyn, A. & Fidler, B. (2002) Advanced Skills Teachers: The emergence of the role. Paper given at the BERA Annual conference, Exeter.

Hattie, J. (2003) Teachers make a difference: What is the research evidence?Auckland: University of Auckland.

Ingvarson, L. & Chadbourne, R. (1997) 'Reforming teachers' pay systems: the Advanced Skills teacher in Australia', *Journal of Personnel Evaluation in Education*, 11, 7–30.

National Research Council (2008) Assessing Accomplished Teaching: Advanced level certification programme, Washington: The National Academies Press.

Ofsted (2001) Advanced Skills Teachers: Appointment, deployment and impact, London: Ofsted.

Ofsted (2003) Advanced Skills Teachers: A survey, London: Ofsted.

TDA (Training and Development Agency for Schools) (2007) Professional standards for teachers. Advanced Skills Teacher, London: HMSO.

# 9

## THE FIRST YEAR OF HEADSHIP

A cross-comparison of the experiences, challenges and successes, expressed by newly appointed headteachers during their first year in post

*Dr Karen Lindley*

### Introduction

The role of headteacher within the English state education system can be extremely demanding, particularly given education's changing policy landscape (Higham & Earley, 2013), the current focus on performance (Burnitt, 2016), standards (Burnitt, 2016) accountability (Bristow, Ireson & Coleman, 2007) and performativity (Ball, 2003; Burnitt, 2016), as well as increased competition between schools (Burnitt, 2016), and for those new to post, the 'culture shock' or 'intensity of the job' (Daresh & Male, 2000). For the most part headteachers are well-qualified, trained professionals, but one might well ask whether it is realistic to expect one person to be able to meet all requirements of his/her job description, and more importantly to be able to cope with the unrelenting pressures placed upon him/her to raise standards.

In the literature there seems to be less of a focus on the positives or successes than the negatives associated with headship. This chapter therefore considers the outcomes of a recent study of the firsthand experiences of three newly appointed headteachers during their first year in post, focusing not only on challenges, but on successes also.

### Review of the literature

As the most senior leader in a school with a high degree of power and authority to make things happen, clearly it is very important to take account of what headteachers have to say with regard to important aspects of their job. In a body of literature that focuses on the experiences and challenges faced by newly appointed headteachers, there is consensus among researchers that challenges for newly appointed headteachers include: difficulties caused by the style and practice of the previous head (Earley & Bubb, 2013; Hobson et al., 2003; Weindling & Dimmock, 2006); communication and consultation with staff (Weindling & Dimmock, 2006); dealing with incompetent staff (Earley & Bubb, 2013; Hobson et al., 2003; Weindling & Dimmock, 2006); low staff morale (Weindling & Dimmock, 2006); managing time and priorities (Earley & Bubb, 2013; Hobson et al., 2003; Weindling & Dimmock, 2006); managing the school budget (Earley & Bubb, 2013; Hobson et al., 2003); problems with school buildings (Earley & Bubb, 2013; Hobson et al., 2003; Weindling & Dimmock, 2006); working with governors (Earley & Bubb, 2013; Weindling & Dimmock, 2006); feelings of professional isolation and loneliness (Earley & Bubb, 2013; Hobson et al., 2003; Earley et al., 2011); how they are prepared for headship (Earley et al., 2011); training, development and support of newly appointed heads (Earley et al., 2011); mentoring and other forms of support (Earley et al., 2011); issues associated with change – including standards, speed, accountability, competence and capability of existing staff (Earley & Bubb, 2013; Earley et al., 2011); and poor work–life balance (Earley & Bubb, 2013).

The challenges can be distilled into 'three main factors' (Bolam, Dunning & Karstanje, 2000):

- the complexity of the headteacher's role and its tasks;
- external pressures and demands;
- poor access to training and support, both before and after appointment.

## Methodological approach

The specific research objectives of the study that was undertaken were:

- to determine how the headteachers understood their first year as headteacher and how their previous experience prepared them for this role;
- to determine the main challenges experienced;
- to determine the key successes experienced;
- to ascertain how well prepared the headteachers were for headship, and how well supported they were during the course of their first year in post.

Of the headteachers:

- 'Jack', aged 45, was in his first headship of a middle school transitioning to a secondary school. He had previously taught in three secondary schools, and had held the position of deputy headteacher.
- 'Katie', aged 50, had also taught in three secondary schools, had experience of being a vice principal, director of alternative provision in a further education college, and was in her first headship of an all-through Pupil Referral Unit (PRU).
- 'Mark' had held numerous teaching posts in primary schools, had been a local authority subject adviser and school improvement officer, and was starting his third headship in a large primary school.

The sample for this study was opportunistic as the researcher had worked with the participants herself, and they had all taken up post within six months of each other in 2017.

The study was planned to be qualitative in order to access data of sufficient depth. These data were collected by means of semi-structured interviews (Simons, 2012), thus securing fidelity to the nature of qualitative research approaches. Furthermore, the researcher considered that discussion between the newly appointed headteachers and herself during the interviews would encourage the participants to 'open up'. This in turn would enable 'thick description' (Lincoln & Guba, 1985). Semi-structured interviews specifically offered the researcher the advantage of combining a structure that was not too rigid, and allowed for probing for further information if not offered by the participants (Busher & James, 2003; Lindlof & Taylor, 2002), with the flexibility for the participants to feel able to express their views freely. This also enabled topics, unanticipated by the researcher, to be raised for discussion by the participants (Newby, 2010). Strict adherence to issues of ethics, in particular confidentiality, anonymity, and assurance that the participants could stop the interview at any point in the proceedings and withdraw permission to use their own interview transcripts, fostered trust between themselves and the researcher. With regard to ethical considerations, the researcher followed the BERA Guidelines for Educational Research (2011) and ethical procedures required by the University of Bedfordshire (2015). Although the three headteachers were offered the opportunity to co-author the current chapter, none chose to do this and requested that both they and their schools should remain anonymous, hence pseudonyms have been used.

The interviews were completed at three points in the first year of headship – one in the first term, one in the second term, and one in the third and final term. The interview schedules consisted of a series of questions to be asked of the three participants, which were drawn from literature on the topic of newly appointed headteachers, particularly Weindling and Dimmock (2006), Hobson et al. (2003), Earley et al. (2011) and Earley and Bubb (2013). The aim was to compare issues raised in the data collected to those in the existing literature in the field. In summary:

- In the first round of interviews the participants were asked about themselves, reasons for applying for a headship at the particular point in time, feelings about their preparedness for doing so, positives and challenges they anticipated in the new role, experience of workload and work–life balance in the new role to date, and their expressed need for further training and development.
- In the second round they were asked whether previous experiences had supported with the new role, what might have been useful, what support was available to them, experience of positives and negatives in the job, relationships with governors, and, again, workload and work–life balance.
- Questions in the third round reflected those asked previously, and also included a focus on strategies they had developed over the year and advice they would give to newly appointed headteachers.

As noted above, the researcher was known to the participants, having worked with each of them in a professional capacity previously, though not in the same school. However, the participants were not known to each other. The researcher felt that, because she had previously gained credibility and rapport with the participants, this would, 'engender a greater level of candour than would otherwise be the case' (Mercer, 2007, p. 7). Although there is a disadvantage to 'familiarity', such as the risk of bias, in terms of influencing the research process (Simons, 2012; Hawkins, 1990), the researcher is certain that her position afforded access to data that other researchers may not have been able to access due to issues of access, trust or understanding.

## Findings and discussion

The interviews were transcribed, and a thematic analysis of the data was carried out. The following themes emerged from the analysis: understanding of the role of the headteacher, reflections on themselves as headteacher, preparation for headship, key challenges, key successes, and ongoing training and support.

### *Understanding of the role of headteacher*

In discussion with the three headteachers, and in line with the findings of Earley and Bubb (2013) and Earley et al. (2011), it was clear that their primary focus was on teaching, learning and positive outcomes. For example, Mark indicated that his role was 'about school improvement', specifically in terms of moving the school from an Ofsted grading of 'Requires Improvement' to 'Good'. Similarly, Jack indicated that the role of headteacher was about 'understanding your school's strengths and pushing from there', whilst 'keeping the quality of the education as good as it can be'; whereas for Katie, her understanding of her role was to do with 'high expectations'. Thus, all three headteachers focused on the change required of the school in their new role, specifically with regard to accountability, or the performance of their school (Burnitt, 2016; Earley & Bubb, 2013; Earley et al., 2011).

However, it is important to note that the three headteachers were at different career stages and had taken up post in three very different types of school: a middle/secondary school, an all-through Pupil Referral Unit, and a primary school. Indeed, the nature of the school context varied significantly, and early on in the study was highlighted as an important factor in that their experiences were context bound; indeed, Mark commented,

> Every school is unique, but boy is this school unique! [...]The LA say 'yes, we've never known a school like it' – it's good to know that because when you start to think this is normal you need to go – it's a sign that you need to get out.

Moreover, because of the demands of the role, all three headteachers indicated that they needed to be seen as a strong figurehead for their schools; indeed, Jack indicated that staff were 'looking for you to be strong' regarding external pressures.

Jack also indicated that he understood that he needed to be a 'visible presence' in the school, who needed 'to be smiling, you can't be the one who's shattered and down-hearted each day – you've got to be the one who says "right, new day, come on staff, keep going"'.

An important factor highlighted early on in the study by the three headteachers was the heavy toll of their workload; in line with the findings of Earley and Bubb (2013), all three headteachers agreed that their working day on the school site was between 7.30/8 am to 5 pm, plus they had work to complete at home in the evening and at weekends. All three headteachers highlighted the amount of emails they received at all times of the day and night. In terms of the school day, both Jack and Mark indicated that they 'walked the school' every day, described as a 'temperature check' by Jack. These two headteachers also talked about needing to be visible to the school community, and they indicated that they were always on duty at breaktime, lunchtime and for the bus queue (Jack), or end of school (Mark). Jack and Mark in particular indicated that strategic leadership time or tasks came in chunks during the working day, whereas day-to-day management responsibilities drained 'little snippets of time' constantly (Jack) (Earley & Bubb, 2013; Hobson et al., 2003; Weindling & Dimmock, 2006). Of the three headteachers, only Jack indicated that he could see opportunities associated with his role in terms of autonomy (see Higham & Earley, 2013), as well as room for 'innovation'.

## Reflections on themselves as headteacher

With regard to reflections on the role of headteacher, all three research participants acknowledged moments of self-reflection and self-doubt, starting before they took up post. These initial concerns were described as 'anticipation and nerves' by Jack. Interestingly, Katie focused on the broad range of the role initially, stating that, 'no single part of taking on a headship worried me – it was the whole thought of being the head of something and being the one that all the decisions came from and responsible ultimately for leadership of it'. Therefore it is clear that the notion of performance (Burnitt, 2016) loomed large in the headteachers' minds prior to even undertaking the role.

The two headteachers taking up their first headship post also acknowledged that they had reflected on their leadership styles and how this may have changed during their first year in post. For example, Jack described himself as a 'pacesetter', who aimed to be collaborative, but also authoritative, stating, 'I expect this and I want this'. Katie also highlighted the changeable nature of her leadership style, 'according to who you're with/what you're doing', but still 'consistent and professional'. Katie also reflected on past mistakes she had made earlier in her career with regard to her leadership style, stating, 'When I first went into senior leadership, I felt I was the big I am, and what I said went. It took me quite some time to work out that to get the best out of people that's not how you deal with them'. Overall, it seems that the headteachers adopted what they felt was the best style of leadership for each situation (Earley et al., 2011), and also adopted a more collaborative, emotionally intelligent approach where possible (see Bullock, 2009).

Jack also reflected on the 'rollercoaster experience' of being a new headteacher, commenting that there had been 'ups and downs – I think there's been some really fantastic experiences, some key moments, but it has been incredibly challenging and I'm not sure that's really going to change'. Moreover, Jack questioned whether the role of headteacher ever becomes any easier – 'It's managing your time through these lows – do I get better at it?' However, it is interesting to note that Jack was headteacher of a middle school transitioning into a secondary school, which had been graded as 'Outstanding' by Ofsted, and he was the one headteacher of the three who reflected on the relentless pace of headship, stating that, 'You move from one thing to the next – if you complete a project or get a member of staff in place, then you're straight onto the next thing. It's a continual process.' However, in line with Gabarro's (1987) five stages of 'taking charge', Jack also highlighted the notion of 'growing into' the role of headteacher, indicating that, 'It takes 12–18 months to feel you're getting anywhere close to where you want the school to be', and, 'I need another 3 years into the journey'.

## *Preparation for headship*

The Department for Education (DfE) and the National College for School Leadership (NCSL) both emphasise the importance of adequate preparation for headship, and courses such as the National Professional Qualification for Headship (NPQH) are ever popular, as were previous programmes including the Leadership and Management Programme for New Headteachers (HEADLAMP) and the Leadership Programme for Serving Headteachers (LPSH). However, is it possible to provide a 'one size fits all' training approach, which develops new headteachers and equips them with the knowledge and experience of all the areas required of them, or is it true to say, as argued by Earley et al. (2011), that 'no preparation programme could be sufficiently bespoke or comprehensive to cover very eventuality' (p. 5)?

Furthermore, all three headteachers in the present study indicated that they were well qualified academically for their role, yet all three denied that having a first class bachelor's degree, an MA, a PhD, or the NPQH helped regarding their preparation for the role. Indeed, Mark indicated that his previous experience of headship, and what he had learnt by making mistakes previously, was the key to succeeding in his new headship:

> It's not like I've not been a head before, but I would have to say that there's been more this time round. The first time I probably just got through on complete naivety. I did stuff then because I just didn't know any better. I got away with it because nobody challenged you really.

Furthermore, in line with the findings of Earley and Bubb (2013), Mark indicated that his work was 'being driven by inspection judgements' (p. 789), and therefore his previous experience was essential in terms of working in a very challenging environment and moving his school from Ofsted's grading of 'Requires Improvement' to 'Good'. Indeed, he confided that, 'If I hadn't been a head in other schools, I couldn't have done this job'.

Mark in particular acknowledged that he was all too aware of the challenge of headship before taking up his new post, stating, 'I knew headship was a challenge – I got out of it for a bit because I just needed a break from it', and, 'even though I'd been forewarned, I didn't think it was going to be quite like this. You don't really know'. Similarly, in line with the findings of Earley et al. (2011), both of the participants new to headship, Jack and Katie, indicated that their previous 'wealth of experience' (Earley et al., 2011, p. 5) as deputy headteacher or vice principal had been most helpful in preparing them for their new role, particularly with regard to dealing with parents, and preparing for their new roles and new responsibilities, including finance, curriculum, data, assessment, SEND, and pastoral issues. However, there is a question about whether new headteachers can ever be fully prepared when taking up a new headship; as Katie said, 'Having never done it you don't know if you can do it – it is a bit of a leap into the abyss.' Furthermore, in line with Mark's earlier comments, Katie argued that:

> I think the challenge of leadership is knowing what you don't know. You go into it not really knowing what you don't know, so you can't fully know that you are prepared because you don't know until things come up. It's only through a lot of experience that you get to be prepared.

## *Key challenges*

Although some of the literature on the topic of challenges experienced by new headteachers indicates differences between heads in different sectors; for example, Hobson et al. (2003) argue that primary headteachers 'encounter more problems with managing time and priorities, improving consultation and communication, getting staff to work as a team, implementing teacher appraisal, and deciding whether or not to teach' (p. ii), whereas for secondary heads, 'Dealing with existing staffing structure was seen as more problematic' (Hobson et al., 2003, p. ii; see also Bolam et al., 1993; 1995), the present study identifies key similarities between the three research participants.

In line with the findings of Earley et al. (2011), the three headteachers highlighted a number of key challenges experienced during their first year in post. The first of which they encountered was their school's Ofsted inspection grading. Because of the rise of, and current focus on, performativity (Ball, 2003; Burnitt, 2016), Clarke (2012) argues that headteachers have had to become proficient at succeeding in Ofsted inspections, and it is this which shapes their work. Indeed, Katie had her first Ofsted inspection as headteacher within six days of taking up post, and her provision was graded as 'Requires Improvement'. Unfortunately, as Katie stated, she 'saw that as a failure [although] the academy chain felt it was a success given the mess it was left in'. Understandably however, there are implications associated with perceived negative Ofsted gradings, as Katie explained, 'It had RI with my name underneath it and that wasn't what I wanted.' Clearly, it can be argued that having been in post for just six days, there was little change that Katie could have effected as the new headteacher, but Ofsted takes no account of staffing changes, and, as Jack indicated, 'as a headteacher you stand or fall by your results'.

The second key concern highlighted by the headteachers was that of their school context, and the issues within this area, in line with the findings of Earley and Bubb (2013), Hobson et al. (2003), and Weindling and Dimmock (2006), were complex and numerous, including concerns about premises, the learning environment, student progress tracking, the quality of teaching and learning, safeguarding and school systems; indeed, Katie said, 'there was nothing that we were doing well'. She went on to explain that, 'The previous head had left the building, and the place was shambolic, absolutely shambolic' with very few effective systems in place, no Single Central Record, and serious safeguarding concerns.

Another major area of challenge for all three of the headteachers was that of leading and managing change, regardless of whether the school had been graded 'Outstanding' (Jack's school), or 'Requires Improvement' (Mark's and Katie's schools) by Ofsted. In line with the findings of Earley and Bubb (2013), Hobson et al. (2003), and Weindling and Dimmock (2006), each of the headteachers had inherited issues with staffing, and, at times, staff negativity; as Jack outlined:

> [T]here's been some incredibly challenging times – in terms of staffing and moving the school forward because the direction of school – you want to take the staff with you but that's not always possible, so there have been some very challenging times.

Similarly, Mark outlined concerns to do with unrealistic staff perceptions of the school's performance, when he discussed 'the staff who have been here a long time, when the school was outstanding, and have still not taken on board that they're requires improvement'. Furthermore, Mark explained that he had inherited a 'poisoned chalice' with his school staff feeling that, 'It's everybody else's fault and not ours.' He further explained that this was 'tough [...] negotiating your way round that, negotiating your way round a school that was just vindictive and deliberately hounded the last head out – there's no point pretending anything else – they did'. It is perhaps fortunate therefore, that Mark was already an experienced headteacher when he took up his new post.

One of the ironies for new headteachers is that leadership theory (see Weindling & Dimmock, 2006) advocates that in a change situation, where possible, 'you've got to bring staff with you' (Jack). In a similar vein, Mark explained that he 'had to pick [his] way very carefully through that to get people on board. I think a new head coming in here – heaven help you – I've had to really pick my way through, and that's been frustrating' (see Earley & Bubb, 2013, and Earley et al., 2011). Furthermore, the new headteachers expressed doubts with regard to how they dealt with staffing issues, with Mark explaining that 'you think have I done this right, or this could come back and bite me on the backside?', and Katie outlined how difficult it can be to 'win over' all staff: 'The difficult member of staff, that no matter what you do, you just can't get them on board – that caused me real concerns.'

Contrary to the findings of Earley and Bubb (2013), who highlight the support that can be offered to the new headteacher in the form of positive relationships with other senior members of staff, challenges actually came from the new headteachers' senior leadership teams (SLT), largely because this was an issue inherited from the previous head (see Earley & Bubb, 2013; Hobson et al., 2003; Weindling & Dimmock, 2006). Indeed, Jack explained that, 'you've got to watch and look carefully at your leadership team; you're balancing their strengths and looking at how they perform', which could provide an element of threat to the existing team, whereas Katie indicated that, 'It's a learning curve because you do make mistakes in the way that you deal with people.' Furthermore, there is a 'separation' between the SLT and the head; as Jack explained, 'It is your decision, nobody can make that decision for you,' and 'You can talk to people but it's your decision. That's where the weight on your shoulders and sleepless nights can come from.' Furthermore, in line with the findings of Hobson et al. (2003), Mark indicated that he felt that as a headteacher, he was expected to be the 'font of all knowledge', and, as he explained,

> Although it's almost nonsensical to think of it like that, if you're the headteacher, you should always get it right. There is a sense that people believe you know everything because I'm asked the most ridiculous questions. You're expected to know, and you've got to get it right every single time.

Therefore, could it be argued that some members of some existing SLTs, or staff or parents could be waiting for a new headteacher to make mistakes from which they could profit or benefit?

Challenges certainly presented themselves in the form of parents and children for the three headteachers. Both Mark and Katie highlighted the difficulty of dealing with children whose behaviour is challenging, most particularly Katie as head of a PRU: 'That was a learning curve for me because I'd never seen it,' and, 'As a head I was having to restrain students which was horrendous.' Mark also talked about some of the very challenging parents he was dealing with, explaining that the nature of some of the exchanges meant that 'your own professionalism and expertise is challenged [which] undermines your authority'.

As indicated by Earley and Bubb (2013) and Hobson et al. (2003), managing the school budget while continuing to improve educational provision is a challenge – Mark stated, 'That's quite draining. We got away with it because of a supportive PTA who topped up the budget by £5K.' Similarly, Katie highlighted that working with people whom she perceived to be focused on financial outcomes rather than the children was difficult, as 'you can be butting heads with the powers that be over educational intent'.

Recruitment and retention was another challenging area highlighted by all three new headteachers, despite their different school contexts. Katie explained that initially in her school '50 per cent of staff were supply', and Jack explained that due to the 'Outstanding' nature of his school,

> Being able to get the best quality teachers [was] a real issue because I can't drop the quality of learning and teaching in this school. I can't just put a body in front of a classroom who I know is going to be struggling, and that's a real challenge.

Indeed, Jack found himself in a position of not being fully staffed; he explained:

> As a headteacher the holy grail is to be fully staffed with specialists and I wasn't fully staffed in September. As a head you've got to step back and be quite brave really, and say, actually I'm not just going to appoint. I'm going to have to hold back.

As identified by Earley and Bubb (2013), Hobson et al. (2003), and Earley et al. (2011), professional isolation was highlighted as a challenge, particularly by Jack and Katie, both of whom were new to headship. For example, Jack said, 'You can feel on your own,' and Katie said, 'It can be quite a lonely position because the buck does stop with you,' although she did indicate that this was 'more of a challenge at the beginning'. Interestingly, there appears to be a period of 'silence' when new headteachers take up post; indeed Jack stated that, 'you go through a starting phase where nobody will talk to you', and although new heads need early feedback to support their development, Jack indicated that, 'nobody tells you as a head' although there is a need for 'validation'.

In common with Earley and Bubb (2013), the final key challenge highlighted by the three headteachers was that of a poor work–life balance, which, at times, caused worry and additional stress. In particular, Jack and Mark highlighted the intrusive nature of emails, particularly in terms of 'making sure email doesn't become all pervasive' (Mark). However, the key issue here was the notion that the work never ends; as Jack said, 'There's always more I could be doing' (see Earley & Bubb, 2013). In line with Earley et al.'s (2011) findings, the high volume of workload and fast paced nature of headship can become stressful, and where a heavy workload became a problem in the current study, the headteachers talked about worry and how this impacted on both their personal and professional lives; as Jack said, 'It's only when you become headteacher that you truly worry about everything.' Indeed, Jack went on to describe a phenomenon he called the 'worry butterfly' – 'you've got all of these different flower heads that are all of your different worries, your butterfly tends to pop on each one, and the size of the flowerhead can reflect how big the problem is'. The issue for the new headteachers is that the 'worry butterfly' is ever present and can lead to significant amounts of stress, which can impact on the headteachers' personal and newly formed professional identities (see Earley et al., 2011), and also on their families.

Mark discussed all of these above issues, and in particular talked about how the stress of the role of headteacher impacted him negatively: 'It's really caused me stress and grief, and middle of the night – I got into such a tizz about it.' Fundamentally, it appears that some of the stress experienced by the heads new to post comes from a place of self-doubt, which can be exacerbated by others; indeed, Mark described one exchange with a parent thus: 'You've done it wrong. You've not lived up to what you wrote in that letter. You're a fraud really.' He went on to say: 'That was a horrible feeling,' and, 'I've not lived up to expectation – you always feel you're just a failure away from getting it wrong.' In terms of stress upon the professional headteacher self, Mark described the disabling effects of severe stress as follows:

> This past week, because I've been snowed under with stuff, all that's happened actually is that I've done nothing. I've got to do this. I can't do that. I've got to do this … I'm almost blankly staring at the screen going I've got to do something!

Interestingly, all three new headteachers agreed that their family acted as a support mechanism for them (see Bristow et al., 2007), however, Mark in particular outlined how his work stress impacted negatively upon his family and described it thus:

> It impacts on me personally – it impacts on me physically, mentally. It affects family as you take it home. Your family become what they're really not meant to be – I need to off-load – I almost need you to say 'it's alright'; 'if you mention that one more time I'm going to get really cross', 'yes, but I need to talk it through'.

Given that Cooper and Kelly (1993), in their study of occupational stress in headteachers, identified that work overload was one of the predictors of job dissatisfaction and mental ill health, this issue becomes a real concern for those who are responsible for the health and well-being of headteachers. Indeed, it is easy to see why Flintham (2003), in a study of headteachers who had chosen to leave the profession, identifies 'stroller' heads, 'who walked away from headship … as a result of concerns over work–life balance, change pressures or philosophical issues' (p. 3) and 'stumbler' heads, 'who suffered burn out through the failure of their sustainability strategies to cope, resulting in stress-related or ill-health retirement' (p. 3).

## *Key successes*

Despite the numerous challenges highlighted in the literature for headteachers new to post, clear successes were also indicated by the three headteachers involved in the present study, during the course of their first year in post. Interestingly, although a visit from Ofsted is an undeniably stressful experience, particularly for a headteacher new to post, two of the headteachers, Mark and Katie, emphasised the positive feedback that they had received from Ofsted/HMI. For example, Mark indicated that HMI had 'confirmed and acknowledged the work and improvements that [he] had brought about in [his] new school'; as did Katie, 'I had made some significant changes, and some points raised in the Ofsted inspection I'd obviously addressed'. This therefore confirms that an important part of headship is to celebrate success and for heads new to post to access feedback, as outlined in discussions about mentoring new headteachers (see Hobson et al., 2003, and Hobson & Sharp, 2005). Mark also indicated that he had found his appraisal to be a very positive experience, which provided some welcome feedback; indeed his Chair of Governors told him, 'you couldn't have done more as a head'. Mark also pointed to the positive comments detailed in a parents' survey.

Jack and Katie meanwhile highlighted their so-called 'quick wins' – easy and quick changes that they put in place shortly after taking up post, which were already providing some positive feedback. For example, both Jack and Katie mentioned the importance of putting effective data systems into place, and both Jack and Mark emphasised that, in line with pupil requests, more rugby had been provided for their students. Indeed, interaction with the children was highlighted by all three of the headteachers as a real success, whether that was in terms of positive feedback to HMI, where one student said that the head 'makes the rules fun' (Mark); or in securing a sponsored rugby kit (Jack); or in successfully transferring a student back into mainstream education (Katie).

There were also key successes to be found in terms of inheriting a challenging school context, particularly where there has previously been failure. For example, Katie said,

> I think in a way that makes it easier because it's easier for you to have an initial impact because you're not trying to live up to an outstanding head who's leaving and trying to fill their boots. You've got very clear direction of where you need to go because there's massive gaps in what's required.

Indeed, staffing and staff appointments was a theme that was revisited during the interviews, because it is so important to get it right. Initially, Jack particularly focused on creating a senior leadership team and explained this as follows:

> As a headteacher you can't do everything on your own – you need a really effective senior leadership team, you want to mould it to your shape and you want the highest calibre people, and that's certainly changed, the dynamic, and using secondments has been incredibly powerful – that's been very powerful for staff to see too – a new staffing structure that's created opportunities for people at all levels.

Furthermore, Jack highlighted the positive atmosphere that these changes had inspired, 'The new appointments we've made have provided a huge amount of energy, so you can feel that energy and buzz.' Moreover, as the only headteacher in the study with a 'first very good set of results', Jack emphasised the 'high morale' this had inspired in the teaching staff.

In line with Hobson et al.'s (2003) findings with regard to school buildings, Jack and Katie also spoke about the need to improve the learning environment. For example, Jack detailed a dance studio upgrade and indicated that 'the member of staff [was] over the moon', as well as the fact that it gave him 'a buzz'.

Furthermore, in line with the findings of Earley and Bubb (2013), Hobson et al. (2003) and Weindling and Dimmock (2006), Jack talked about accessing funding to improve the school buildings, for example replacing the school windows during his first year in post. Similarly, Katie explained that she had dramatically improved her school's learning environment as, initially, 'it looked like Beirut', but a few months later 'you wouldn't have recognised it'.

Furthermore, Mark and Katie indicated that they had built very positive relationships and accessed support from external bodies – particularly with the Local Authority (LA) (see Earley & Bubb, 2013) or other providers of alternative provision (AP) (Katie).

Finally, Katie highlighted the new experiences she had had as a result of her new role. For example, she had worked with the DfE to secure free school status for her school, which she described as 'scary but exciting' and a 'huge achievement', and she had been involved in the development of the plans, the architecture of the new school, parking on a temporary site, and creating a new curriculum. Katie also indicated that a personal mark of success for her had been her status with regard to day-to-day decision-making as, 'People come to you for decisions and you can really positively impact' and 'I got a real buzz being in charge and making decisions – being the head'.

## *Ongoing training and support*

Despite the documented pressures and challenges of the role of headteacher, there is rarely a formal transition process in place to support the incoming head. Indeed, despite headteacher training programmes, including the NPQH, and Hobson et al.'s (2003) list of recommended methods of providing support for new heads, support is not always accessible or put into place, and little was experienced by the three new headteachers in the present study. Hobson *et al.* (2003, p. iii) recommend:

- detailed documentation for the appointee prior to them taking up the headship;
- preparatory visits to their new schools prior to the heads' start date;
- bringing local headteachers together to provide peer support;
- mentoring by more experienced headteachers;
- training in specific skill areas, such as finance and personnel issues;
- a needs assessment process that is acted upon.

Fortunately, as detailed above, and in line with the recommendations of Earley et al. (2011, p. 7), Jack outlined the very positive handover process that he experienced, indicating that he met the previous head over a period of six weeks before taking up post. However, the other two headteachers were not offered the same experience, and few of the remaining recommendations were experienced by any of the three new headteachers.

However, with regard to support and in line with the findings of Earley and Bubb (2013) and Weindling and Dimmock (2006), all three headteachers indicated that they had committed time to 'building relationships and working with governors' (Earley & Bubb, 2013, p. 790), particularly with regard to meeting with their Chair of Governors every week, although, as Mark indicated, the relationship is 'not one where you'd be spilling the beans completely really'. Both Mark and Jack indicated the 'hint of threat' that there is in terms of working with the Chair of Governors, and, as highlighted by Earley and Bubb (2013), both Mark and Katie indicated that their support came from LA advisors – therefore, with regard to support, as Mark said, 'that is it'. Indeed, Mark particularly appreciated the half-termly visits by his assigned advisor, saying, 'I do find those supportive – we do learning walks, and I can do some off-loading to her, but that's not particularly her role'.

However, as indicated by Jack, and depending on the school context, surely support can also come from the CEO or Executive Headteacher of the school's multi-academy trust (MAT)? Given the rise of executive heads, described as 'an increasingly important part of the school leadership landscape [who] can provide strategic capacity and oversight across more than one school or equivalent responsibility' (Lord et al., 2016, p. 3), this could appear in some cases to be a solution. However, could this lead to conflict between heads of school and executive headteachers? Interestingly, one of the key recommendations for national system policy arising from Lord et al.'s (2016) study is that, 'More research is needed to explore the role of Head of School (HoS) and CEO to further understand how they relate to EHTs' (p. 1). Unfortunately, Katie indicated that her experience with an executive head was that they were, 'worse than useless because they are so far removed from what you're doing, it's almost like platitudes rather than actual support', and 'I felt they were otherwise engaged with their whole role rather than being focused on what I needed'. Indeed, Katie gives a very clear warning to new headteachers with regard to who they can truly talk to within their academy chain: 'Ultimately the support I got was not very good. I think you've got to be very careful about what you say, and how you operate.'

One of the most supportive measures for a new headteacher is undoubtedly the role that mentoring can play in their development. In a systematic review of the literature on the topic of mentoring new headteachers, 'the most widely reported benefits of mentoring arrangements for new headteachers concerned the psychological well-being of the mentee' (Hobson & Sharp, 2005, p. 34). Drawing on the work of Grover (1994), Bolam et al. (1993, 1995), Bush and Coleman (1995), Monsour (1998), Pocklington and Weindling (1996) and Draper and McMichael (2000), Hobson and Sharp (2005) argue that mentoring 'enables a reduction in feelings of isolation' (p. 34), and 'increased confidence and self-esteem for the new head teacher' (p. 35). Hobson and Sharp (2005) also highlight the 'reported associated therapeutic benefits of mentoring, including reductions in stress and frustration' (p. 35), and argue that head teachers themselves appreciate 'mentors who provide emotional support and reassurance within an informal and friendly relationship' (p. 35). Hobson and Sharp (2005) also indicate that new headteachers 'also value mentors who are able to provide practical advice and assist them in problem-solving' (p. 35), and that 'Some use their mentors as a sounding board, taking opportunities to share ideas, discuss concerns and uncertainties' (p. 35), and 'to let off steam' (p. 35). However, issues regarding mentoring are highlighted to do with 'the availability of time', 'the matching or pairing of mentors and mentees', 'the qualities and attributes of mentors' and 'mentor training' (Hobson & Sharp, 2005, pp. 36–38).

It is argued that 'Such [mentoring] programmes have been effective', although there are 'notable gaps in the evidence base' (Hobson & Sharp, 2005, p. 25). However, the literature also highlights the notion of new headteachers having the support of a mentor as a 'very important form of support and critical friendship' (Earley et al., 2011, p. 5; see also Earley & Bubb, 2013). As Katie indicates,

> I don't know if I've ever found that to be happening – to actually see that critical bit and actually have that conversation where someone is able to say to you 'you know I don't think this is working how you need it to be – why don't you try A, B and C?' Not just somebody who is saying to you 'this isn't working'. I see the friend bit as somebody who says to you 'OK this is happening, but why don't you try this?' to add that support. I feel that people can be very critical but without that support.

Earley et al. (2011) and Earley and Bubb (2013) indicate that mentor headteachers are often allocated to support headteachers new to post, although this was not the case in the present study. However, as Jack argues, 'there's stuff you can say to them and stuff you can't because they're operating in a similar political context'. On the other hand, other, perhaps more experienced, headteachers are in a position to offer unofficial rather than official support. Jack indicated that it is possible for new headteachers to 'share stuff with them – really valuable', but is this always the case? As Mark says, 'Loneliness and professional isolation is very, very, challenging because of politics. It's challenging to find someone you can offload to truly and talk about your concerns.' Indeed, in line with the findings of Earley et al. (2011), the present study identifies a need for 'a range of people on whom [headteachers] could call depending on the need or issue in question' (p. 5).

Therefore, the findings of this small-scale study indicate that there is some way to go in providing effective support for new headteachers. Indeed, Jack stated, 'You're not provided with any support. You seek out your own methods of support – there's nothing there for you.' Moreover, Mark emphasised that this is a real issue for some headteachers new to post: 'The whole issue of support is quite a worry really, and it makes me emotional – there needs to be something because it's not sustainable.' Furthermore, as outlined previously, the present study found that, in reality, there is little in the way of 'one size fits all' training for newly appointed headteachers, which can be an issue, particularly for those who are new to headship. As highlighted by Earley et al. (2011) and, as stated by Jack, 'There is no training that takes you further or prepares you as new headteacher – training stops.'

Overall, if there is a lack of training or support for newly appointed headteachers, perhaps they need to be largely self-reliant. As Jack said:

> Headteachers really have got to look after themselves in terms of health and well-being, mental and physical because it's physically draining. I think carefully about diet, exercise – probably the hard bit is more that mental side – how do you cope or manage the worry butterfly because it is incredibly challenging and it doesn't go away – it's just always there.

As identified earlier in this chapter, the one consistent supportive factor identified by all three of the headteachers was their family. However, as a 'lack of time for self and family' is highlighted by Hobson et al. (2003, p. 10), is this appropriate, or could this high level of support come at a high cost to the headteachers and their families?

A clear solution to this problem, in line with other professions that offer weekly professional supervision sessions, is to put some form of external and confidential coaching or therapeutic provision in place for new headteachers. Indeed, Mark said, 'What I almost need is a therapist in here every now and then – I need to say that to you, is that ok? What do you think?' because, 'What you don't get in headship unfortunately is enough space and time to step back and understand, ok it was a bit crap, but it isn't the end of the world because there'll be another thing for you to deal with, and another thing.'

## Conclusions

The present study set out to gain a deeper understanding of the experiences, challenges and successes of three newly appointed headteachers during their first year in post. The three headteachers had a clear understanding of their roles, which were largely context bound and informed by policy and the headteachers' previous experiences. There was no one clearly identified pathway to prepare for headship, although qualifications, previous training and previous experience were all involved to a lesser or greater degree.

The key challenges identified by the present study included Ofsted inspections and gradings, school contexts, leading change, issues with staffing, issues with funding, the recruitment and retention of teachers, student outcomes, a sense of professional isolation, heavy workload, poor work–life balance, worry and stress.

However, and although these are not clearly identified in the literature, the key successes identified by the present study included Ofsted/HMI inspection feedback, 'quick wins' identified by the headteachers, positive staff appointments, improving the learning environment, building relationships with external bodies and new learning experiences.

Ongoing training and particularly support for new headteachers were very interesting themes deemed to be lacking by the present study. Indeed, there was no clearly identified effective support mechanism in place for any of the newly appointed headteachers and this is an issue given the advent of academy chains, school federations and executive headteachers with regard to whom headteachers can truly trust to be able to offload. Is this scarcity of support a sign of the times, and a response to the ever-dwindling authority and presence of local authority advisors? Or is this an issue associated with the current levels of competition amongst neighbouring schools? As Hobson et al. (2003, p. iv) argue, although:

> New headteachers tend to experience similar kinds of problems, it is important to recognise that individual headteachers will also have varying needs and be at different stages of development. The recommended support strategies are not necessarily equally applicable or effective for all new heads. It would seem important to ensure that support provision is flexible, individualised and negotiable.

Unfortunately the present study indicates that Bolam et al.'s (2000) 'three main factors' are still an issue for newly appointed headteachers:

- the complexity of the headteacher's role and its tasks;
- external pressures and demands;
- poor access to training and support, both before and after appointment.

Furthermore, it seems that little has changed with regard to Ofsted's (2002) findings of 'inconsistency in the quality of support provided by LEAs for newly appointed headteachers' (p. 5), although this is a broader issue now given the changes in the English education system since that report was written. Moreover, given the current crisis in the recruitment and retention of teachers in the English education system, it is high time that policy makers, school leaders and responsible bodies started to take seriously the toll of high work pressures, a poor work–life balance and insufficient support in newly appointed headteachers if they are to be retained. Given the current pressures on headteachers, and in line with other high-pressure professions, there is a need for independent and confidential external support for newly appointed headteachers, if only for their first year in post. School leaders ignore this at their peril, as the loss of good headteachers is to the detriment of the children and their education, and to society as a whole.

## References

Ball, S. J. (2003), 'The teacher's soul and the terrors of performativity', *Journal of Education Policy*, 18(2), 215–228.
Bolam, R., Dunning, G. and Karstanje, P. (Eds) (2000), *New Heads in the new Europe*. Munster: Waxmann. Bolam, R., McMahon, A., Pocklington, K. and Weindling, D. (1993), National evaluation of the headteacher mentoring pilot schemes. London: DFE.
Bolam, R., McMahon, A., Pocklington, K. and Weindling, D. (1995), 'Mentoring for new headteachers: recent British experience', *Journal of Educational Administration*, 33(5), 29–44.
Bristow, M., Ireson, G. and Coleman, A. (2007), A life in the day of a headteacher: a study of practice and well-being, dera.ioe.ac.uk/7066/2/download%3Fid=17101&filename=a-life-in-the-day-of-a-headteacher.pdf (accessed 19 September 2018).

Bullock, K. (2009), The importance of emotional intelligence to effective school leadership (research associate summary report). Nottingham: National College for School Leadership.

Burnitt, M. T. (2016), Primary headteachers: perceptions on standards, accountability and school context. Unpublished PhD thesis. University of Manchester.

Burton, D. (Ed.) (2000), *Research training for social scientists*. London: SAGE.

Bush, T. and Coleman, M. (1995), 'Professional development for heads: the role of mentoring', *Journal of Educational Administration*, 33(5), 60–73.

Busher, H. and James, N. (2003), Interviews and interviewing, Leicester: The University of Leicester.

Clarke, J. R. (2012), A study into headteachers' perceptions of the extent to which Ofsted influences how a school is led. Unpublished EdD thesis. Institute of Education, University of London.

Cooper, C. L. and Kelly, M. (1993), 'Occupational stress in head teachers: a national UK study', *British Journal of Educational Psychology*, 63(1), 130–143.

Daresh, J. and Male, T. (2000), 'Crossing the border into leadership: experiences of newly appointed British headteachers and American principals'. *Educational Management Administration and Leadership*, 28(1), 89–101.

Draper, J. and McMichael, P. (2000), 'Contextualising new headship', *School Leadership and Management*, 20(4), 459–473.

Earley, P., Nelson, R., Higham, R., Bubb, S., Porritt, V. and Coates, M. (2011), Experiences of new headteachers in cities (Executive summary). Nottingham: National College for School Leadership.

Earley, P. and Bubb, S. (2013), 'A day in the life of new headteachers: learning from observation', *Educational Management Administration and Leadership*, 41(6), 782–799.

Flintham, A. (2003), When reservoirs run dry: why some headteachers leave headship early (Full Practitioner Enquiry Report). Nottingham: National College for School Leadership.

Gabarro, J. J. (1987), *Dynamics of taking charge*. Harvard: Harvard Business School Press.

Grover, K. L. (1994), 'A study of first year elementary principals and their mentors in New York city public schools'. Paper presented at the Annual Meeting of the American Research Educational Association, New Orleans, 4–8 April.

Hawkins, B. S. R. (1990), The management of staff development in a contracting education service. Unpublished PhD. thesis. Birmingham Polytechnic.

Higham, R. and Earley, P. (2013), 'School autonomy and government control: school leaders' views on a changing policy landscape in England', *Educational Management Administration and Leadership*, 41(6), 701–717.

Hobson, A., Brown, E., Ashby, P., Keys, W., Sharp, C. and Benefield, P. (2003), Issues for early headship – problems and support strategies. Nottingham: National College for School Leadership.

Hobson, A. J. and Sharp, C. (2005), 'Head to head: a systematic review of the research evidence on mentoring new head teachers', *School Leadership and Management*, 25(1), 25–42.

Lincoln, Y. S. and Guba, E. G. (1985), *Naturalistic inquiry*, Beverly Hills, CA: Sage.

Lindlof, T. R. and Taylor, B. C. (2002), *Qualitative communication research methods*, Beverly Hills, CA: Sage.

Lord, P., Wespeiser, K., Harland, J., Fellows, T. and Theobald, K. (2016), Executive headteachers: What's in a name? A full report of the findings. Slough, Birmingham and London: NFER, NGA and TFLT.

Mercer, J. (2007), 'The challenges of insider-research in educational institutions: wielding double-edged sword and resolving delicate dilemmas', *Oxford Review of Education*, 33(1): 1–17.

Monsour, F. (1998), 'Twenty recommendations for an administrative mentoring programme', *NSSP Bulletin*, 82(594), 96–100.

Newby, P. (2010), *Research methods for education*, London: Pearson.
Ofsted (2002), Leadership and management training for headteachers, dera.ioe.ac.uk/4525/1/Leadership%20and%20Management%20Training%20for%20Headteachers%20(PDF%20format).pdf (accessed 15 September 2018).
Pocklington, K. and Weindling, D. (1996), 'Promoting reflection on headship through the mentoring mirror', *Educational Management and Administration*, 24(2), 175–191.
Simons, H. (2012), *Case study research in practice*, London: SAGE Publications.
Weindling, D. and Dimmock, C. (2006), 'Sitting in the 'hot seat': new headteachers in the UK', *Journal of Educational Administration*, 44(4), 326–340.

# 10

## PRIMARY HEADTEACHERS' PERCEPTIONS OF SCHOOLS' ROLES IN TRAINING TEACHERS WITHIN A CHANGING LANDSCAPE OF TEACHER TRAINING

*Dr Elaine Barron*

### Introduction

In recent years there have been a number of reforms to teacher training in England which have focused on giving schools a more prominent role in the training of teachers. One of the architects of these reforms, the then Secretary of State for Education, Michael Gove, suggested this would allow trainee teachers to 'learn and train in schools, working with experienced teachers and putting their lessons into practice from day one' (Gove, 2012: online). In 2014 the then head of the National College of Teaching and Learning (NCTL), Charlie Taylor, declared September 2016 as the target date in the responsibility for teacher training for 'an irrevocable shift from the centre to schools' (Taylor, 2014: online). To achieve this target it is obvious that the willingness of schools, and particularly school leaders, to accept this responsibility would be paramount. There appeared, however, to be little evidence of any substantial research exploring how school leaders perceived such a move.

As this policy shift was being undertaken, the current author was conducting a small-scale research project associated with one of the reforms, the Graduate Teacher Programme (GTP). The GTP was an employment-based teacher training programme where a school employed a trainee as an unqualified teacher during their training year. She was investigating factors in school which were reported as contributing to a trainee teacher on the GTP in a primary school attaining the grade of 'outstanding' on completion of the training year. The research findings identified a number of factors but one crucial factor, which underpinned many others, was the strategic leadership of the headteacher. This leadership created a climate where success was possible and where those involved in the training year were given the resources and support to undertake their roles effectively. At one point during this period the author attended a meeting of local primary school headteachers where the subject of the government's intentions to increase the involvement of schools in teacher training was being discussed. She noted the headteachers' concern that this was not something they had been pressing for. Indeed one of the headteachers, when told that the Secretary of State for Education had said headteachers up and down the country were urging him to take such measures, exclaimed: 'Well nobody asked me!' This remark, the ensuing discussion and the findings from the research project prompted the author to undertake research in which she would ask a number of primary school headteachers for their views about the changing landscape of teacher training to allow their voices to be heard.

## Methodology

As the research study aimed to investigate primary school headteachers' views on the changing landscape of teacher training without making any prior judgement about what they would all say, no hypothesis could be made. Rather an approach which required listening to their views was adopted by means of constructivist grounded theory. This, Charmaz (2014: 239) suggests, is research which is the 'study of how – and sometimes why – participants construct meanings and actions in specific situations'. Individual semi-structured interviews were selected as the method of data collection to try to capture what, in terms of teacher training, the headteachers had 'seen, heard and experienced' (Rubin & Rubin, 2005: 13). As Seidman (2006: 10) notes, interviews are particularly relevant to educational research because they permit the investigation of 'educational organisation, institution or process through the experience of individual people'.

It was important to select these individual people carefully as they would come from a 'limited universe' (Miles & Huberman, 1994: 27). Creswell (2007: 118) advises a search for 'a sample group of people who will best inform the researcher about the research problem under investigation'. To achieve this, 12 primary school headteachers were invited to participate in the research. The headteachers were identified through three criteria: that they were current leaders of a school educating pupils aged 3 to 11; that the school held an Ofsted grade of 'good' or 'outstanding', as it was these schools the government had identified as those to take the lead in teacher training; and that the headteacher had direct experience of the three main routes into primary school teaching: the Bachelor of Education (BEd); the Post Graduate Certificate in Education (PGCE); and the replacement for the GTP, the School Direct Salaried route (SDS).

Each headteacher was asked to reflect on the teacher they believed was fit to practise. They were questioned about their perceptions of the current routes into primary teaching, the roles and responsibilities of those involved in the training and their perceptions of government moves to place greater responsibility for teacher training with schools. Each interview was transcribed and data were analysed by means of a three-stage process: initial coding; focused coding; and theoretical coding (Charmaz, 2006). The findings emerged from the final stage of the research and these were entitled using phrases taken directly from the transcribed interviews to ensure the voices of the headteachers were represented authentically.

## Overview of findings

The findings of the research are presented below under four headings summarising the theoretical codes arrived at through the recursive analysis process:

- 'Beyond the standards': an exploration of the headteachers' perceptions of teachers fit to practise.
- 'I know it when I see it': the headteachers' perceptions that they can spot fitness to practise in trainee and qualified teachers.
- 'A journey to get them to where it is you want them to be': discussion of the headteachers' views on routes into teaching.
- 'If you've said they can learn how to do their job in your school, then you have to give them the opportunity to succeed and make sure this happens': investigation of the headteachers' perceptions of the roles and responsibilities of schools in teacher training and their views on the potential impact on schools of changes to this training.

### *'Beyond the standards'*

The headteachers were asked to identify characteristics demonstrated by teachers fit to practise and they responded with descriptions of attributes and actions which covered the job of the teacher as well as predispositions required to become a teacher. There were strong links to Sockett's (2009: 295) 'disposition to teach', which he described as comprising the attributes of character, intellect and care. Character could be seen in the headteachers' perceptions of the ways in which teachers demonstrated their commitment to teaching. The identification of the attribute of critical thinking illustrated intellectual attributes. The attribute of care was seen reflected in many of the verbs the headteachers used to describe their best teachers: 'encouraging', 'motivating', 'sharing' and 'supporting'. In addition, the headteachers believed that it was not sufficient for teachers to just possess these attributes; they needed to have the ability and judgement to apply them appropriately and independently in a range of contexts (Sockett, 2009). This demands a great deal of teachers and may explain why the identification of critical thinking was the category to which the headteachers' descriptions of the actions of teachers fit to practise most contributed. These teachers were identified as able to think independently and, from this, to be able to take actions appropriate to the context: the teachers, Hattie (2012) believes, have the potential to become 'expert teachers', able to reflect on the impact they have on outcomes for their pupils.

Identifying critical thinking as crucial suggested the headteachers perceived that to be such a teacher required a predisposition of intellectual capacity. This created some tension when viewed against the headteachers' perceptions of potentially fit-to-practise teachers, because only a third suggested they looked for academic qualifications. It may be argued that academic qualifications do not necessarily wholly represent critical thinking, but three of the headteachers noted high grades and studying a subject degree indicated that they identified fitness-to-practise in teachers who were capable of applying themselves academically. However, as noted above, this was not a view shared by all the headteachers, with others being more sceptical of the value of the qualifications and preferring to look for what they perceived to be practical intelligence or wisdom (Lunenberg & Korthagen, 2009). Nonetheless, for some of the headteachers, there was the tension that they identified intellectual capacity in their descriptions of 'good' teachers but appeared to put less emphasis on this when considering their selection of those with the potential to teach. This apparent lack of clarity in thinking may have unfortunate implications if schools assume greater responsibility for teacher training to include the selection of trainees.

A commitment to the job of being a teacher was the second most popular identifier of teachers fit to practise. Kyriacou and Coulthard (2000) identified commitment to teaching as a key motivation factor for those entering teaching, with this being altruistic in terms of a wish to contribute to society by means of a worthwhile job and intrinsic in terms of working with children and undertaking the role of the teacher. There was a greater synergy between this identification and the headteachers' views on potential teachers, as a commitment to teaching was the main indicator that the headteachers looked for in aspiring teachers.

These were the views of leaders in the front line, as the government chooses to describe them, so it might be expected that their perceptions and those of government on what constitutes the teacher fit to practise would be homogenous. A review of the standards suggested this was not the case. The route to Qualified Teacher Status (QTS) for trainee teachers is through meeting the Teachers' Standards (DfE, 2011) and thus these can be seen to be used to regulate teachers. These standards appear to be less demanding of teachers than the attributes identified by the headteachers, suggesting they could be viewed as setting the minimum standards for attaining QTS. The headteachers perceived the standards to be a series of tick boxes, or an audit, to be completed in an administrative process to demonstrate the competence of the trainee (Trotter, Ellison & Davies, 1997). However, the headteachers appeared to be seeking much more than competence in the teachers they wanted to employ in their schools; they were seeking the predisposition to do the job rather than simply the competencies (Trotter, Ellison & Davies, 1997). Thus the headteachers seemed to be endorsing the views of those such as Ball (2003), Beck (2009) and Taubman (2009) that the standards represent a narrow vision of the role of the teacher by reducing it to that which can be measured.

## *'I know it when I see it'*

Eight of the twelve headteachers interviewed believed they had the ability to identify good teachers, or potential teachers, early on in the process of meeting them, believing this was about the teacher having a *presence*. For potential teachers this was about the headteachers identifying them as the *right person* or the *person who fits*. The headteachers found it difficult to explain how they identified presence or fit. Indeed two of the headteachers felt the need to defend their views because they perceived that expressing such views did not appear to be professional. There is a tension here as the headteachers could be looking for teachers and potential teachers who align with their own beliefs and this could have a number of implications if schools, and their headteachers, take the lead in the recruitment of trainee teachers.

One implication is concerned with equality of opportunity. If, as the government intend, schools play the lead role in teacher training this is likely to lead to headteachers being actively involved in the recruitment of trainee teachers. But having this choice brings with it the responsibilities associated with ensuring fair recruitment practices. Headteachers, and wider school personnel, are already involved in recruitment in the appointment of all staff to the school and thus should be aware of the need to demonstrate and apply all legal requirements associated with equal opportunities. In terms of the recruitment of potential teachers, headteachers would need to ensure the same procedures are demonstrated and applied. But headteachers who believe they have the ability to judge early on the teaching potential of a candidate, and who perceive they are looking for applicants who fit their view of the school, may be looking through a narrow, perhaps prejudiced, lens.

In looking at literature on how headteachers approach recruitment and selection, there is evidence that it appears to be common practice for headteachers to rely on their own perceptions and experience. A study by Rhodes, Brundrett and Nevill (2008: 313), for example, identified that when recruiting staff for schools there was a 'reliance on the tacit knowledge of educational professionals, such as heads, gained through years of service'. Blake and Hanley (1998: 21) also noted the headteachers in their study being 'quietly confident in their own insights into potential' and this was seen in the headteachers in this study. In a similar vein, Raynor's (2014: 40) research found that headteachers faced with appointing staff looked for 'new staff [who] shared the mission and ethos of the school'.

In the findings only three of the twelve respondents made reference to training teachers in their own schools to join the teaching profession. Yet six of the respondents described their views that training allowed them to 'grow their own' teachers, with five respondents noting this as a strategy to support their schools in the recruitment of teachers. This may be particularly attractive to headteachers who struggle to attract applicants to their school and to those concerned with teacher shortages. It may also be attractive to those headteachers who perceive that their school has a way of teaching that needs to be replicated by every teacher in the school – a one-size-fits-all approach. Thus participating in in-school teacher training will permit a trainee to be trained in the ways of the school and thus *fit* the school as a teacher after completion of their training. Headteachers may consider the government approach as one which endorses their right to select the kind of trainee teacher they believe will fit their school because the current government approach assumes this signifies the trainee would also fit the teaching profession as a whole.

One potential consequence for the trainee in this approach may be that they are identified to be trained to be a teacher only for a particular school. This could narrow a trainee's training to that which the school, and the headteacher, perceive to be good practice. Harris (2011: 29) warns that such perceived good practice may lack transferability for trainees because it is 'highly situated and context bound' and this could limit trainee teachers in developing their own ideas and style of teaching. This approach suggests that there is little for trainee teachers to learn outside of the school but this was not what the headteachers believed, to be discussed further later in this chapter. Yet the most important factor to the headteachers was that the prospective trainee was the *right person* for their school and this is understandable because, in terms of recruitment, most of their experience has been gained in employing qualified teachers for their school. The headteachers' starting point has thus been post-qualification selection of teachers, but changes to teacher training imply that this automatically means the headteachers are competent to select pre-qualification teachers and to provide the training which leads to qualification judged against the Teachers' Standards (DfE, 2011). This reflects the views promoted by Gove (2012), Wilshaw (2014) and Taylor (2014) that schools are fully equipped to undertake teacher training because they are already running as institutions which educate pupils – a move that endorses Ball's (2003) view of governments believing a national curriculum approach is both for pupils and for teacher training. The headteachers in this study did not agree with this but, if given greater opportunities to select trainee teachers, the headteachers may rely on their personal beliefs that they can identify the *right person* to train in their school.

Thus headteachers taking on more responsibility for selecting trainee teachers may benefit from greater consideration of how they might approach recruitment to teacher training. Recently available figures for completion of teacher training show that 91 per cent of trainee teachers on a postgraduate route were awarded QTS, with 87 per cent awarded on undergraduate initial teacher training (DfE, 2015a). These figures were similar to those for previous years, demonstrating that a significant majority of those recruited to teacher training go on to qualify as teachers. There were, however, differences in outcomes for some groups, with male trainees, those of minority ethnic backgrounds and those with a declared disability recording lower success rates in being awarded QTS (DfE, 2015a). Addressing issues of equity for these groups has been a focus for teacher training policy, but the move to place responsibility on headteachers in primary schools to recruit entrants to teaching has the potential to weaken any progress. The headteachers in this study were most concerned with identifying potential teachers to fit in their schools. With this being their uppermost concern, and with primary schools likely to be only taking a few trainees each year, opportunities could be narrowed.

## *'A journey to get them to where it is you want them to be'*

The majority of the headteachers wanted to see a range of routes into teaching in which they should have opportunities both to practise teaching and to study teaching, identified as theory, and that they should do these in appropriate locations. Teacher recruitment was of concern to some and they were keen to see different routes offered in order to attract as wide a pool of potential primary school teachers as possible, what Rafferty (2010: 13) refers to as 'opening the door to a glorious mix' to ensure the needs of all pupils were met by their teachers and which may go some way to address issues about diversity and equality of opportunity.

In comparing current routes into teaching, the headteachers perceived the BEd route attracted those who had a commitment to teaching and who wanted to study education, suggesting this gave trainees the time to study theory and to practise teaching in schools. Negative perceptions expressed about this route were about trainees starting at a young age when they may not have clear views about their choice of career and the perception that applicants to the BEd route may have lower qualifications than those applying to study subject degrees.

The one-year PGCE was viewed slightly less favourably, with only those whose own route was the PGCE seeing benefits to the route, and these were largely concerned with the more academic nature of PCGE trainees who would have studied a subject degree prior to commencing teacher training. The main objection to the PGCE was that it gave trainees insufficient time to study theory and to practise teaching, something the headteachers identified as contributing to the development of teachers fit to practise.

Although the School Direct Salaried (SDS) route is also a one-year course, the concerns about the PGCE route were not replicated. One reason for this was that the trainee was an employee of the school and thus immersed in school practice. The headteachers perceived this gave them a level of control over the choice of the trainee and the training of the trainee. This may align well with government moves to situate teacher training predominately in schools and suggests some headteachers may well be swayed by such arguments. If the government could allay the headteachers' concerns about the SDS route, which were largely about the financial costs, they might be able to persuade headteachers to participate. If, however, the government's premise is that training teachers falls seamlessly into what a school already does and that additional funding is not required, then headteachers may be less willing to consider this type of school-centred route. Thus the final decision may be a financial one rather than a philosophical one.

The headteachers perceived that the opportunity to practise being a teacher was the central core of teacher training, subscribing to Beck and Kosnik's (2002) concept of primacy of practice. Practice was needed to lead teacher training, believed the headteachers, because teaching was best learned *on the job* where trainees could have the opportunity to practise 'professional craft knowledge' (Hagger & McIntyre, 2006: 35). These opportunities to practise needed to take place in environments where the job was actually being undertaken – in authentic settings. The headteachers' use of terms such as 'what teaching really looks like', 'warts and all' and 'the reality of teaching' suggested that they were looking to ensure trainees became classroom ready before going on to employment as Newly Qualified Teachers (Hayes, 1999).

One of the main means of sharing the realities of teaching with trainees was through being trained by staff who were actually doing the job of teaching, identified by Murray and Male (2005) as first-order practitioners. The headteachers perceived that this allowed practitioners to act as role models who could support trainees to observe, practise, discuss and refine teaching through which they might acquire the professional knowledge of the teacher. What the headteachers considered in less detail was how an approach like this, in one school, might also narrow trainees' acquisition of professional knowledge. Black-Hawkins and Florian (2012) warn that this could result in the trainee acquiring learning that is heavily situated and which may not transfer to other contexts. Indeed Murray and Male (2005) caution that trainees require more than just practice; they need to be able to conceptualise their learning and this should be undertaken by practitioners skilled in turning a critical lens on the study of core teaching practices, identified as second-order practitioners.

The headteachers concurred with this concern as they perceived that, in order to become teachers fit to practise, trainee teachers needed opportunities to study teaching. Theory, according to the headteachers, consisted of academic work, theoretical study and reflection, and this required time away from practice in school. The headteachers gave some examples of what this might look like – studying appropriate subject knowledge, pedagogical approaches, child development, undertaking research and being given time to reflect on these to explore how they underpinned practice in school. These examples echoed Browne and Reid's (2012) identification of the need for trainee teachers to be given opportunities to view practice through a critical lens and to reflect on what they find.

The tension between practice and theory was evident in the headteachers' views about the locations of training. The tension appeared to be about what the headteachers perceived to be the dichotomous nature of teacher training: the practical training, which they believed was best done in schools; and the theoretical training, which all but the headteacher of the teaching school perceived was best done outside of schools. In order to develop to be a teacher fit to practise in a primary school, a trainee required both practical and theoretical training. The headteacher of the teaching school believed skilled practitioners could undertake the entire practical and some of the theoretical training he perceived trainee teachers required. This is not unsurprising, perhaps, as this is a tenet of being a teaching school, but he also acknowledged a role for experts outside of his school in areas he felt the school was unable to cover, which might involve working with outside bodies.

This was not, however, a view shared by the other headteachers. These headteachers were in accord with the views of Hagger and McIntyre (2006: 64) who noted that the prime reason for involving bodies outside of schools in teacher training was 'the access they can provide to bodies of theoretical and research-based knowledge, and even more their tradition of independent, critical inquiry central to the development of student teachers' thinking'. The headteachers were looking for academic and pedagogical study beyond the school, which would inform the trainee teachers' understanding of teaching and learning, what Mansell (2010: online) refers to as 'education as well as training'. For some of the headteachers this linked to their views on the acquisition of critical thinking skills as they believed these bodies should act 'as an alternative voice, challenging trainee teachers to critique what they see' (Harris, 2011: 30).

This requires a relationship between the school and the outside provider and the nature of this relationship was of concern to the headteachers. They expressed their desire to work in a partnership, ideally with universities, and there was a sense that this was not what they believed they had experienced. This is an important point to consider as the headteachers believed school to be the place where trainee teachers learned about the practice of teaching yet they perceived that schools were not seen as equals to the trainees' providers or perhaps by the trainees' providers. This may explain the headteachers' responses, which focused on the need for an equal partnership where each partner's role was distinct and complementary (Burn, 2006). It also demonstrated how important it was to the headteachers that their voice had the same prominence as that of their partners.

The possibility of teaching schools leading other schools in a teacher training partnership was mentioned by the headteachers. They, with two exceptions, were hesitant, and some even hostile, to the idea of working with teaching schools in teacher training. Indeed, the headteacher of the teaching school acknowledged this to be true, perceiving one reason to be the manner the government portrayed teaching schools as an elite. Hargreaves (2012) believes local schools working together in partnership could create a collective purpose – the training and supply of good teachers to work in local schools – and the head of the teaching schools concurred with this view. Although the other headteachers wanted a supply of good teachers to employ in their schools they appeared unconvinced that schools working together under the leadership of a teaching school would serve this purpose.

## 'If you've said they can learn how to do their job at your school, then you have to give them the opportunity to succeed and make sure this happens'

The final theme reflected the headteachers' perceptions about the responsibilities and roles of the school in teacher training. The headteachers considered the type of school which they believed could participate in teacher training should include a school's Ofsted grade, ethos and climate. The roles and responsibilities of headteachers, school-based mentors and other staff were considered. The headteachers also reflected on the external pressures which they perceived might prevent or limit a school from participating in teacher training. A discussion of these pressures concludes this section.

At the point of interview all 12 headteachers were leading schools graded at least 'good' by Ofsted and this was, according to the Institute for Fiscal Studies (2014), a typical picture of primary school involvement in teacher training. Eight of the headteachers believed that the Ofsted grade a school held should be taken into account when considering participation in teacher training. This affirmation may be attractive to the headteachers as a method of validating their leadership of their school. An issue arising from the premise of using a school's Ofsted judgement as the entry criteria to teacher training is that it may prove to be a difficult measure to sustain. School circumstances can alter; headteachers and staff leave; performance measures can be changed, leading to changes in Ofsted grades. These were factors noted by the headteachers interviewed and link to Ball's (1997: 317) proposition that schools were organisations which 'change, drift, decay and regenerate'.

Bitan, Haep and Steins (2014: 5) suggest headteachers are 'particularly responsible for the school's climate' and this was evidenced in responses where the headteachers noted their strategic responsibility in creating a climate in their school where trainee teachers could succeed. The headteachers believed this required leadership from them to include judgements on key staff to support trainees, maintaining a strategic overview of the training, monitoring progress and stepping in if there were problems. The overriding sense from the headteachers' responses was that they wished to ensure a climate where learning was at the centre of what the school did; a community where trainee teachers, as novices, could be exposed to an articulation of the complexities of teaching in what Wenger-Trayner et al. (2015: 15) describe as 'a respected community of practice'.

One of the key decisions the headteachers made was in the selection of staff to be school-based mentors. They selected a mentor carefully and made judgements about the mentor's own practice. In a recurring theme it appeared they were looking for a teacher that they wanted the trainee to strive to be like. The headteachers chose their 'best person' to be the mentor who could demonstrate best practice to the trainees, who in turn might take this on in their own practice. Mentoring trainee teachers had professional development opportunities for mentors as it created opportunities for the mentors to reflect on their own practice in teaching and learning (Carney, 2003). There was an appreciation from the headteachers that engaging in teacher training was not a one-way activity for schools where they were simply playing the role of host to trainees but that there were continued professional development benefits to the school staff from participation.

A concern for some headteachers was that mentors should have the skills to work with adults. There were particular mentions of the skills involved in teaching adults and judgements on the possession of these skills were made by headteachers in identifying mentors (Turner-Bisset, 2001). These skills were particularly about the ability to provide feedback to trainees, which allowed them to improve their practice as this was seen as crucial to success. The headteachers highlighted the need to have an organised programme in school which created regular time during the school week for the trainee and the mentor to meet. Lofthouse and Hall (2014) suggest that timetabling such meetings is crucial to creating a climate in which productive professional dialogue is seen to be highly valued. Such in-school organisation features in literature as one of the most variable aspects of teacher training (Jones & Straker, 2006; Webb et al., 2007), with the Carter Review (DfE, 2015b) identifying it as a key aspect on which to focus in teacher training reforms. Webb et al.'s (2007) study of the specific training programme of a group of school-based mentors suggested mentors needed time and training to fulfil their role but that owing to the constraints of time and funding any training given to mentors was often only about familiarisation with the procedures and paperwork. If more teacher training is moved to schools this may be something headteachers will need to consider.

Trainee teachers need to work with staff beyond their mentor, according to the headteachers, to access their expertise (Brooks, 2000). There were assumptions by the headteachers that other staff should be willing to engage in teacher training, something Hobson (2003) noted was not always the case. The challenge will be to create a climate within the school which enables all staff to be able and willing to contribute to teacher training, as there is a danger that otherwise it could be viewed as increasing teachers' workload and they may not perceive any benefits from doing this (Carney, 2003). Additional responsibilities allocated to school staff at a time when the government is claiming action to reduce teacher workload may not be welcomed by all teachers (Menzies et al., 2015).

The headteachers perceived they had a choice of whether they, and their school, participated in teacher training. There were external pressures on school, which they identified as having the potential to limit their participation in teacher training or increased teacher training: the Ofsted inspections regime; whether schools should be expected to take on more responsibility for teacher training; and resources issues, which were largely concerned with finances. There was an additional issue that the headteachers perceived impacted on teacher training – that prospective teachers were being put off applying for teacher training by the way teaching was portrayed in some areas of society.

The role of Ofsted was highlighted as a negative force even though these headteachers, in Ofsted terms, could be described as leading successful schools. The headteachers were concerned that Ofsted inspections required so much focus on their school and their existing staff that this could limit them in participating in teacher training – especially in a year where an inspection was expected. The headteachers perceived part of their role to be one of defending or protecting their staff against Ofsted, something seen in Courtney's (2013) study of headteachers' responses to Ofsted. It may also suggest that, in preparation for inspections, the headteachers are engaged in what Ball (2003) describes as performativity, doing what they need to do to meet external measures and expectations, to enable good outcomes – what one of the headteachers called the 'Ofsted game we play' (Jeffery & Woods, 1998).

The level of scrutiny of schools and the narrowness of the focus to that which could be measured contribute to a lowering of the status of teachers in society, suggested the headteachers. This links to Brown, Ralph and Brember's (2002: 11) views that there is a perception amongst teachers that 'the general community does not value or appreciate, in either sense of the word, what teachers and schools do'. Ozga (2000: 26) has a similar view, suggesting political and media criticism has created a poor public image of teaching and left teachers feeling undervalued. This type of criticism has, however, served successive governments well in creating a public climate which allows their reforms to be seen as justified to meet the criticisms expressed. For some of the headteachers there was the belief that recent government policy initiatives in teacher training demonstrated a lack of understanding of the demands of teaching and suggested teaching was easy. Ozga (2000: 26) suggests that successive government reforms have made teaching 'unattractive to graduates looking for intellectual challenge'.

The issue of the resources required to enable teacher training was raised, with some of the headteachers perceiving that increased teacher training in schools was linked to government efforts to save money – teacher training on the cheap – rather than a consideration of how best to train teachers fit to practise. It is difficult to escape this conclusion in some ways, particularly when considering the ideology which prompted the current government policy of more training in schools – that teaching is best learned on the job. This seems to suggest that apprenticing trainees to a teacher, or school, will mean they will learn everything they need to become a good teacher. A fortunate by-product of this, from the government's point of view, is the suggestion that the schools will need few additional resources to achieve this because they will themselves be the prime resource. The headteachers in this study disagreed. None of the 12 headteachers interviewed believed training in school was sufficient to produce teachers fit to practise and several perceived it was not, and should not, be their sole responsibility to train teachers. They looked to trainee teachers having much wider experiences, going to other schools, working with training staff not based in schools and having the chance to discuss, debate and reflect on their experiences away from the school.

## Conclusion

In considering the training of teachers fit to practise, the headteachers looked for attributes in teachers which went well beyond those detailed in the Teachers' Standards (DfE, 2011), particularly in terms of critical thinking skills. Yet some of the headteachers believed they had the ability to spot good teachers early on in the process of meeting them, and they extended this to spotting potential in prospective teachers. The headteachers believed that trainee teachers should spend the majority of their training in schools where they could practise being teachers. However they also wanted to work with academic partners who would provide the theoretical training and reflective opportunities needed to allow the trainees to reach their full potential. Academic partners were most frequently described as universities and there was a level of mistrust exhibited by some of the headteachers of the idea that teaching schools could assume this role, when in practice the headteachers believed trainees needed to be placed in good schools where a climate existed that supported their training. The trainees needed to have opportunities to engage in professional dialogue with skilled mentors and expert practitioners. Headteachers perceived senior leaders, most usually themselves, needed to maintain a strategic overview of teacher training in schools. External factors, such as Ofsted inspections and funding, put pressure on schools and the headteachers believed such pressures might cause them to reconsider participation in teacher training.

## References

Ball, S. (1997) 'Good school/bad school: Paradox and fabrication'. *British Journal of Sociology in Education*, 18(3), 317–336.

Ball, S. (2003) 'The teachers' soul and the terrors of performativity'. *Journal of Education Policy*, 18(2), 215–218.

Beck, C. and Kosnik, C. (2002) 'Professors and the practicum: Involvement of university faculty in pre-service practicum supervision'. *Journal of Teacher Education*, 53(1), 6–19.

Beck, J. (2009) 'Appropriating professionalism: Restructuring the official knowledge base of England's 'modernised' teaching profession'. *British Journal of Sociology of Education*, 30(1), 3–14.

Bitan, K., Haep, A. and Steins, G. (2014) 'School inspections still in dispute – an exploratory study of school principals' perceptions of school inspections'. *International Journal of Leadership in Education: Theory and Practice*, 18(4), 418–439.

Black-Hawkins, K. and Florian, L. (2012) 'Classroom teachers' craft knowledge of their inclusive practice'. *Teachers and Teaching: Theory and Practice*, 18(5), 567–584.

Blake, D. and Hanley, V. (1998) 'The views of recently qualified primary PGCE teachers and their headteachers on effective initial teacher education'. *Journal of Further and Higher Education*, 22(1), 15–24.

Brooks, V. (2000) 'School-based Initial Teacher Training: Squeezing a quart into a pint pot or a square peg into a round hole?' *Mentoring and Tutoring: Partnership in Learning*, 8(2), 99–112.

Brown, M., Ralph, S. and Brember, I. (2002) 'Change-linked work-related stress in British teachers'. *Research in Education*, 67, 1–12.

Browne, L. and Reid, J. (2012) 'Changing localities for teacher training: the potential impact on professional formation and the university sector response'. *Journal of Education for Teaching*, 38(4), 497–508.

Burn, K. (2006) 'Promoting critical conversations: The distinctive contribution of higher education as a partner in the professional preparation of teachers'. *Journal of Education for Teaching: International Research and Pedagogy*, 32(3), 243–258.

Carney, S. (2003) 'Learning from school-based teacher training: Possibilities and constraints for experienced teachers'. *Scandinavian Journal of Educational Research*, 47(4), 413–429.

Charmaz, K. (2006) *Constructing grounded theory: A practical guide through qualitative analysis*. London: Sage.

Charmaz, K. (2014) *Constructing grounded theory*, 2nd ed. London: Sage.

Courtney, S. (2013) 'Head teachers' experiences of school inspection under Ofsted's January 2012 framework'. *Management in Education*, 27(4), 164–169.

Creswell, J. (2007) *Qualitative inquiry and research design: Choosing among five approaches*, 2nd ed. Thousand Oaks, CA: Sage.

DfE (2011) Teachers' standards. London: DfE.

DfE (2015a) ITT performance profiles management information: 2013 to 2014. Available at: https://www.gov.uk/government/statistics/itt-performance-profiles-management-information-2013-to-2014 (accessed 5 April 2016).

DfE (2015b) Carter review of Initial Teacher Training (ITT). Available at: https://assets.publishing.service.gov.uk/government/uploads/system/uploads/attachment_data/file/399957/Carter_Review.pdf (accessed 11 February 2015).

Gove, M. (2012) Speech to the National College Annual Conference on 14th June. Available at: https://www.gov.uk/government/speeches/michael-gove-at-the-national-college-annual-conference (accessed 5 April 2014).

Hagger, H. and McIntyre, D. (2006) *Learning teaching from teachers: Realising the potential of school-based teacher education*. Maidenhead: Open University Press.

Hargreaves, D. (2012) *A self-improving school system: Towards maturity*. Nottingham: NCSL.

Harris, R. (2011) 'Learning how to be a teacher – lessons the government needs to learn'. *Prospero*, 17(3), 28–33.

Hattie, J. (2012) *Visible learning for teachers: Maximising impact on learning*. London: Routledge.

Hayes, D. (1999) 'Opportunity and obstacles in the competency-based training and assessment of primary teachers in England'. *Harvard Educational Review*, 69(1), 1–29.

Hobson, A. (2003) 'Trainee teachers' conceptions and evaluations of 'theory' in initial teacher training (ITT)'. *Mentoring and Tutoring: Partnership in Learning*, 11(3), 245–261.

Institute for Fiscal Studies (2014) The cost benefits of different initial teacher training routes: IFS Report R100. London: IFS.
Jeffery, B. and Woods, P. (1998) *Testing teachers: The effect of school inspections on primary teachers*. London: Falmer.
Jones, M. and Straker, K. (2006) 'What informs mentors' practice when working with trainees and newly qualified teachers?' *Journal of Education for Teaching*, 32(2), 165–184.
Kyriacou, C. and Coulthard, M. (2000) 'Undergraduates' views of teaching as a career choice'. *Journal of Education for Teaching*, 26(2), 117–126.
Lofthouse, R. and Hall, E. (2014) 'Developing practices in teachers' professional dialogue in England: Using Coaching Dimensions as an epistemic tool'. *Professional Development in Education*, 40(5), 758–778.
Lunenberg, M. and Korthagen, F. (2009) 'Experience, theory and practical wisdom in teaching and teacher education'. *Teachers and Teaching*, 15(2), 225–240.
Mansell, W. (2010) 'Train or educate teachers?' *Kappan Magazine*, 92(2), 90–91.
Menzies, L., Parameshwaran, M., Trethewey, A., Shaw, B., Baars, S. and Chiong, C. (2015) *Why teach?* London: LKMCo/Pearson.
Miles, M.B. and Huberman, A.M. (1994) *Qualitative data analysis: An expanded source book*. 2nd ed. Thousand Oaks, CA: Sage.
Murray, J. and Male, T. (2005) 'Becoming a teacher educator: Evidence from the field.' *Teaching and Teacher Education*, 21(2), 125–142.
Ozga, J. (2000) *Policy research in educational settings: Contested terrains*. Buckingham: Open University Press.
Rafferty, F. (2010) 'Just how well qualified should teachers be?' *Education Journal*, 121, 13.
Raynor, S. (2014) 'Playing by the rules? The professional values of headteachers tested by the changing policy context'. *Management in Education*, 28(2), 38–43.
Rhodes, C., Brundrett, M. and Nevill, A. (2008) 'Leadership Talent Identification and development'. *Educational Management, Administration and Leadership*, 36(3), 311–335.
Rubin, H. and Rubin, I. (2005) *Qualitative interviewing: The art of hearing data*. 2nd ed. Thousand Oaks, CA: Sage.
Seidman, I. (2006) *Interviewing as qualitative research: A guide for researchers in education and the social sciences*, 3rd ed. New York: Teacher College Press.
Sockett, H. (2009) 'Dispositions as virtues'. *Journal of Teacher Education*, 60(3), 291–303.
Taubman, P. (2009) *Teaching by numbers: Demonstrating the discourse of standards and accountability in education*. Abingdon: Routledge.
Taylor, C. (2014) Speech to the North of England Education Conference on 17th January. Available at: https://www.gov.uk/government/speeches/charlie-taylor-speech-to-the-north-of-england-education-conference (accessed: 10 January 2015).
Trotter, A., Ellison, L. and Davies, B. (1997). Determining and developing competencies in schools. In B. Davies and L. Ellison (eds), *School leadership for the 21st century: A competency and knowledge approach*. London: Routledge, pp. 54–67.
Turner-Bisset, R. (2001) *Expert teaching*. London: Fulton.
Webb, M., Pachler, N., Mitchell, H. and Herrington, N. (2007) 'Towards a pedagogy of mentor education'. *Journal of In-Service Education*, 33(2), 171–188.
Wenger-Trayner, E., Fenton-O'Creevy, M., Hutchinson, S., Kubiak, C. and Wenger-Trayner, B. (eds) (2015) *Learning in landscapes of practice: Boundaries, identity, and knowledgeability in Practice-based learning*. Abingdon: Routledge.
Wilshaw, M. (2014) Speech to the North of England Education Conference on 15th January. Available at: http://webarchive.nationalarchives.gov.uk/20141124154759/http://www.ofsted.gov.uk/resources/north-of-england-education-conference-2014-hmci-speech (accessed 2 January 2015).

# 11

# LOST IN TRANSLATION

A discussion of a small scale study of South Asian non-English speaking parents' experiences of negotiating their children's primary schooling

*Anna Graham and Rumisaa Shabir*

### Introduction

In the last decade, immigration has been the subject of intense debate in the UK raising particular concerns about segregated communities and schools, the exclusion of immigrant families from access to services and opportunities and the broader societal implications of ethnically segregated communities for integration and social cohesion (Cantle, 2001; Osler, 2009; Statham, Harris & Glenn, 2010; Hasmath, 2011). Within education, there has been particular focus on schools with high proportions of children speaking English as an Additional Language, specifically in relation to refugee and asylum seekers and EU migration from Eastern European countries. However, while research has focused on school funding, EAL pupil experiences and attainment (Arnot et al., 2014; Evans & Liu, 2018; Hutchinson, 2018) there has been a lack of recent research that generates greater understanding of the cultural and linguistic barriers faced by non-English speaking parents from established British South Asian communities in supporting their children's education. The latest UK census (Office of National Statistics, 2011) shows that adults of Pakistani (18.9 per cent) and Bangladeshi (21.9 per cent) origins self-identified as having poor levels of English language proficiency, amongst whom, women were disproportionately represented. As children's primary carers, women are at the forefront of relationships with schools and teachers and carry the principal emotional, practical and economic burdens of meeting school demands. As Reay (1998) and Byrne (2006) have argued, it is through the informal day-to-day interactions of dropping off and collecting children, and discussions at the school gate and classroom doors, that information is exchanged, mutual understandings of home and school life reached and parent–teacher partnerships established. These are the important and often brief but illuminating moments when mothers can ask questions, intervene in academic and pastoral care decisions and advocate for their children.

While a wealth of research has identified the ways in which social class, gender and ethnicity intersect to constrain the capacity of parents to meet school prescriptions of involvement (Reay, 1998, 2000; Lareau & McNamara Horvat, 1999; Lareau, 2002; Crozier, 2001; Abbas, 2007; Byrne, 2006; Bhopal, 2014; Vincent, 2017), few studies, with the notable exception of Crozier and Davies (2006, 2007), explore the lived experiences of specifically non-English speaking parents living in established British South Asian communities. The importance of parental involvement in schooling and more particularly in children's learning (Goodall & Montgomery, 2014) takes on particular significance in the context of government withdrawal in 2011 of the Ethnic Minority Achievement Grant (EMAG) funding dedicated to raising attainment of children with EAL in schools and its subsequent replacement with Direct Grant Funding which is not ring fenced for EAL provision. Therefore, amid new calls for the engagement of parents of EAL learners in positive support for their children's language development including language support for parents, commitment by schools to enhance communication through clear strategies such as language awareness policies, timely information and plain English information on school uniform, school meals, homework clubs and guidance from teachers about the ways in which parents can help children's learning, there remains a significant lack of understanding amongst teachers about the barriers to engagement for non-English speaking parents. While Goodall and Montgomery (2014) argue that a model for parental engagement in their children's learning should not be equated with or judged on the basis of interaction with school, Rudney (2005) highlights that teachers make assumptions about parents' commitments, aspirations and expectations based on limited evidence.

Often characterised as a 'hard to reach' group (Crozier & Davies, 2007), this chapter draws on in-depth interviews with a small sample of parents, to explore family negotiations of their children's primary schooling in a disadvantaged British South Asian community in the South East of England. It highlights the ways communication barriers operating between home and school disrupt information exchange, obscures teachers' recognition of parental efforts to support their children's learning and inhibits understanding of the socio-economic and cultural sensitivities surrounding family–school–community relationships. It also examines the challenges posed for children, extended family and community members who act as language brokers between parents and teachers.

## The study

The study was undertaken as a series of semi-structured, in-depth interviews with parents of Pakistani and Bangladeshi descent living in a South Asian community in the South East of England. The research sought to investigate the challenges confronting non-English speaking parents' negotiations of their children's primary schooling across family, community and school contexts. The respondents were accessed through the community and were conducted in participants' own homes in Urdu, Punjabi and Pahari-Pothwari by a female researcher of Pakistani origin. All of the respondents, with the exception of one (Mr Iqbal), were mothers and had at least one child attending the local primary school.

## The community

All the families in the study lived in 'Highfields', a large social housing estate on the outskirts of 'Oakington', a town with a population of 135,000 residents in the South East of England. Surrounded by pleasant countryside and adjacent to affluent commuter towns to London, 'Oakington' had once been a prosperous area known as a base for specialist crafts and light manufacturing. Throughout the latter half of the twentieth century, chain migration saw the establishment of South Asian communities on the town's social housing estates, particularly 'Highfields' and 'Willington'. As predominantly low-skilled agricultural workers originating from rural areas of Pakistan, Bangladesh and India, these families were disproportionately affected by the gradual decline of the town's traditional industries and, since the 1980s, the area has become noted as a pocket of intense disadvantage with high unemployment, a low-skilled, low-paid local labour market, environmental decay and poor housing conditions. By 2018, 7.6 per cent, approximately 13,000 residents, were of Muslim, South Asian origin and were living in predominantly segregated areas of the town, with 'Highfields' an area noted for its mosques, Asian food markets and clothing stores. Demographically the town had a youthful population with 57 per cent aged between 18 and 39 years. However, only 58 per cent of pupils attending local schools achieved five or more A*–C grade GCSEs, with the national average being 68 per cent. While English was the first language of 66 per cent of children in the town, 19 per cent spoke Punjabi, 7 per cent Urdu and 2 per cent Bengali (Office of National Statistics, 2011; 'Oakington' Community Partnership Plan, 2017–20; 'Oakington' District Local Plan, 2018).

## The families

Aysha Khan and her husband Karim were 34 and 36, respectively. They had two sons, aged 5 and 12. Aysha was a housewife and Karim worked in a local takeaway restaurant. Both participants had been educated to primary level in their native Bangladesh and spoke very limited English. They had moved to the UK in 2015 after one of their children was diagnosed with a serious medical condition and was referred for specialist medical treatment. Neither Aysha nor her husband had relatives in the country, and they spoke Urdu and Bengali at home.

Mrs Haleema Ali was 29 years old and married to Hassan Ali, aged 32. They had three children: two daughters, aged 3 and 5, and one son, aged 8. Mrs Ali moved to the UK from Pakistan in 2010, after an arranged marriage, and spoke no English. Although Hassan was born in the UK and was a qualified accountant, Haleema had not attended school in Pakistan and described herself as uneducated. Haleema had never worked outside the home and cared for her husband, children and elderly in-laws. The family spoke Pothwari, although Hassan spoke English with their children.

Mr Safir Iqbal was 45 years old and his wife Javeria was 39 years old. They had five children: four daughters, aged between 5 and 14, and one son, aged 3. Mr Iqbal was originally from Pakistan and came to live in the UK following his marriage, 18 years ago. Javeria Iqbal was a well-respected member of the community, having been born and brought up in the area and, while she had completed secondary education in the UK and spoke English fluently, her husband was a non-English speaker. Safir Iqbal had studied up to class 11 in Pakistan – the equivalent of primary school and the first year of secondary school in the UK, and worked locally as a taxi driver. Therefore, in the family home, they spoke three languages – Urdu and Punjabi, and Javeria spoke English with the children. However, a recent family crisis had meant that Safir had taken over from his wife as the key contact with the school in order for her to undertake further caring responsibilities

## *Language culture and community*

> Being actively involved within the community has been key for me .... Whether it is a big or small favour, we are always there for each other .... There have been times when everybody's needed help .... Without the community I would be lost...
> *(Aysha Khan, 2018)*

'Highfields' was described by the respondents as a 'traditional' close knit community consisting of extended kinship networks and friends who had the status of family. It was a place where individuals felt safe, surrounded by people who shared their cultural values, traditions and religious beliefs. For women, these relationships were particularly important, providing a sisterhood of reliable, trusted help and advice. Aysha Khan recalled how, after her arranged marriage, she arrived in 'Highfields' unable to speak English, alone and frightened. She struck up an enduring friendship with a woman whom she described as her 'surrogate' mother: 'I was so scared when I came to England ... I have a mamoh gi (mother) who helps me with everything .... Mamoh gi has filled in my children's school applications, doctors' forms and enrolled me in adult learning' (Aysha Khan, 2018).

Within the community, Asian culture and tradition meant that the division of domestic labour was highly gendered, whereas men were the main breadwinners and often worked long and unsociable hours, particularly as taxi drivers or in the restaurant trade, few women worked outside the home and instead were the principal carers of children and older relatives. Therefore, whilst men were working in the night-time economy in occupations that required little English, women who were charged with the day-to-day responsibilities of running a home and caring for their families felt the most disadvantaged by their inability to communicate. Yet, attending English language classes could be difficult, as Haleema Ali explained:

> I am not learning English but would like to learn it .... There are extra support classes provided by the school but I cannot attend them [as] I have too much going on at home ... I am looking after my auntie and uncle who are also my in-laws and I am their full time carer. It is hard as my children are missing o⸴ because of me but I cannot do anything about it, I am helpless.
> *(Haleema Ali,*

All the female participants regarded a lack of English fluency as a hindrance to integration and worried about the implications this had for their children, particularly with regard to communicating with teachers or accessing services. However, women's agency was also constrained by the traditional patriarchal values of their husbands. Men exercised most of the decision making for their families, including prioritising household expenditure, children's education, and organising the family's social life. Therefore, men tended to exercise authority in the home and women were expected to accede to their husband's wishes. Therefore, for women, attending adult education classes could be difficult if consent was required from their husbands, specifically where a chaperone ('mahram') was needed or where it was necessary to arrange childcare and find time for language practice and study. Haleema Ali explained:

> I have asked Mr Ali several times to let me go to adult learning [...] He told me I married as my parents wish ... not to come to England to study .... You do not need it .... If I do not listen to my husband I will be viewed as a bad wife [...] I already have the label 'bad mother' by the community.
> *(Haleema Ali, 2018)*

The community, whilst a resource for practical help and advice, especially for assistance with translation, was also a significant barrier for women. Aysha discussed the unequal exchange value of favours asked and rendered.

> I get my friends to help. In return I have to do a lot more to receive a small favour [...] as I do not want them to count back .... It is hard but that is the principle of life, you take with one hand and give with the other.
> *(Aysha Khan, 2018)*

Requests for help left women obligated to assist others even when the time and effort to reciprocate far out-weighed the initial kindness requested. The notion of 'izzat', or family honour, is central to South Asian culture. Maintaining the family's reputation is deeply embedded within ideas of reciprocity and operates across religious Hindu, Muslim and Sikh communities. Izzat requires individuals to aid those that have been rendered assistance earlier and any failure to do so could result in a loss of family respect and reputation within the community. Therefore, for respondents, the intricate network of social relationships, whilst supportive and enabling, also presented a delicate d complex web of diplomatic negotiations borne out of duty and obligation as well ction. Failure to conform to traditional cultural values risked the family's reputa- good standing within the community. Therefore, for all the respondents, the represented a continuum which at one end they felt able to draw from the edge and skills of family, close friends and neighbours, but at the other, hat these social relations were fragile and their continued social e on these communal assets was dependent upon their capacity with community norms and values. Any disrespect or action that caused offence, whether real or unintentioned, had the potential for women to be regarded as 'bad wives or mothers'. Of particular concern to all the respondents was a continued anxiety about the ways in which family problems, particularly in relation to children, could become the subject of community gossip, reproach or speculation. Therefore, for some respondents there was a constant anxiety about being subject to the surveillance of relatives and their wider social circle and the repercussions of bringing 'sharam' (shame) on the family through their own or their children's transgressions. For some women, managing this complicated web of social relationships became increasingly difficult. Haleema Ali recalled how her obligations to respect family privacy meant that she had few friends and felt isolated and alone: 'I am always at home with the in laws …. They do not like other people knowing our business …. So I do not bother [to make friends] as I need to respect their decision '(Haleema Ali, 2018).

Mothers recognised and were particularly sensitive to the constant surveillance of their lives and the ways their actions and decisions left them vulnerable to the admonishment of family and community. However, it was in the context of schooling where parental competence was most open to professional scrutiny and respondents were unable, because of their lack of English, or unwilling, through fear of family or community censure, to explain their circumstances.

## Talking to the teacher

> I do not need to learn English … I know a bit which is good for me, it does the job … I do taxis so only need few words to communicate with the customers … but school is a different process.
>
> *(Safir Iqbal, 2018)*

Safir Iqbal's wife had been the main contact with the school until his young son became seriously ill. His wife, Javeria, who had grown up on the estate and spoke fluent English, had to spend most of her time at the hospital, where her communication skills were vital to the family. Therefore, for the first time since he moved to the UK, Safir had to manage their daughters' schooling and found himself struggling to explain his circumstances and monitor his children's progress. As teachers rarely initiated conversation, he had to take his own translator to school to communicate with staff. This left him feeling isolated and frustrated and anxious about his daughters.

> It is so annoying I cannot get to voice my opinions …. They think I do not know my rights because I cannot communicate with them … which makes it ok … for them to exclude me from the educational process.
>
> *(Safir Iqbal, 2018)*

Both of Safir's daughters were performing well academically but his son's illness had resulted in domestic upheaval and prompted real concerns about the girls' emotional well-being. Keeping in touch with the children's teachers through the casual interactions at classroom doors and the school gates had become an important aspect of pastoral care for the family during a difficult time. However, a lack of school translation services meant that conversations with staff had become confined to the stiff formality of academic reporting at the Parent Teacher evening, and the spontaneity of informal support offered by casual encounters with teaching staff was lost.

> They do not want to include me …. At first I thought I am new to all this as I only got involved actively [with the school] last year …. But as time went on, they only spoke to me on parents evening with a teaching assistant to translate …. What about the rest of the academic year …?
>
> *(Safir Iqbal, 2018)*

Respondents' regarded their inability to speak English as a key part of teachers' reluctance to approach them or initiate conversation. This meant that parents rarely heard positive reports of their children's progress and the small learning gains and major triumphs, which are the subject of family celebration, went unrecognised outside school. As Haleema Ali explained:

> They only communicate with me when my children are behind or they have not completed their homework …. It is always for the bad stuff … which makes me look like a bad mother in front of the rest of the community.
>
> *(Haleema Ali, 2018)*

The lack of a free flow of information enforced a separation between the children's worlds of home and school and, for all the mothers in this study, initiated a sense of alienation from their children's school lives. Parents, particularly mothers, were deeply resentful that teachers only reported issues that required parental sanction and, where teaching assistants were used as translators, the possibility remained that these problems could become more widely known in the community with all the implications this held for generating shame or damaging their reputation as good mothers. This sense of exclusion was further reinforced by respondents' descriptions of the ways they felt that teachers marginalised their maternal knowledge. As Haleema explained, school staff tended to focus their discussions with the English-speaking spouse. Therefore, while mothers, as children's primary carers, understood their children's needs and were in a position to advocate, challenge or explain, they were rarely included or called upon to give their opinions in discussions.

> I do not have a voice …. I thought I was an equal partner …. It does not feel like it as decisions get made without me …. I am not allowed to have my say. Is it because I am illiterate and that it is harder to communicate with me? My husband comes to the parent evening with me as I cannot speak English […] Mr Ali and the teacher speak English, I sit there quietly and smile … I do not really understand anything. I just shake my head …. When we get home Mr Ali tells the in laws. That's when I find out!
>
> *(Haleema Ali, 2018)*

To a greater or lesser degree respondents allied themselves to the patriarchal values of the community, and for some mothers, teachers' marginalisation of their knowledge of their children's educational and welfare needs painfully reinforced the unequal gender relations within the family.

> My children are noticing that I am being treated differently compared to their father, despite me being their primary carer, knowing everything about them because I am always with them [I know] their strengths, weaknesses everything … I may not be educated but I do value education (but no-one wants to hear my point of view).
>
> *(Haleema Ali, 2018)*

Respondents often thought that their silence was misinterpreted as evidence of ignorance about the educational system, school practices and processes, a lack of care or disinterest. This was particularly painful for women when they had invested their time, resources and emotional energies in their children's schooling and were keen to share their knowledge and expertise. In this study, parents were acutely aware of the discourses of partnership and their shared responsibilities.

> It is a joint responsibility of both parents and teachers to ensure the child maximises their potential. We are both experts, me on my child and teachers in terms of educational knowledge.
>
> *(Aysha Khan, 2018)*

## *Resources, support and expectations*

This pervading sense of alienation from children's schooling, especially when respondents felt they were not being regarded by teaching staff as an authority on their children, was particularly evident when mothers had children with Special Educational Needs. Women spoke of their struggles to advocate on behalf of their children and the frustrations they felt in not being heard by schools who were also juggling competing demands for their reduced resources. For mothers desperate to access support and co-ordinate services, their inability to communicate with professionals was a source of guilt and frustration.

> Parents that can speak English fluently have it easy! …. Unlike myself …. They know how to use the system, they get heard and do not get looked down at like me …. I am trying … I really am … They do not believe me …. [but] I am engaged in my children's education.
>
> *(Aysha Khan, 2018)*

Aysha Khan, like many parents with children who had Special Educational Needs, battled to get an Education Health and Care Plan (EHCP) for her child but found herself increasingly marginalised from the process. Attempts to convey both the complex medical diagnoses and her child's needs to a broad range of education, welfare and medical professionals left her exhausted and angry. Translation services, particularly within the school, could often be reduced to any member of staff who was available and not necessarily the most suitably qualified. Consequently, Aysha was constantly worried that her concerns were not being translated accurately or delivered with any sense of urgency and that her difficulties in communicating meant that she was excluded in any meaningful way from the decisions affecting her child and family.

> They [the teachers] do not involve me in anything, as they need a translator ... I receive very little support from the teacher and school ... I have never been consulted about my son's EHC plan .... Nothing .... Then they have falsely stated that I have been included in the decision making process and my son's needs are being met. I have not received any resources or specialist equipment that are in that EHC plan .... Nothing – I am not lying ... [she hands over the report] if that's true, where is all this equipment and the support? [...] They are failing to meet the needs of my child, so am I .... I need help now before it is too late .... my son does not deserve this .... His rights are being neglected. My children's educational needs are not getting addressed as I have nobody to advocate for him ... there are times when my friends cannot help ... that's when things get very problematic between me and the teacher ... [If] only they could try harder – we have the same goals.
> 
> (Aysha Khan, 2018)

Aysha Khan was attending English classes, but learning whilst meeting her domestic responsibilities meant that progress was slow. She felt that she was in a race against time and, unable to advocate for her child, press for the resources she needed or work with teachers to bring about improvements meant that window of opportunity for her child to make progress was diminishing.

> [I want to be] included in the decision making ... before it's too late ... and my children miss out because decisions get made without me .... I am learning to speak English .... It is difficult for me but I cannot give up.
> 
> (Aysha Khan, 2018)

A sense of powerlessness in the face of professional authority pervaded respondents' accounts of their struggles to have their children assessed or additional support provided. Yet, these stories were also the accounts of women who had to overcome their cultural conditioning and challenge the patriarchal values of their families and communities in pursuit of their claims on behalf of their children. In continuing to contest in a public domain professional expertise and demand action and explanation meant that they risked the censure of their families and their wider community who often had poor expectations of the potential of children with disabilities. Nevertheless, while respondents were anxious to press their children's entitlements to resources and support, they also recognised their own responsibilities to support their children's learning and spoke about their willingness to meet school demands.

> I do not read with my children .... My husband supports the children when he come back from work ... with the homework, reading everything the school wants us to do.
>
> *(Haleema Ali, 2018)*

Engaging with children's learning, however, could be problematic. All of the respondents stressed the importance of ensuring that their children completed homework tasks, but few felt able to help them. Parents discussed not only their poor English language proficiency, but also that the homework set went beyond their own level of education. As a result, they would designate other family members to help but even if they had the pre-requisite skills, adult helpers (particularly men) worked long and unsociable hours and could not be relied upon to meet school deadlines for completion. However, parents were determined that their children should avail themselves of every opportunity that living in the UK afforded them and for some, like Mr and Mrs Khan, this meant making considerable economic sacrifices. When they found themselves unable to assist their child, they decided to employ a private tutor.

> I am worried that he will not achieve his potential, as I struggle to meet the demands due the communication and language difficulties ... he complains to us that he does not enjoy school [...] We cannot help him with the homework as it is in English and harder now ... so we have got him a private tutor, but this is only for two hours a week.
>
> *(Aysha Khan, 2018)*

As Karim Ali was a low-paid restaurant worker, the two hours of private tutoring for his son represented a significant amount of the weekly household budget. Nevertheless, this was regarded as an important investment in his child's future. Education, while being highly prized by families and the community, represented a ladder of opportunity that parents had been denied in their own childhood and all of the respondents were keen to see their children succeed. Safir Iqbal had moved from Pakistan to marry his English-born wife in the 1990s and took pleasure in recounting how family and community support and hard work had led him to owning his own home and the pride he now felt in his daughter's ambition to become a doctor.

> It was hard integrating into a new country, culture, language and community .... With the support of my family I have settled in ... I own my house, got a good job and most importantly my children are getting a good education. Even though I cannot speak English ... I make sure my children are achieving academically .... By the grace of God all my daughters are in top sets .... I do everything in my power to ensure they get the life I did not have.
>
> *(Safir Iqbal, 2018)*

For Safir Iqbal, education provided opportunities for social mobility, but for other respondents educational success was deeply rooted in a desire that their children gain employment, which gave them sufficient economic resources to fulfil their cultural obligations to meet the future care needs of their family members. Aysha Khan was particularly concerned that her eldest son would be able to provide for his severely disabled brother. Therefore, employing a private tutor was an investment in both their children.

> I am so grateful to be in England. I want my sons to receive the opportunities I did not have [and] my eldest to be successful and take care of his younger brother.
> *(Aysha Khan, 2018)*

Respondents felt that teachers rarely lived in the community in which they taught and had little understanding of the complex socio-economic and cultural constraints that shaped their interactions with schools. Mothers described being represented as 'hard to reach' or 'disengaged' but, while they argued that teachers thought that the onus was on parents to 'integrate' and demonstrate their commitment to their children's education, some respondents argued that schools did not promote a sufficiently inclusive ethos. Haleema Ali argued that schools needed to be more open, welcoming and attuned to the needs of the community:

> Teachers need additional support to ensure they can integrate within the community which can create a welcoming atmosphere for all. Teachers do need additional training to work with Muslim parents as they are viewing us 'hard to reach' but we have several obstacles that are to do with cultural belief and communication .... If they understood us .... Things would not be this hard .... Parents like myself are struggling, they do not know my situation and have never tried finding out .... If they knew they would understand and help.
> *(Haleema Ali, 2018)*

## Lost in translation

Haleema Ali, like several of the mothers in this study, felt that teachers lacked sufficient cultural awareness of Asian communities, particularly a sensitivity to the traditions, customs and values that constrained maternal agency. Of particular concern was the ways insufficient care in communication or translation could hold real and enduring repercussions for mothers beyond the classroom. Haleema angrily recounted an incident when her daughter went to school without her glasses for a few days.

> They [the teachers] were going to call social services because that was seen as a form of neglect. Her glasses were broken and her prescription had changed but none of the teachers asked me – probably because I do not speak English. But that one morning a teacher got a parent to translate to me, I felt so embarrassed and annoyed that parents were discussing my business.
> *(Haleema Ali, 2018)*

Haleema was affronted by the teacher's assumption of ignorant or neglectful parenting, and she, like other parents in the study, was angered by the use of other parents to translate. Teachers' reliance on passing parents to interpret breached their confidentiality and potentially exposed their private circumstances to the scrutiny and judgement of others in the community. Respondents were fearful of bringing shame on the family and guarded their privacy zealously, with the result that they were extremely wary of anyone who translated for them. Schools rarely had an interpreter available and teaching staff tended to enlist the help of anyone on school premises who happened to be free to assist. This casual practice with all of the attendant risks of wider condemnation and embarrassment undermined trust in teachers. To preserve their confidentiality, parents often invited close family or friends to accompany them to meetings, but if they were unavailable they had to rely on the professionalism of teaching assistants who frequently lived in the community and were not always regarded as providing accurate translation. Often parents were at a loss to know who to trust. As Safir Iqbal remarked:

> Even with the teaching assistant there, I do not understand the teacher […] The facial expressions always look different to the information I get … I confirmed this at the end of last year when the teaching assistant told me different [to] the report sent home.
> 
> *(Safir Iqbal, 2018)*

The unreliability of translation and the lack of availability of translators meant that parents occasionally and somewhat reluctantly, used their children as language brokers. Aysha Khan recounted:

> There have been times when my son has translated for the teacher but the information he reported back was not accurate-he was lying … which make me look like a bad parent … but the teaching assistant that can speak Urdu is never there …. When she is, that's when I find out the truth.
> 
> *(Aysha Khan, 2018)*

Parents recognised that their children may not necessarily be honest brokers with regard to translation and could often be seeking to use their parents' ignorance of the system to avoid the repercussions of poor performance, but they could also be seeking to protect their parents from embarrassment or uncomfortable truths. Aysha Khan thought that asking her child to translate placed him in a compromising position. By bridging the language gap between home and school, children became privy to the intimate worries of adults and had to convey the professional judgements of teachers. Yet, in the absence of reliable professional interpreters, Aysha felt she had no other option available to her.

> I want my son to live a stress free childhood – not to be a translator, for me and the teacher … I have no choice, otherwise I am viewed as a parent that does not care …. I want to give him his childhood back.
> 
> *(Aysha Khan, 2018)*

## Conclusions

The purpose of this chapter was to capture the experiences of non-English speaking British South Asian parents in negotiating their children's primary schooling. However, it is important to note that the voices of teachers were absent from this account and the challenges and, indeed, rewards of working in an economically disadvantaged and ethnically segregated community were not represented here. Instead, this study focused on the experiences of non–English speaking parents who have traditionally been regarded as a 'hard to reach' group (Crozier & Davies, 2007). The female field worker accessed the respondents through established social networks in a predominantly Muslim Pakistani heritage community and her cultural cognisance, together with her ability to speak four languages, provided the basis for the trust and rapport that underpinned the interviews.

A recurring theme throughout respondents' accounts was the ways in which the school as an institution was a site of struggle, particularly for mothers, in which there were few effective or trusted pathways for communication. However, parents were acutely attuned to discourses of partnership and were highly motivated to engage with their children's learning. Amongst all respondents, education was regarded as vital to social mobility and the enhancement of family prestige, and essential to safeguard the future welfare of the family. Nevertheless, despite the value parents placed on their children's education, in the silences and miscommunication that ensued between parents and teachers, respondents felt that their actions were misconstrued, their efforts to support their children went unrecognised and deficit discourses flourished. Consequently, mothers felt at best marginalised and at worst alienated from their children's schooling. Their accounts of their experiences of language barriers, the struggles to voice their children's needs and advocate on their behalf and the casual breaches of confidentiality occasioned by the ad hoc nature of translation, were also infused with a deep concern that schools and teachers lacked sufficient cultural sensitivity to the traditions and religious values embedded within the community and the ways they shaped their abilities to meet their parental responsibilities for their children's education.

Studies of British South Asian neighbourhoods have highlighted the importance of social capital operating within such communities. Social capital has been criticised as an ambiguous concept with contested definitions (Schuller, Field & Baron, 2001; Bankston & Zhou, 2002). Nevertheless, while theorists such as Bourdieu (1997), Coleman (1994) and Putnam (1995, 2000) approach the concept from different perspectives, common themes emerge. Essentially social capital can be described as the social glue that binds families and communities together. Putnam (1995) describes it as embedded within dense networks of family and community relationships with shared norms and values, active civic engagement and high levels of social trust. In this respect, the community acts as a resource with members able to draw upon the different social, economic and cultural assets inherent within the social networks of family and wider associations of friends and neighbours and predicated on mutual understanding of shared cultural values and reciprocity. Indeed, respondents in this study valued community as a place of safety and stability and reported that friends and family offered emotional and practical support from helping with translation to registering their children with GP practices. This ability to draw upon the skills and knowledge of family and friends was deemed by most respondents as essential. In the absence of direct conversations with teachers, school information was shared, disseminated and confirmed through the informal but highly relied upon, communication networks of parents – predominantly mothers. Similarly, help and advice, particularly with regard to supporting homework completion was devolved to anyone within the family's social network who had the knowledge and skill to assist. However, social capital is not unproblematic, and while it highlights the significance of associational links in promoting community cohesion, individual capacities to access and utilise different forms of social capital, 'bonding' and 'bridging' (Putnam, 1995, 2000) are dependent on cultural capital and positionality, not least in relation to gender, social class, cultural norms and ethnicity and the complexities of caste. As Garmarnikow and Green (1999) have argued, social capital can be seen on a continuum with the capacity to empower and enable at one end and surveillance and regulation at the other. For the women in this study, the ability to access community support was highly dependent on their compliance with the customs and values of the family and community as a whole. Being regarded within the community as a 'good wife' or a 'good mother' meant adhering, to a greater or lesser extent, on the values and cultural strictures of the family. Haleema Ali found her ability to undertake English classes, or mix more widely within the community, was constrained by the patriarchal values of her husband and her in-laws. Therefore, while she recognised the importance of acquiring greater English proficiency, Haleema was compelled to comply with the wishes of her husband and refrain from activities that could lead to disapproval and reproach. For Haleema, her sense of powerlessness was confirmed by teachers' reluctance to communicate with her without her English-speaking husband present. This denied her opportunities to work with teachers and advocate on their behalf, reduced her status and maternal authority in front of her children and challenged her own identity as a caring mother.

Crozier and Davies (2006), in their study of two communities of Bangladeshi and Pakistani origin in the North of England, describe how negotiating schooling requires parents to pursue their own self interests in acting strategically within an education market to compete for school places or resources. In this respect individualism works against the collective nature of community. In this study, respondents were dismayed and frustrated by the lack of teachers' understanding of the social consequences of being seen to act outside of community norms and values. The potential to bring 'sharam' (shame) on their families meant that mothers were highly conscious of the ways fighting for additional learning support or assessment of their children's needs required them to ignore their communal attachments and promote the interests of their own children. For mothers like Aysha Khan, who was dependent on the translation services of her friends and family, the constant pressure to pursue her child's needs meant that her struggles to challenge professional judgements were conducted in a public arena where her concerns about her child's educational progress and well-being were also subject to the scrutiny and opinions of other community members who would not necessarily share her belief in her right to fight to secure her child's entitlement to school resources, or support her desire to challenge professional expertise.

The operationalisation of social capital, particularly the notion of mutual exchange and reciprocity, places huge demands on the unpaid and invisible labour of women. The ability to draw upon and contribute to community resources, to support the demands of schooling, was dependent on women negotiating a complex web of social obligation in which the principle of mutual exchange could often be felt as unequal. Drawing on the advice or expertise of other mothers could lead to complex negotiations and obligations that increased their domestic and caring burdens. Nevertheless, failing to render assistance to others could cause offence and social disgrace. Parents reported that the day-to-day realities of engaging with children's education not only required huge investments of time and planning, particularly in terms of face-to-face encounters with teachers and all the necessary arrangements for ensuring someone could interpret, but also the accessing of help with instructions for homework, deadlines and the necessary support to complete the task. Al-deen and Windle (2017) have pointed out the hidden emotional, economic and physical realities of women's work in relation to schooling, particularly feelings of maternal failure when their actions or priorities were misunderstood by teachers. This lack of contextual understanding of the cultural complexities, particularly the social and emotional risks experienced by non-English speaking parents, had particular resonance for mothers in this study. Respondents' accounts of their interactions with teachers repeatedly indicated that teachers were unaware of the extent of their involvement and assumed that they were uncaring, complacent or disinterested in their children's school lives.

The absence of reliable channels of communication operating between home and school was a key factor in creating a sense of parental marginalisation and alienation. Of central importance was the lack of trust this engendered between parents and teachers, particularly as respondents felt that there were few honest language brokers available to them. Teaching assistants, unlike teachers, frequently lived in the community and parents often felt uncertain about the accuracy of the translation or worried about the maintenance of confidentiality. In the same way, doubts existed about the language competency of friends or neighbours, particularly when it came to conveying and understanding the subtleties of meaning. The possibilities of disclosure of individual circumstance were also problematic when, as a last resort, parents asked their children to translate with all the implications this could hold for opening up new frames of reference for the child about home or family circumstances. While Bauer (2016) argues that children acting as translators can have positive benefits for the parent–child relationship, other researchers (Love & Buriel, 2007; Martinez, McClure & Eddy, 2009; Cline et al., 2017) have expressed concerns about adult–child role reversal and the introduction of adult anxieties and responsibilities in children's lives. Aysha Khan, in this study, was similarly exercised by this and was concerned that her son's childhood should be protected from adult concerns. It should be noted that child language brokering is also infused with the wants and desires of all parties not to cause embarrassment or offence, or in the case of children as translators to protect their parents from the shame of uncomfortable truths about their behaviour or performance.

Recent government concerns about social integration, specifically with regard to ethnically segregated communities, have focused on the role of schools and teachers as key to overcoming cultural dissonance and promoting community cohesion (Ofsted, 2010; Housing, Communities and Local Government, 2018). These anxieties are not new. Bhatti (1999), writing about British South Asian children's home and school lives discussed the ways in which teachers had little understanding of Asian culture, especially the role of tradition, religion and values. Two decades later, respondents in this study were critical of the ways in which they faced pressures to integrate but had little acknowledgment by schools of the barriers they faced. Therefore, if schools are to develop culturally responsive ways to improve educational outcomes for pupils, it is important that strategies are developed in conjunction with families and communities and implemented as an integrated whole school approach that aligns with parental values and aspirations. Goodall and Vorhaus (2011) and Goodall and Montgomery (2014) advocate a shift from parental involvement with schooling to parental engagement in children's learning. For them, parental engagement in learning provides a more dynamic interpretation of the parent–teacher relationship based upon a shared vision of improved performance and educational outcomes. In this respect, strategies to meet the needs of parents and pupils would be implemented through shared understandings of family and community needs and the recognition of parents as active agents in their children's education. Consequently, collaboration and communication lie at the heart of such an approach from simple implementation of a 'pictorially literate' school with photographs that provide information about school lunch menus, uniform requirements, staff photographs and classroom layouts to routine notices and letters written in other community languages. However, while such approaches may promote a more inclusive culture, strategies also need to be outward facing, linking the family–school–community relationship in direct and sustainable ways. This can include opportunities to work collaboratively with parents through family literacy or numeracy initiatives, or support homework and curriculum enrichment through after-school homework clubs (Walker, 2014). Nevertheless, while such approaches can provide opportunities for the development of trust, their sustainability depends on teachers' abilities to understand the cultural context in which they are working and to develop confidence in their interactions with parents (Maylor, 2010). Of central importance is the allocation of resources to translation and the development of trusted, open channels of communication that allow parents and teachers to develop a more holistic view of children and their needs. Therefore, it is essential that schools invest in skilled interpreters that are available to parents and regarded as trusted communicators. Accurate and sensitive translation works to benefit both schools and teachers in which the free flow of information challenges discourses of parental deficits and creates new opportunities for schools, communities, parents and teachers to develop collaborative partnerships.

This was a very small scale study and its inception was borne out of a recognition that there are few sociological accounts of ethnic minority families and communities and their relationships with schools. While this research provided a glimpse of the issues facing families and communities, it is limited, and further research is required to draw more definitive conclusions particularly in relation to the operationalisation and analysis of social capital and the intersectionality of social class, race and gender in shaping parental subjectivities, priorities and actions in relation to schooling.

## References

Abbas, T. (2007) 'British South Asians and pathways into selective schooling: Social class, culture and ethnicity', *British Educational Research Journal*, 33(1), 75–90. doi: doi:10.1080/01411920601104474

Al-deen, T. J. and Windle, J. (2017) '"I feel sometimes I am a bad mother": The affective dimension of immigrant mothers' involvement in their children's schooling', *Journal of Sociology*, 53(1), 110–126. doi: doi:10.1177/1440783316632604

Arnot, M., Schneider, C., Evans, M., Liu, Y.Welply, O. and Davies-Tutt, D. (2014) School Approaches to the Education of EAL Students: Language development, social integration and achievement, Anglia Ruskin University/University of Cambridge, Cambridge: Faculty of Education and the Bell Foundation.

Bankston, C. L. and Zhou, M. (2002) 'Social capital as process: The meanings and problems of a theoretical metaphor', *Sociological Inquiry*, 72(2), 285–317. doi: doi:10.1111/1475-682X.00017

Bauer, E. (2016) 'Practising kinship care: Children as language brokers in migrant families', *Childhood*, 23(1), 22–36 doi: doi:10.1177/0907568215574917

Bhatti, G. (1999) *Asian children at home and at school. An ethnographic study*: London: Routledge.

Bhopal, K. (2014) 'Race, rurality and representation: Black and minority ethnic mothers' experiences of their children's education in rural primary schools in England, UK', *Gender and Education*, 26(5), 490–504.

Bourdieu, P. (1997). The forms of social capital. In A. H. Halsey, P. Brown & A. S. Wells (Eds.), *Education, culture, economy, society* (pp. 46–58), Oxford: Oxford University Press.

Byrne, B. (2006) 'In search of a "good mix": "Race", class, gender and practices of mothering', *Sociology*, 40(6), 1001–1017.

Cantle, T. (2001) Community cohesion: A report of the Independent Review Team (Chaired by Ted Cantle), London: Home Office.

Coleman, J. S. (1994) *Foundations of social theory*, Cambridge, MA: Belknap Press.

Cline, T., Crafter, S., Abreu, G. de & O'Dell, L. (2017) Child language brokers' representations of parent-child relationships. In Antonini, R., Cirillo, L., Rossato, L., & Torresi, I. (Eds.), *Non-professional interpreting and translating: State of the art and future of an emerging field of research* (pp. 281–294), Amsterdam: John Benjamins Publishing Company.

Crozier, G. (2001) 'Excluded parents: The deracialisation of parental involvement', *Race Ethnicity and Education*, 4(4), 329–341.

Crozier, G. and Davies, J. (2006) 'Family matters: A discussion of the Bangladeshi and Pakistani extended family and community in supporting the children's education', *The Sociological Review*, 54(4), 678–695.

Crozier, G., and Davies, J. (2007) 'Hard to reach parents or hard to reach schools? A discussion of home–school relations, with particular reference to Bangladeshi and Pakistani parents', *British Educational Research Journal*, 33(3), 295–313.

Evans, M. & Liu, Y. (2018) 'The unfamiliar and the indeterminate: Language, identity and social integration in the school experience of newly-arrived migrant children in England', *Journal of Language, Identity & Education*, 17(3), doi:doi:10.1080/15348458.2018.1433043

Garmarnikow, E. and Green, A. (1999) Developing social capital: Dilemmas, possibilities and limitations in education. In A. Hayton (Ed.), *Tackling disaffection and social exclusion education perspectives and policies* (pp. 46–64), London: Kogan Page.

Goodall, J. and Vorhaus, J. (2011) A review of best practice in parental engagement, London: Department for Education (DfE).

Goodall, J. and Montgomery, C. (2014) 'Parental involvement to parental engagement: A continuum', *Educational Review*, 66(4), 399–410.

Hasmath, R. (2011) *The ethnic penalty, immigration, education and the labour market*, London: Routledge.

Housing, Communities and Local Government (2018) *Integrated communities strategy Green Paper*March 2018, London: HMSO.

Hutchinson, J. (2018) *Educational outcomes of children with English as an Additional Language*, London: Bell Foundation/Education Policy Institute.

Lareau, A. (2002) 'Invisible inequality: Social class and childrearing in black families and white families', *American Sociological Review*, 67(5), 747–776.

Lareau, A. and McNamara Horvat, E. (1999) 'Moments of social inclusion and exclusion: Race, class, and cultural capital in family-school relationships', *Sociology of Education*, 72(1), 37–53.

Love, J. & Buriel, R. (2007) 'Language brokering, autonomy, parent-child bonding, biculturalism, and depression'. *Hispanic Journal of Behavioral Sciences*, 29(4), 472–491.

Martinez, C. R., McClure, H. and Eddy, J. M. (2009) 'Language brokering contexts and behavioral and emotional adjustment among Latino parents and adolescents', *The Journal of Early Adolescence*, 29(1), 71–98.

Maylor, U. (2010) 'Notions of diversity, British identities and citizenship belonging', *Race Ethnicity and Education*, 13(2), 233–252.

Ofsted (2010) Learning together: How education providers promote social responsibility and community cohesion, London: Ofsted.

Office of National Statistics (2011) 2011 Census: Special migration statistics (United Kingdom) [computer file]. UK Data Service Census Support. Downloaded from: https://wicid.ukdataservice.ac.uk

Osler, A. (2009) 'Testing citizenship and allegiance: Policy, politics and the education of adult migrants in the UK'. *Education, Citizenship and Social Justice*, 4(1), 63–79.

Putnam, R. (1995) 'Bowling alone: American's declining social capital', *Journal of Democracy*, 6(1), 64–78.

Putnam, R. (2000) *Bowling alone: The collapse and revival of American community*, New York: Simon & Schuster.

Reay, D. (1998) *Class work: Mothers' involvement in their children's primary schooling*, London: UCL Press.

Reay, D. (2000) 'A useful extension of Bourdieu's conceptual framework? Emotional capital as a way of understanding mothers' involvement in their children's education?' *The Sociological Review*, 48(4), 568–585.

Rudney, G. L. (2005) Every teacher's guide to working with parents, Thousand Oaks, CA: Corwin Press.

Schuller, T., Field, J. and Baron, S. (2001) Social capital: Critical perspectives, Oxford: Oxford University Press.

Statham, J., Harris, A. and Glenn, M. (2010) Strengthening family wellbeing and community cohesion through the role of schools and extended services, London: Centre for Excellence and Outcomes in Children and Young People's Services (C4EO).

Walker, P. (2014) Engaging the parents of EAL learners in positive support for their children's language development. CASS School of Education and Communities, University of East London, British Council/EAL Nexus Research. London: British Council.

Vincent, C. (2017) 'The children have only got one education and you have to make sure it's a good one': Parenting and parent–school relations in a neoliberal age', *Gender and Education*, 29(5), 541–545.

# 12

# A MOTHER'S EXPERIENCES IN THE SPECIAL EDUCATIONAL NEEDS SYSTEM

*Martha Smith*

## Introduction

The right of parents and/or carers to be consulted at every stage of decision-making about their children is enshrined in law across the UK, for example, in the Special Educational Needs and Disability (Northern Ireland) Order, 2005; Children and Families Act, 2014 in England; 1996 Education Act, Part IV in Wales; Education (Additional Support for Learning) (Scotland) Acts, 2004 and 2009. Crozier and Reay (2005, p. 155) suggest that parents' and families' entitlement to have their voices heard during the formal education of their children is the 'centre piece' in 'twenty first century' education policy-making. However, entitlement in law is not always synonymous with experience in practice. In 2009, the Lamb Enquiry into special educational needs and parental confidence in the system, for example, concluded that: 'Failure to comply with statutory obligations speaks of an underlying culture where parents and carers of children with SEN can too readily be seen as the problem and as a result parents lose confidence in schools and professionals' (Lamb, 2009, 1.1)

This chapter focuses on the experiences of the mother of a young autistic boy at home and during her encounters with the education system. Autistic spectrum disorder has been identified as among the most common primary areas of special educational need (SEN) in state-funded primary, secondary and special schools. The Department for Education (DfE) carries out an annual school census in January and compiles data relating to the incidence of SEN in its schools in England in its publication 'Statistical first release (SFR). Special educational needs in England'. The SRF for January, 2017,[1] indicates that 31.1 per cent of boys who were reported as experiencing a SEN of some kind were recorded as autistic, for example (DfE, 2017).

'There are no biological markers in the identification of autism,' as Klin et al. (2000, p. 163) comment. Typically, autism in young people is identified through agreed diagnostic criteria consisting of a profile of symptoms and characteristics of autistic behaviour. Many assessments of autism spectrum disorders in the UK are based on the *International Classification of Diseases* (ICD), published by the World Health Organization. In the *ICD-10* (WHO, 2016, F84.0), autism is described as a 'disorder'; identified, for example, through difficulties in social interaction, communication, 'repetitive behaviour' and 'restricted … interests … and activities'. However, as in the narrative below, many families may well not recognise their children in professionals' descriptions of them as 'disordered', and in formal lists of 'symptoms' and characteristics of autistic behaviour. Use of descriptors such as these may well be experienced as highly negative and damaging to a child and to a family's sense of self-worth, and not at all helpful in considering how most sensitively and effectively to address the developmental needs of an autistic child. Out of such terminology and lists may emerge a stereotype of autism that masks the individuality and humanity of the child so labelled, creates a sense of 'otherness' and distances the child from peers and families from professionals. As Temple Grandin (herself autistic) and Panek (Grandin & Panek, 2013, pp. 4–5), for example, note:

> autism can't be diagnosed in the laboratory [...] Instead, as with many psychiatric syndromes [...] autism is identified by observing and evaluating behaviors. Those observations and evaluations are subjective, and the behaviors vary from person to person. The diagnosis can be confusing, and it can be vague.

This chapter, written from a mother's perspective, describes her own experiences of bringing up her son, the way in which she taught him to communicate, her and her son's relationships with the various professionals, including teachers, they encountered, and the lessons she learnt along the way. Much of what she describes illustrates some of the issues and challenges facing parents and families of children with special or additional learning at the present time, leaving one to conclude that Lamb (2009, 1.1) might well continue to draw the same conclusions that he did nearly a decade ago: 'As the system stands it often creates "warrior parents" at odds with the school and feeling they have to fight for what should be their children's by right; conflict in place of trust.' However, in the midst of negativity from a number of quarters, there is also optimism and joy in the mother's account of her experiences.

The chapter concludes with the mother's personal recommendations for practices that will enable many autistic children to be more effectively included in schools, and their families to be more confident that their children will have the opportunity to thrive, grow and enjoy enhanced life experiences.

## The beginning: identification and assessment

Our first entry into the world of special educational needs and disability was a clumsy affair. A nursery teacher saw patterns in my son's behaviour that concerned her, and after three sessions I was handed a referral form to sign, an invitation for him to return only when there were no other children present and a casual, 'Don't worry, I can give you the phone number of another mother whose child has special needs; she's not OK about it either.' From that point on, life seemed to be filled with practitioners who came, saw, assessed and wrote reports. It was absolutely terrifying. Some expressed concern, some were adamant that there was no cause for alarm. A Health Visitor referred us to the local Child Development Centre and, by the time our appointment arrived a couple of months later, I had convinced myself that there was no need to be worried. Just before we left, my little boy took a pack of shuffled number cards 0–20 and arranged them in order on the floor. He was 2 years and 6 months old.

At the Child Development Centre, we were ushered into a small room where a nurse tried to coax my son onto a scale and attempted to measure him. Eventually the nurse led us to a large room in which the Paediatrician sat behind a desk. There was a student sitting by the door. The Paediatrician addressed the now familiar questions to me: 'What does he like to do?' and my replies: 'Oh, he loves puzzles. He's so clever; he always starts with the same piece and completes the puzzle in the same order.' Or sometimes: 'Oh yes, he is brilliant with numbers.'

But something odd was happening. There were some brilliant toys in the room, lots of numbered things that stacked, toys with letters on them, puzzles and alphabet posters. While I was answering the same old questions about coordination I noticed that the nurse would give him a toy, see his delight and then, while he was mid-play she took it away from him and put it on a high shelf. He was getting more and more frustrated and would point at it in the hope of getting it back. The Paediatrician's gaze was darting between him and her notes. After a while I said: 'Please can you stop winding him up? He was really enjoying playing with the truck, could you give it back to him please so I can concentrate on answering these questions.'

There was an awkward silence. The Paediatrician looked at me. 'How much do you know about autism?' she said. I stared at her. The room seemed to have shrunk in front of my eyes, as if I was looking through the wrong end of a pair of binoculars. 'Enough,' I said, 'to know that I do not want you to tell me that he has it.' She told me that he was showing 'features' of autism but seemed unable or unkeen to give us a concrete diagnosis. 'Is that why he can't talk?' I said. My husband panicked differently. 'Will he ever get married or live on his own?' He was too young, time would tell etc. I looked at my boy and felt a wave of overwhelming guilt. All this time I had been badgering him to talk, thinking that it was because he was too reliant on me. I'd been reading him pretentious poetry while he was in the bath, trying to lure him into a love of language. Stupid woman! He'd been dealing with this all on his own and I had been expecting him to sort it out by himself. I had let him down, failed to protect him and had abandoned him when he needed me.

We thanked the Paediatrician for her time. 'What do I do?' I asked the nurse. 'I have no idea what to do to help him. I need something to read. Please find me something that tells me what to do.' She rummaged around and found a couple of books and some information about a local autism charity and advised me not to let my son form any solid habits, telling me about a girl who loved to run around naked in her garden aged 5 and still does it at 17. Right, I thought, I won't let him do that, and off we went.

We stumbled out of the room, and headed back to the car. What you need at that point is for someone to look into the future and tell you that he is going to be all right. That you are going to be all right. That this is OK. But no one can and no one will. It is terrifying.

We went home. Alone. Without the first idea of what to do.

The feeling of being out of my depth was overwhelming. Autism is a diagnosis and not a description of a person. Nobody could tell us how our son's autism would affect him and I was terribly aware that I didn't know what I needed to know. This put me at a huge disadvantage in meetings as I did not feel I could appropriately advocate for him. People with job titles that I did not understand started rocking up at the house and I couldn't always take in why they had come. Everybody seemed to know more than I did and they were making decisions for us. Everything I was doing seemed to be wrong. I felt that I was a failure as a parent. I had to take direction from people I had never met who were trying to train him to have the skills necessary to cope with pre-school, changes in routine, boundaries, unstructured time, and at times their methods seemed brutal. I had to learn fast.

## Teaching my son to communicate

My son was non-verbal so we were assigned a Speech and Language therapist who assessed his current level of communication and recommended a textbook by Fern Sussman (2012), *More than Words*. She explained everything clearly and gave us homework. First, we had to stop asking him questions. We are all taught to bombard our developing children with questions. 'What colour is that? How many are there? Which one do you like?' Asking a child questions when they do not have the means to respond causes them stress. Instead, we had to 'comment'. When we were together, we would simply say the name of an object. Verbal labelling. We then had to establish a reason for communication because, up to that point, there had been no real reason for him to invest in it. We had to start from object exchange, hand over hand at the beginning. I placed a raisin in a magnetic picture frame on the fridge and tried to entice him to take it and exchange it with me for an actual raisin. No chance. Days passed. As a last ditch effort I swapped it for a picture of a chocolate biscuit (Figure 12.1). Bingo. Before long he would bring the picture to me, I would say 'biscuit please', swap it for a biscuit and he would scuttle off with his prize.

Communication suddenly had a point; there was something in it for him. Within weeks this had become embedded and he started to branch out, bringing me a cup when he wanted a drink or the small plastic banana from his toy food collection.

The next step was photo exchange. I photographed friends outside their houses, the supermarket, the park, the car, the village shop and home (Figure 12.2). Eventually, his fear of leaving the house reduced slightly. He could see that there was a plan and that, at the end of it, we would be returning home. Until that point it had been difficult to visit friends. The fear of what might be on the other side of the front door was

A mother's experiences 195

**FIGURE 12.1** Chocolate biscuit in magnetic frame

overwhelming. Anyone who lived on the route to the park was almost impossible to visit as he'd spend the hour hammering on the front door crying, hoping to finish the journey to the destination he had envisaged. When we left the house we would need to finish the journey to the park before returning home.

Over the following months we introduced simple line drawings to the bottom of some of the photographs to lead into the Picture Exchange Communication System.[2] Over time he learned to assemble a sentence on a velcroed strip of plastic, for example: 'I want a biscuit please' or 'Park please'. He could exchange the sentence for the actual thing and begin to have some form of real control.

**FIGURE 12.2** Laminated photograph of the park

The textbook was an absolute lifeline for me. It provided a way of first identifying my son's level of communication and then making suggestions as to how to positively engage him. Over the weeks and months that followed I could see real, meaningful progress and it raised my spirits. We had no guarantee that he would ever speak but it was clear that he could learn to communicate. We had been told that the inability to speak was somehow linked to the fact that he could not kick a football or pedal a trike so we placed the trike outside his window and endlessly marched around the garden saying '1, 2, 3, KICK', and pushing his foot forward onto a ball. I have no idea whether it ever made a difference.

## The issue of food

Shortly after my son's diagnosis he started self-limiting food. He had been weaned on every fruit, vegetable and pulse under the sun. Everything was steamed, mashed, whizzed and consumed. But suddenly something he had previously eaten would make him gag. I started trying to disguise vegetables so they looked like the ones he would eat, chopping up green beans to make them look like peas, cutting sandwiches into shapes, using every act of encouragement I could. He limited and limited and limited. Eventually we got down to six foods: yogurt, bread, jam, tuna, Weetabix and sausages. Mealtimes were heavily ritualised: correct plates, bowls, cups. It stayed like this for months. He simply couldn't look at some food without retching. I was desperate, reading piles of books on it, trying everything I could to entice him. I mixed miniscule amounts of vitamin drops into his yogurt, all the while risking it changing the flavour and him giving up yogurt too.

The stakes are so high when your child eats next to nothing – losing a food from the list is catastrophic. We leased an allotment to help him touch, grow and hopefully try fruit and vegetables. Every person in his life was instructed to casually offer him things, eat things in front of him while saying how delicious they were. We took endless trips to the supermarket to sniff things and see what he might like to try. I went on a course with a dietician who said: 'Well there's nothing much more you can do, but don't worry, I have seen people who eat nothing but breakfast cereal into adulthood. They are not very healthy but they have survived.' I grimaced. Perhaps she might have told us this before we got in the car in the hope she could help us. Another parent had laminated a picture of a plate on to which she could stick pictures of the food that would be served – it was a good idea and it seemed to help her son. Back at home we pored over pictures of fruit and vegetables in books, read stories about them, all the time trying to disguise the fact that I was panic stricken and had run out of ideas.

For a while he needed the washing machine on in order to eat. Then he needed to eat in a different room. When he finally managed to eat at the dining room table he needed an iPad to keep him occupied and distract him from the stress of eating. Headphones sometimes helped.

Then one day he licked a segment of orange at a friend's house. It was like getting an electric shock. There was a tiny opening, the smallest possibility that he would eat one. We tried again at home, nothing. We tried again at the friend's house. Nothing. We put a slice on the table, near to but not on his plate and started from there. Over the next few months he learned to tolerate it and not throw it. He managed to sniff it and got a sticker every time he did. In all, it took about two years until he took a lick and then a small bite. After another few months he ate a whole piece.

This work carried on with a few target foods. I printed off the major vitamins and minerals and targeted the foods that could help the most: blueberries, grapes, bananas. He got a sticker in his 'Big Food Adventure Book' for every attempt (Figure 12.3). Thank goodness he drank milk. A teacher managed to interest him in a raisin and he was away. Pre-school managed to form an interest in cocktail sausages and my sister got him to try a rice cake after a sustained but stealthy group eating session with her children.

Slowly, slowly over the following years we built up to around 20 foods. Now, at the age of 11, he probably tries and tolerates one new food a year but sometimes giving up an old one in the process. He has eaten the same lunch for seven years. Milk or water are all he will drink but I can live with that. He can now use a knife and fork, despite not seeing the point. He has just started taking liquid vitamins as he originally tried them as a medicine when ill. I've set a daily alarm to remind him to take them. The battle continues, by stealth, persuasion and encouragement.

## Joining a playgroup

A few weeks after his diagnosis we were invited by his keyworker to join a Friday morning group, which would teach him the skills that he needed for pre-school. He had to learn to 'transition' between tasks and understand and use a rudimentary

**FIGURE 12.3** Picture of 'Big Food Adventure Book'

schedule. There were 'now and next' boards and he and three other children gradually learned, via a Makaton sign,[3] to understand that a fun game had finished and that they must move on to the next one.

I had been warned that it took a while for the children to grasp what they had to do. I had not, however, anticipated his extreme reaction to singing. The two keyworkers made a circle of little chairs and hemmed everyone in with tables before starting a vigorous rendition of 'Row, Row, Row Your Boat'. Chaos ensued. All four children started crying and my son made a bid for freedom across the tables. He was caught and restrained. The absolute shock of seeing a stranger firmly holding my son was too much for me. I rose up out of my chair and told them to leave him alone. Is this it now? Is this what we get? No more nice, twee little nursery for us. We get this instead.

It was too much, too horrible, too upsetting. We were never going to return to this awful place, right up until the following Friday when, with reluctance, I loaded my boy into the car. The problem was, I knew that they knew more than me. They had a plan and I did not. We were going to have to get on with it in order to learn what they knew and move forward. I did not do it entirely gracefully.

Over time, the playgroup proved invaluable. He did learn to transition, he did learn some Makaton signs, he did learn to follow a schedule, he did learn to use his PECS book and he could (although only just) tolerate singing. He was ready to move on.

## Learning at home

I had been concerned about scheduling[4] and worried that following a list of tasks on a schedule would make him even less flexible. I was completely wrong. The night before I completed my scheduling course my boy was jumping up and down on our bed at 11 pm. Every night he was late to bed and up in the night. We were desperate. I assembled a long schedule and left it by the door for when he returned from school. It told him when to play, when to have his snack and supper and when to go up for a bath. He followed it diligently. In the bathroom was another schedule telling him, in line drawings, what to do. The end of the schedule was: get into bed, listen to a story, turn off the light, go to sleep. By chance I put another one on the end, a gold star with his name on it saying 'Well done'. It was like witchcraft. I turned out the light and crept downstairs. He stayed in bed. I waited and waited and still he stayed in bed. The next morning he woke me up by bringing me the 'Well done'. All that time he had been working towards it. While I cannot claim that he always remained in bed for the whole night, he certainly went to bed as scheduled and went to sleep quickly. We were so lucky that this method worked for him; it does not work for everyone.

It was clear that he had a good memory so we started playing a phonics matching game. We had an alphabet poster on the wall and a pile of flashcards. We started by matching the letters by finding the same ones in the pile and holding them up to the poster while I said their name and sound. When he had mastered that I would sign 'the name is ayyyy, the sound is a' and he'd find the card and hold it up again (Figure 12.4).

Numbers also came easily to him. I found a plastic grid with the numbers 1–100 on tiles and he learned to match all the numbers and then to find them in the pile of loose tiles (Figure 12.5). He loved the games.

## Help from allies in the education system

It was in the second pre-school that I found my first true ally in the education system. It was a glorious place, children happily playing, toys all over the place, anyone sad

**FIGURE 12.4** Phonics flashcard

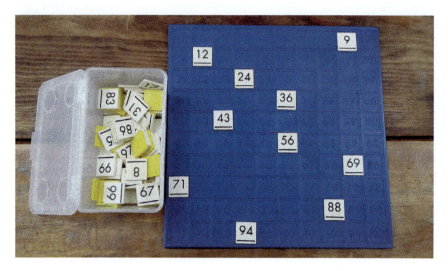

FIGURE 12.5 Number board

being hugged by staff. Everything you could want from a setting. When staff came to meet my son in school, they sent their most experienced teachers. I have spoken to so many parents who have not been so lucky. Their children have been given a terrified 16 year old or the kindly person with no experience or knowledge of autism, who has been used simply to babysit the 'difficult one' rather than work with the child to move things on. We had been afforded one term of funding for one-to-one support to get him started. The special educational needs and disability co-ordinator (SENDCo) and I agreed that it was ridiculous – left alone he would simply move toys from one pile to another, oblivious to anything or anyone else. I was going to have to fight for funding. I did not have access to the decision-makers at the Local Authority; everything seemed to be arranged through the setting. Together she and I produced endless reports and proof that he needed support for the whole year, every half term re-applying for future funding. If a practitioner came to assess my son, we would wear red jumpers in order to look like a force to be reckoned with. I don't think it worked but it made us feel more assertive! We succeeded, even when told no. 'You can't appeal,' they said. We appealed anyway. By the end I think they were so desperate to get rid of us and our endless reports that the funding stopped being questioned.

However, the involvement of all the staff went further than I could have possibly expected. When I was asked to come and teach a couple of teachers the Makaton signs that my son used, every single member of staff turned up. They could not bear the thought that a non-verbal child might be communicating with them and they would not know. As his ability to make himself understood grew, his frustration lessened. When the staff at pre-school read aloud a story with a repeated refrain, those words were recorded onto a little device so he could, with support, push the button and join in with the chorus. Every day they talked to me about his day, his progress, any sounds he was starting to make. I shared the work we did at home with them. We worked in synch. I was happy to hear their ideas and try them – they exposed him to new experiences while working on his strengths. He was happy and relaxed. The DVD of his day at pre-school is one of the most precious things I own.

## Hitting a buffer: resource-led decision-making

I had heard from another parent, whilst at the playgroup, that a similar level of support could be available to some children with additional needs when they move to Lower School. No practitioner had ever discussed this with me. My son's key-worker was less than optimistic and suddenly pronounced him 'borderline'. It is amazing how quickly a child can move from being profoundly affected to being borderline when you are asking for cash. I disagreed. She even tried 'What if another child needs the funding more than him?' That, I said, is not *his* problem. The pre-school SENDCo and I agreed that he would need the extra support and started the process. More reports to try to qualify for an assessment. Several weeks later, permission for an assessment was granted and we had to furnish the local authority with further reports. Reports, reports, reports. It was endless. It is important to recognise that some parents cannot face the struggle. That the thought of having to submit their own evidence as well as gathering reports from other practitioners is simply too much. The law in the UK has changed and the process is supposed to be easier. It isn't always the case. Life is tough when you have a child, or children with additional needs and, as parents, our capacity to take on more work wavers. It does not take much for us to lose heart. There is no disgrace in that. It shouldn't have to be so hard.

An Educational Psychologist arrived at the pre-school on a freezing cold day and was so shocked by seeing the lengths that the staff had to go to in order to get my son to remove his hands from a tray of ice-cold water in the garden that she suggested we apply for a place in a Special School. One practitioner saying borderline, one saying Special School. We had to assume that the truth lay somewhere in between the two extremes. At the very end of the summer term we were sent a draft copy of a Statement of Special Educational Needs, affording my son 21 hours per week of one to one support. It was hard won.

## The shock of entry to Lower School

Lower School was a horrible shock, despite the best efforts of our Early Years Keyworker, who spent three days at the school setting up schedules and helping to train my son's Learning Support Assistant (LSA). His entry to Lower School meant that I lost all the useful professionals we had had and the relationships that I had built up. We had to wait another half term before we could move up as the Statement had taken so long to produce. Luckily the school had found a fantastic LSA, despite the job being advertised at the same hourly rate as a lunch-time supervisor. She and I worked well together and she was an invaluable support, despite being afforded very little say in the classroom activities. My relationship with other teachers was more challenging as some insisted on using 'time out' as a punishment, even though it was not something my son even vaguely understood. Despite my protestations it only stopped when they realised he was doing the same thing wrong at exactly the same time every day and then putting himself on the Time Out beanbag in order to have a cry. He'd built the punishment into his own schedule so committed the crime on cue. He made progress due to the enormous (and undervalued) efforts of his Teaching Assistant but I felt the loss of my previous collaborators keenly. I felt alone and unable to advocate effectively for my son for that whole first year. No one seemed interested.

I didn't meet the school SENDCo until the following year. I had been invited to my son's annual Statement Review, which was concerned with his provision for extra help. She explained that she didn't know much about autism and asked whether I had considered getting him a pet. Shortly into the meeting I brought up my battle with the new Speech and Language therapist (SALT). My son had started school able to say only three random words and yet the SALT felt that another appointment would not be necessary for another six months. I had been battling alone and was getting nowhere. His new form teacher spoke up. 'I'll take that on, you do not need to do that on your own. I will help.' A new ally. What a tremendous relief.

## Effective, and not-so-effective, professionals

In the following years, this trusted new ally became the SENDCo and my son's form teacher for two years. She was and remains passionate about children with SEND and she and I work together well. Along with excellent LSAs who learned quickly how to get the best out of my son, his progress at school was exciting. Bumps in the road were resolved, everything I sent in from home was read and I was involved in every IEP (individualised education programme) meeting, every informal target, absolutely everything that affected him. We were a team, working together with a common goal and it was massively beneficial to my son's development.

Over the years he has had so many teachers. Not every teacher 'gets it'. It is hard to describe how crushing it is to come across someone who will not listen to you, usually because they believe themselves to be an expert; a person who seems to think that inclusion starts and finishes with providing your child with a chair inside the classroom. Little bumps become mountains, providing constant proof that their lack of knowledge stymies development. Meetings become more frequent and more fraught. I find myself thinking, 'If you knew what you were doing you would not even have to ask me that' or, 'If you had read what I sent in you would know the answer and things would not have gone so badly wrong.' Worried parents gain a reputation for being difficult, aggressive, ones to avoid. It is deeply unfair. The parent's anxiety goes through the roof and the academic year feels like a right-off. Two separate parties working separately. Pointless.

I once met a teacher who was quite happy to tell me that he didn't know enough but was keen to learn. I found him a course, which he took over the summer holidays in preparation for the new school year. He didn't mind meeting afterwards so I could hear about his training (code for me checking that he had done it!), and did his own research as well. He had an open mind and a genuine interest and took the time to get to know my son and understand the way he thought. It was a tremendous year and we rarely needed to meet; I knew that my son was safe and understood and the teacher could ask me a speedy question in the playground in the morning, negating the need for a formal meeting. When I once joked at an IEP meeting that for the four targets on his list, I had about 500 at home, he told me to give him some of mine, however random. It remains one of the best examples of inclusive practice I have ever enjoyed.

It is also important to note that not every practitioner will be useful. Some have been in their jobs for so long that they can lose empathy. Our children become a name on a list to be worked through and stock responses are meted out, regardless of the individual circumstances and needs of the child and their family. I once had the misfortune to encounter a practitioner who had become so lost in herself that she spent the first few minutes of our meeting describing how her back complaint made it painful to use the toilet. I continued the rest of the meeting fighting with an unwelcome image in my head. She then launched into phase two 'Tell me how you would describe your son if you were to sell him on Ebay.' I responded in glowing terms only to be met with irritation. 'Well, most parents tell me what disappoints them about their child and I help them look at the positives.' I had clearly not followed the script. She went on to tell me about those other parents, who clearly needed a bit of a boost, in order to fill the time that I had so flagrantly failed to use. Lastly, she asked what I would like to know. I was keen to hear her findings, as she had spent well over an hour observing my son. The report would follow but the general upshot was that he was young for his year (having been born two weeks before the cut-off for the next academic year) and that he was autistic. Neither conclusion had escaped my notice. The school got a huge bill and we had absolutely nothing of use to push us forward. It transpired that, over the years that this psychologist had been visiting the school, no member of staff had ever sat in on a meeting to gauge her effectiveness.

By contrast, I met another Educational Psychologist some years later. He was so keen to get things right for my second child that he told me he had read every report I had sent him three times before our meeting. He had already observed her and his carefully considered recommendations filtered into a document full of potential outcomes that will make a huge difference to her future. He shared his observations with me and wished to know what I felt my child needed for support. He spent a long time talking to her about her future aspirations. I was immensely grateful for the time he spent and the care he took.

## Transition to Middle School

Transition to new schools is a dangerous affair and, handled badly, can be devastating for children. As they grow older, contact between staff and parents becomes more formal and less personal. Transition to Middle School was handled well by the Lower School, which knew my son well, and poorly by the next school. They had not prepared any schedules for him, insisting that he would simply have to get used to his written timetable. I cannot emphasise enough how important it is not to inflict change during transition. Stick with what the child knows and make the necessary adjustments when they feel comfortable and safe. His Lower School Teaching Assistant turned up in desperation at reception with a pile of schedule cards and was patronisingly assumed to be having difficulty 'letting go of her baby'. He was later told off by a teacher who did not understand the behaviour he exhibited in order to handle the stress of a completely new environment. He started to be frightened of being told off and, to this day, finds it almost impossible to ask for help from a teacher. Children quickly picked up on this weakness, and played on it, and now he will sprint away from any member of staff that approaches him in the fear that he is going to be spoken to harshly. This has prevented him from accessing help during sustained periods of bullying.

The Middle School's perceived lack of preparation meant that my initial meetings with them were testy. I had to request meetings myself as none were initiated by the school. I came across as officious, irritable and difficult. I questioned the qualifications of the staff, their experience and their will to get things right. I felt let down and angry, and I feared that they would ignore the needs of my child and therefore fail to keep him safe. Better communication would have prevented ill-feeling on both sides and ensured that we formed a trusting and effective partnership sooner.

## Break-through, home and school

Over time, my son settled in to Middle School and formed a solid and positive relationship with the SENDCo and some other members of staff. I now have a great relationship with the SENDCo, which means that we work well together to ensure that my son has the support that he needs to access different aspects of his school life. During unstructured time he was a lone figure in the playground, engrossed in his imaginary world, the hero saving the world from attack. No one else knew the rules of the game and, although it was an effective and enjoyable coping strategy, it meant that he spent every break time playing alone. The overwhelming need for the comfort of routine prevented him from accessing clubs either at break time or at lunchtime until we devised a plan to help him to branch out. He is a helpful child who will always assist people in need. When he was younger he would step out into the road to protect his classmates if he felt that they were too close to the traffic. Two teachers approached him and asked for his help. They were setting up clubs that they could not possibly run without him. He had the skills that they needed to help them and the other children. Could he please come and help? Of course if he wanted to actually join in he was welcome to... That year he took part in tennis club after school (having never before held a racquet) and Nature Club during lunchtime. It was a seismic change and left the door ajar for future opportunities.

My son is happy, kind, loving and fun. He enjoys school, has a plan for his future and is looking forward to growing up. His academic successes are *because* of the support he has received and *in spite* of the hurdles that have been put in his way. He has started to navigate his way through the joys and horrors of young friendships and has emerged with his sense of self intact. He is proud of himself, despite starting to become frustrated with his brain and the differences that he perceives. I cannot begin to express how proud I am of him.

## Advice from experience

If I could advise the legion of practitioners that we parents encounter, it would be to view every child and their family as unique. Take the time to understand what matters to our children, how they feel and think and give us the tools we need to help move our children forward happily. Understand that the advice you give may not be the only advice we are asked to follow and that some of it may conflict. Remember that we love our children deeply and are proud of them and that sometimes we get frightened. Know that those that are prickly are so for good reason – they, like me, may well have simply come across too many people who sit in judgement and add nothing positive to their situation. Consider that, while you may have mastered your own field, we must become experts in them all. At school most parents can count on the fact that the teachers have been taught how their child learns effectively. For our children, every year is a lottery for us as to whether our child's teachers have had the necessary additional training. It can take immense effort to get our children to school in the morning, all the while trying to ensure that those tasked with teaching them do so in a way that they can access. Try to imagine the barriers we face every day and how hard we work to minimise their impact on our children. Most of us are too tired to pick a fight with anyone – we only bite when we feel let down. We need the best of you – please work with us.

## Notes

1 This is available at https://www.gov.uk/government/uploads/system/uploads/attachment_data/file/633031/SFR37_2017_Main_Text.pdf (accessed 20 May 2018).
2 The Picture Exchange Communication System (PECS) is a form of Alternative and Augmentative Communication (AAC) in which a child is taught to communicate with an adult by being given a card with a picture on it. In PECS, the adult teaches the child to exchange a picture of something for an item s/he wants, for example, to exchange a picture of a drink for a drink. Pictures can be used progressively to make whole sentences or express preferences, but it may take a long time to reach this stage of development in communication.
3 Makaton is a sign and symbol language designed to support spoken language. Signs are used with speech in spoken word order to help children and adults to communicate.
4 Visual scheduling is a visual timetable of events that are to take place during the day.

## References

Crozier, G. & Reay, D. (2005) *Activating participation: Parents and teachers working towards partnership*, London: Trentham Books.
Department for Education (DfE) (2017) Statistical first release, SFR 37/2017, Special educational needs in England: January 2017, Darlington: DfE.
Grandin, T. & Panek, R. (2013) *The autistic brain: Thinking across the spectrum*, Boston, MA: Houghton Mifflin Harcourt.
Klin, A., Sparrow, S., Marans, W. D., Carter, A., & Volkmar, F. R. (2000) 'Assessment issues in children and adolescents with Asperger syndrome'. In A. Klin, F. R. Volkmar and S. Sparrow (Eds), *Asperger Syndrome*, pp. 172–209, New York: Guilford Press.
Lamb, B. (2009) Report to the Secretary of State on the Lamb Inquiry Review of SEN and Disability Information, London: DCSF.
Sussman, F. (2012) *More than words* (2nd edn.), Toronto: Hanen.
World Health Organization (WHO) (2016) *The International Statistical Classification of Diseases, ICD-10*, Geneva: WHO.

# 13

# STUDENTS', TEACHERS' AND FAMILIES' VIEWS ON HOMEWORK

*Dr Wendy Edwards and Professor Janice Wearmouth*

## Introduction

Homework has been discussed since 'payment by results' for teachers was introduced in 1883 following the Elementary Education Acts (1870, 1880). These two Acts established universal primary education; one important argument for which, at the time, was to enable Britain to remain in the frontline of manufacturing and industry with an educated workforce.

A number of reviews of research literature on homework (Gordon, 1980; Department for Education and Science, 1987; MacBeath and Turner, 1990; Weston, 1999; Sharp, Keys & Benefield, 2001; Hattie, 2009; Higgins et al., 2014) indicate that particular issues have recurred since the nineteenth century. These include the purpose and type of homework, concerns about the home environment and, as Hallam (2004) in particular notes, the national and local political, economic, social and educational contexts influencing homework policy and practice. This chapter focuses on a research study that elicited views about these recurring issues from four groups of stakeholders: students, families, teachers and governors, in six secondary schools in one town in the East Midlands of England. As Gladman (1885), and Hallam (2004) over a century later, noted, if homework is to be effective in supporting learning and achievement in schools, teachers need clear guidance on what is its purpose and what type might be set. They need to take into consideration the workload of students, resources available at home, and the school–life balance. Students need to know what the relevance of the homework is and how it will improve their learning. As is discussed in this chapter, this was not always the case in the policies and practices of the schools where the research was carried out, however.

The text below begins by discussing the recurrence of these issues in their historical and contemporary contexts, and goes on to outline the research study in question, together with its findings and implications in the current educational context.

## Historical and current context

Questions about the purpose homework should serve, whether or not it can be shown to be effective in supporting improved learning and achievement, whether families can support completion of work set by schools in the home, and the influence of political, economic, social and educational factors have surfaced repeatedly in research. From the outset no political party in office seems to have been willing to take a stand on whether the setting of homework should be compulsory. Currently there are Government guidelines on setting homework but they are still only recommendations, as homework has never been made statutory.

In terms of purpose, one recurring argument is that it can supplement the curriculum in order to increase students' academic development and examination results and, thus, support the UK to compete economically with other countries. 'A Lady' (c.1870), cited in Gordon (1980), explained that it was reasonable for teachers to be concerned about the academic development of their pupils with so few hours spent at school. Nearly 60 years later, the Board of Education (1937) Educational Pamphlet no. 110 argued that pupils would be living in a competitive economic world and in order to compete they would need to have well trained intelligence and the development of self-reliance and initiative. Towards the end of the twentieth century a Department for Education and Science (1987) report on homework concluded that many schools were using it to increase study time and improve study skills.

Over the years, concerns have been expressed about the lack of resources and inadequate home environment for many children to complete homework, the tensions home conditions have created in this regard, and the necessity to privilege working for money above homework in some households. From the late nineteenth century, once almost all children, often from diverse social backgrounds, were receiving education, home lessons were difficult for some students as a result of their living conditions. Dr Crichton-Browne wrote in the School Guardian (1884) that some parents would forbid home lessons and that they would put books on the fire. In other homes parents might not object to 'home lessons' but the children found it difficult to complete their work owing to overcrowding in the home. 'A one roomed house with five or six restless and noisy inmates is not the best place for the calm exercise of the intellect' (School Guardian, 1884, p. 646). On 3 July 1934, during a Parliamentary debate, Fielding Reginald West (Labour MP for Hammersmith North) asked Sir Hilton Young (Conservative Minster of Health and MP for Sevenoaks) how children could do their homework in homes where there were no sanitary conveniences and water had to be carried up three or four storeys (*Hansard*, 1934b). The Minister of Health did not give a specific reply to this. Homework has also been in and out of favour with families when children have been needed to work to supplement the family income when not at school (Martin, 1979).

The type and amount of homework have been discussed in Parliament on a number of occasions. On 16 June 1884, discussion over Dr Crichton-Browne's

Elementary Schools Report included remarks that overpressure existed in schools and if left unchecked could result in serious consequences for future generations (*Hansard*, 1934a). According to Hansard (1934c), 50 years later, on 11 December 1934, Edmund Radford, Conservative MP for Manchester Rusholme, asked the Conservative Parliamentary Secretary to the Board of Education, Herwald Ramsbotham, whether he would set up a committee to look into homework. He had concerns over the excessive amount of homework some children were receiving. The reply came that excessive homework was a matter best left to local education authorities, governing bodies, teachers and school inspectors.

In terms of political considerations, no political party seems to have been willing to make homework statutory and all stakeholders responsible for it. Homework guidelines were eventually established through David Blunkett, the Education Secretary in England during the Labour government, in 1998 (DfEE, 1998). In 2012 Michael Gove, another Education Secretary, reflecting the Coalition government's political decision to move decision-making and, thus, accountability more to schools, announced that homework guidelines in schools would be dropped and that schools would be given the freedom to decide how much homework was set.

## Current research study

The study discussed here investigated a number of questions drawn from the research literature from the perspectives of four groups of stakeholders: students, teachers, governors and families:

1. What is the purpose of homework?
2. What type of homework is seen as most effective in supporting students' learning in the various areas of the curriculum?
3. To what extent does the home environment support students to complete homework, what kind of resources do students need, and do they have access to these resources at home?
4. What political, economic, social and educational factors (Hallam, 2004) are important in understanding the context in which homework policies and practices are developed?

The intention of the study was to address these questions as they relate to the purpose and relevance of homework in state secondary education at the current time in six secondary schools in one urban area. This study was carried out at a time when particular factors in the national context had very clear implications for schools and homework, including:

- The effect of the marketisation of education following the 1988 Education Act and the issues that such marketisation has brought about: competition between schools to achieve the highest possible examination results on league tables,

accountability mechanisms, free parental choice of school for their offspring, and as a consequence the desire of schools to present themselves publically in the most favourable light, pressure on schools during inspection through the government inspection arm, the Office for Standards in Education (Ofsted), to achieve the highest possible grading, and so on.
- The increased encouragement of private provision and autonomy within the state system, together with a sustained level of accountability for students' progress and achievement.
- Ambivalence over parental rights and responsibilities with regard to education. On the one hand, parents and families have considerable rights in terms of decision-making about their children's education, for example choice of schools, and so on. On the other hand, there are particular expectations placed on families, as exemplified in the home–school agreement, which may appear to be a legal requirement. While schools are required to take 'reasonable' steps to ensure that parents understand and sign the agreement, there is no absolute requirement to do so. 'Breaches of the terms of the agreement will not be actionable through the courts […] parents should not face any sanction for either not signing the home-school agreement or failing to abide by its requirements' (DfE, 2013: 4). Homework is one of those areas that seems to have no basis in law, although mention of it appears in the home–school agreement.

## Participants

The study involved six secondary schools in one town in the East Midlands of England. The sample included a faith school, a new school, an academy, a school with an Ofsted grading of 'notice to improve', one with a grading of 'outstanding' and a school with teaching school status in a variety of socio-economic circumstances.

In each school one Year Ten tutor group, their families, teachers and the governors were selected by the school and invited to participate in the research.

## Research methods

The study included questionnaires given to the four main stakeholders: governors, teachers, families and students. Broadly, the questions asked were based on previous research and current government homework guidelines. They covered the rationale for setting homework, knowledge of the home environment, provision for completing homework at school, the type and amount of homework and the feedback given, stress levels on students that were associated with homework, rewards and sanctions, and policy issues.

Schools' documents were scrutinised, including the home–school agreement, homework policies and homework guidelines for students, families and teachers, to understand the schools' public stance on homework.

Interviews were conducted with senior teachers at the schools, with responsibility for implementing the homework policy. Again, areas for discussion related to previous research, but also included outcomes of analysis of information on school policy document. Areas of questioning covered organisation of homework and homework policy, school provision, the rationale for setting homework, sanctions for non-completion, impacts of homework on students and families, and views of the future of homework.

## Findings

### 1 Purpose of homework

Given the apparent importance attributed to homework in the schools' public statements it would seem that students, families, teachers and governors all have a clear idea about the purpose of it. In the current context where schools, since the 1988 Act, have been increasingly in competition with each other, it is essential that the school maintains a clear public focus on learning and achievement. Schools in close proximity to each other, and with similar catchment areas, could be undersubscribed or oversubscribed and attempting to attract the same families and students. In the current study there is very close agreement between schools' homework policies, home–school agreements and planner documents about the various purposes of homework. These include developing organisational, study and independent learning skills, reinforcing work carried out in class, preparing for future classwork, developing research skills for future study and promoting home–school communication with homework as the link between them. However, there may be a difference in families' perceptions of what they want and what policy makers in schools think families want and/or expect. Although the majority of participants across all schools agreed that homework improves grades, is a valuable aid to learning, and helps the understanding of classwork, the situation was not as simple as it appeared. There were degrees of difference between respondent groups regarding the issues of whether homework should be set, why it is set and the impact it has on learning, grades, understanding classwork and the levels of stress it causes students, which largely reflected the socio-economic backgrounds.

In rank order, the most common reason with the highest level of agreement between all groups about why homework is set was to 'reinforce what the students had done in class'. Next came to 'help students to work independently', which is a skill that all schools had reported they would like students to develop, not only for working in school but for future employment and study. Next came the response from all groups that homework is set to 'help students learn more'. 'To finish classwork' was a response from proportionately more families and students (around 18 per cent) than teachers and governors (around 8 per cent).

In this study a large majority of teachers and governors took the school's policy view that homework is so important to students' learning and achievement that it should be set, but only a minority of families (44 per cent) and students (39 per cent) took the same view. When comparing schools, proportionately more families, teachers and governors in the higher achieving schools in the more affluent catchments areas of the town agreed with this compared with the much lower proportion of families (14 per cent) and students (5 per cent) in the lowest achieving school.

## 2 Effectiveness of homework

School documents including the homework policy, the home–school agreement and the planner all outlined expectations of homework: tasks should be achievable, suitable for the subject, age range and ability of the students and should take into account the resources and support required to complete the work. However, this was not always happening when teachers actually set homework.

In relation to effectiveness, teachers and governors were much more likely to say that homework 'improved grades' than were families and students. In all but the lowest achieving school the majority of the groups thought homework is a valuable aid to learning and to understanding classwork, with around 60 per cent of students responding positively even though half had said it does not improve grades and only a minority supported its setting. When comparing responses across schools it could be seen that it was proportionately more families, teachers and governors at the three higher achieving schools who gave the more positive responses compared with responses from the two lower achieving schools. Only one thirds of students and families from the lowest achieving school saw homework as a valuable aid to learning, for example.

Only teachers were asked what evidence they had that homework improves grades. In rank order, their responses were: 'improved grades', 'improved independent work' with, equally ranked, 'improved classwork', 'improved memory' and 'improved study skills'.

There was a clear disjunction between students' perceptions of 'finishing off classwork' as the most commonly set kind of homework, and teachers' perceptions of it as the least useful and effective. In rank order, students' reports of what was set most commonly was 'finishing off classwork', 'revision', 'preparation for classwork' and 'coursework'. Around two thirds of all groups agreed that 'revision' is a very effective type of homework, but only 7–8 per cent of teachers viewed 'finishing off classwork' as both the most useful and the most effective.

The guidelines for homework, introduced by David Blunkett in 1998 and scrapped by Michael Gove in 2012, suggested that Year Ten students should receive between 90 and 150 minutes each night. In the current study, the amount of homework set was reported to vary across the schools, with two thirds of both students and families reporting an average of 30 to 60 minutes each night. Across all schools, around 60 per cent of both families and students agreed that the amount was 'about right'. However, in two of the highest achieving schools over half the students stated that they thought they received too much homework. The majority of students from the lowest achieving school stated that they did not receive any homework. Most teachers responded that the students completed their homework either 'usually' or 'sometimes'. Teachers from the highest achieving school stated that over 90 per cent 'always' or 'usually' completing it. The highest 'sometimes' or 'never' teacher responses were from two of the lowest achieving schools.

All respondent groups were in agreement that homework caused the students stress, but the proportions were rather different: over 80 per cent of students, two thirds of families, and just over half of the teachers. The highest proportions of positive responses came from students and teachers from the highest achieving schools. With schools in competition with each over student numbers, league tables, Ofsted and external perceptions, it may be that higher achieving schools may be putting more pressure on their students to complete homework in order to achieve and maintain grades, with the result that the students felt more stressed over homework. Although students at the highest achieving schools felt that they received too much homework and they were stressed about it, a larger proportion than in the other schools reported that they still completed it. In rank order those perceived by teachers as most stressed were boys, girls, 'Special Educational Needs' students, those who had 'English as an additional language (EAL)' and 'Pupil Premium' students. Mathematics was reported by students as the most difficult subject in which to complete homework.

Teachers were also asked which of the students they thought would have more difficulty than their peers in completing homework at home. The responses, in rank order, largely reflected the responses to the previous question: 'students with Special Education Needs', 'boys, 'children with EAL' and 'Pupil Premium students'. Two thirds of the teachers reported that they made allowances for those students who were having difficulty, half that they supported the students in school, around 40 per cent that they gave extra time, and a very few, 3 per cent, that they provided extra resources, or gave students their email address. The majority of teachers reported that they 'sometimes' differentiated homework, the majority by task, but, in two of the lowest achieving schools, by resources also (50 per cent of teacher responses).

The issue of the quality of feedback and length of time between submission of work and feedback is an important one. Homework policies across the schools included statements about teachers giving feedback, which should be constructive and given within set time limits. The majority of students in the current study felt that it was useful to receive comments from their teachers so that they understood if the work was correct and where improvements could be made, although a quarter of the students, including over half from two of the lowest achieving schools, stated that no one looked at their work. No teachers in any school reported that no feedback was given. Across the schools there was a wide variation of answers in reply to the question about speed of feedback. Three quarters of teachers stated that they gave feedback one week or less after homework was handed in, but only one third of students agreed. The majority of students at the highest achieving school agreed with their teachers who all stated that they gave feedback in less than a week, however.

All schools had sanctions in place for non-completion of homework, but over 90 per cent of teachers and students perceived that these only 'sometimes', 'rarely' or 'never' worked. Around one third, the biggest proportion, of all groups reported that 'detention' was the type of sanction given more than any other, even though most effective in the view of teachers was 'families informed'.

The importance placed on homework may be seen in part as reflected in the provision of facilities on site for homework completion. All the schools in the current study offered homework clubs, but a number of issues were reported with their effectiveness. Over half of students knew there was a club, but only 5 per cent reported actually using it. Interviewees reported that negative peer pressure might prevent attendance, and that the timing of after-school clubs might not be suitable when students had transport issues getting to and from school, or clubs clashed with extracurricular activities. Only one third of teachers agreed that the availability of subject specific support at homework clubs matched the homework timetable. Some homework clubs were supported by non-teaching staff. In a few cases, teaching staff supported students with homework in their own subjects in these clubs, or subject departments organised sessions. Only one quarter of teachers, across all schools, responded that they had this as part of their workload, however.

All schools were reported to use a form of planner to communicate with home and for students to write down their homework. The majority of respondents from five schools stated that they used the planner, but the majority of families and students from the lowest achieving school stated that the planner was not used. This was in contrast to the teachers at the school who thought the planner was being used.

## 3 Home environment

School documents suggested that teachers should set homework tasks that were achievable and should take into account the resources and support required to complete the work. Two important issues arose in the response to the questions about homework and the home environment: issues related to the availability of resources at home, both physical and human, and the effect of homework on family life.

School documents scrutinised in the current study indicated that resources were expected to be provided at home. There was an assumption here, not always well substantiated or grounded in reality, that the students had access to those resources and, if they did, that this access was at a time suitable to complete the work. Teachers were asked if their students would need computer and Internet access at home in order to complete their homework. Two thirds stated that their students would need both, because many homework tasks required computer or Internet access. However, one third of the total number did not know if their students had such access. Families with only one computer expressed concern that it caused a problem at home if more than one of their children were set homework that required computer use. Schools were compared to see what resources were available at home. More students from higher achieving schools had access to more resources at home, including computers and books than students from lower achieving schools. The lowest achieving school had the lowest percentage of students who had access to a computer at home, 42 per cent compared with the average of 82 per cent. The same school also had the lowest percentage of students who had access to books at home, 16 per cent, compared with the students from the other schools, on average 41 per cent.

Home–school agreements expected families to make space available for students to complete homework at home. Around two thirds of families and students reported that the majority of homework was completed at home, and half of each group stated that this was in the bedroom. The other half responded that it was completed in communal areas of the house: dining room, living room, kitchen or study. The highest proportion of students working in their bedrooms came from the highest achieving schools.

Legally, both students and families should sign a home–school agreement, but two thirds of the students and half the families reported not knowing if there was an agreement. The lowest achieving school had the lowest overall positive responses from students and families of one fifth.

School documents in the current study expected some family involvement in supporting their children with their homework. The overwhelming majority of students (82 per cent) at all schools reported that they needed some help either 'always' or 'sometimes', with 88 per cent of the student respondents at the highest achieving school stating 'always' compared with the average across all the other schools of 20 per cent. Across the schools one quarter of families stated they 'always' had time to support homework, and two thirds 'sometimes'. Families at two lower achieving schools reported that they did not give the same level of support as did families at the three highest achieving schools. While over 90 per cent of families at the higher achieving schools gave help at some point, 90 per cent in the two lower achieving schools either 'sometimes' or 'never' had time to help. One quarter across all schools responded that they should not be expected to help their children.

School documents and interviews showed that in some cases it was expected that the completion of homework should be a joint activity. There was no pattern of confidence in supporting homework from either higher or lower achieving schools, however. Around two thirds of families stated that they felt confident in supporting homework, implying that one third were not confident. Some teachers said they were not aware of who was at home to help the students.

Most students and families agreed that homework adversely affected family activities due to the time involved in completing it. Three quarters of families who responded stated that there was no time for family activities, the students could not take part in family events, and weekends and evenings were governed by homework. The negative effects on family life were exacerbated by the frequent clash of deadlines when different subjects did not coordinate these. Three quarters of students felt that homework did encroach on family time. The biggest majority of these students were from the higher achieving schools and, again, this could be due to the pressure placed on them by their schools to achieve. There is clearly a balance to be achieved here in how much time is reasonable for homework, and how much might be reserved for interactions with the family, including involvement in important family events.

## 4 Political, economic, social and educational factors (Hallam, 2004) in the educational context

There seems little doubt that the following factors are highly influential over current policies and practices in schools in England: the current national political context; economic considerations of supporting young people to achieve as much as they can to give themselves the best possible chance of finding profitable employment; social aspects relating to relationships between families and children and families and schools; and, finally, educational factors related to the requirements of the National Curriculum.

## Political factors

In the current research the political factors are understood as factors in the national context, the local context and within the schools, which act as facilitators, constraints or pressures on policy and practice relating to homework. Since the introduction of the 1988 Education Reform Act in England and the marketisation of education, schools have been operating in a climate of accountability, competition, inspection and parental choice of school for their offspring. What might be called the 'public face' of schools is clearly very important in this context and at this moment in time. In addition, legal requirements to publish policy documents related to learning have been imposed on schools as a framework against which the quality of what they offer can be judged by outsiders. All in all, therefore, the policy documents published by the six schools have to be written for an audience that includes families looking for the 'best' school for their child and Ofsted.

Since 1992 schools have been subject to inspections by Ofsted. The frequency of inspections at present appears to depend, at least in part, on the extent to which, in secondary schools, achievement levels in external examinations are maintained and/or improved (Ofsted, 2015). According to the DfE (2014), it is not a statutory requirement to have a discrete homework policy, perhaps because what a student does at home cannot be legally enforceable by schools (DfE, 2013). Schools therefore find themselves in a considerable dilemma here. Homework is viewed officially as a 'good thing' per se, but students' activities at home cannot be regulated by law. This means that schools are heavily dependent on the goodwill of families to support their homework policies.

In the current study, all the schools had a policy that included reference to homework. The policy documents outlined what was expected from homework and stated why homework was set, the type of work set, the support needed from school and home and, in some cases, what sanctions would be set for not completing homework. The questionnaires showed that teachers and governors knew there was a policy but, interestingly, the majority of students and families were unaware of this. The gap between teachers' and governors' knowledge of the policy documents and that of families is potentially very serious where homework can, potentially, add so much to the learning and achievement of young people but students' activities at home cannot be enforced by law. It is obvious that, in order to enable families to share understandings of homework policy with those officially responsible for policy development within a school, families and young people, as well as school staff, should be involved and, as far as possible, support it. This is particularly important where the setting of work that is intended to be carried out outside the school setting has no basis in law.

In these schools, many governors were not from an educational background. According to the *Governance Handbook* (DfE, 2017: 4), governing bodies are 'vision setters and the strategic decision makers for their schools' but nowhere in this handbook does it state that governors must have an understanding of educational matters. Neither does the document make reference to homework. Again, no guidance is given to governors by government agencies on homework. Given the strategic importance of the governing board in schools' decision about the curriculum this may, perhaps, seem surprising. However, given the non-statutory status of homework a question might be asked about guidance that might be given in a public document, when homework is officially viewed as beneficial to students' learning but has no basis in law.

## Economic factors

Economic factors most specifically relate to an assumption that homework is supportive of improved achievement and study skills and, therefore, has the potential to contribute to enhanced future life and work opportunities. The school documents and interviews tended to assume that completion of homework was related to improved grades and, by implication, enhanced life and work chances. There was a difference, however, in the responses between schools in the different catchments areas with regards to the value of homework, with proportionately more respondents in the higher achieving schools stating that there was a value to homework, compared with those in the lower achieving schools. There is a clear issue of equity when the homework that was set required specific resources that were not available in some homes. Work patterns of family members may be such that they may not be able to help with homework when that help is needed. Schools need to be more aware of home circumstances and make allowances for this, including supporting those supporting students. Families in lower achieving schools gave less support than families from higher achieving schools and yet those students possibly required more support. Some schools actively encouraged families to help and the majority of families felt that they should be expected to do so. However, if collaboration was encouraged, a further issue of equity arises here for students who either have no support available from their parents, or have no support available when they need it.

## Social factors

Factors associated with social aspects include those related to family life, peer pressure, the attractions of alternative forms of entertainment outside school, and so on. There appears to be a disconnection between rhetoric around the importance of the family and the setting of homework. David Cameron, then Prime Minister, spoke of the importance of family life and how the government would strengthen and support family life (Prime Minister's Office, 2014). However, families themselves reported that homework affected family activities.

In the current study, as outlined above, the majority of families supported their children when they were asked to but would have liked more guidance from schools. With so many changes in the curriculum since some members of the family were at school they were likely to question their own ability.

Homework was reported to affect family life and caused students stress in the higher achieving schools more than in the lower achieving schools. As Hallam (2004) previously explained, pressure could be caused by homework in family and social relationships and activities. Teachers in the current study stated they realised that homework caused stress, but, even so, still set it and students reported that were stressed as a result. Given this finding, it seems reasonable that the issue of stress might be discussed at a high level in these schools, for example by senior management and in meetings of the governing board. Teacher awareness should lead to setting more appropriate homework and reduce that stress in the first instance.

In terms of peer pressure and attractions outside school that reduce the amount of time available for homework, these six schools are located in an urban area with a wide range of amenities and facilities: cinemas, theatres, sporting venues, nationally successful sports teams. There is a very efficient transport system that enables easy movement across the whole area and nationally by young people. These pressures and alternative attractions may compete for a student's time outside school and explain, at least in part, why the vast majority of students were not in favour of the setting of homework.

### Educational factors

Educational factors link very closely with factors relating to economics: the assumption that improved grades will result from the completion of homework, and that improved grades will result in enhanced job prospects. In the current study, proportionally more governors and teachers than families and students thought homework improved grades as did proportionally more families, teachers and governors at the higher achieving, than at the lower achieving, schools.

Schools in England have to meet the demands of the National Curriculum and the assessment of the students, and in managing this they put pressure on all involved, including students, families and teachers. However, there is an educational value to homework only if the student understands the work in the first place. In this respect it is noteworthy that homework was not differentiated by all teachers in all subjects, neither was it differentiated by the task set or by how the students completed the task. Sanctions were rarely seen by students as effective and there was inconsistency between what the school documents stated and what actually happened. Once again, there is a clear case here for, first of all, ensuring that the homework given is effective in supporting learning, which itself implies that the school is aware of what type of work this may be. In no schools was there any evidence that there had been any kind of evaluation of this.

In the publicly expressed view of homework in the current study, homework may be seen as a valuable aid to learning and developing a range of skills. Schools offer students support in completing homework through homework clubs, but evidence from the six schools in the current study indicates little use of them.

There has long been an understanding of the importance of formative feedback in supporting students' learning (Black & William, 1998). Homework should be marked and feedback given in line with school policy, and it should be monitored, but as can be seen from the documents, interviews and questionnaires, this was not always the case.

## Discussion

Similar issues and concerns about homework have echoed down the years since the nineteenth century. The findings from the current study bring to the surface some of the contradictions inherent in schools' expectations as required by central government, and what actually takes place. The same political stance pertains as it always did: no political party will take a stand on homework and make a decision on whether a school should set it or not. In the current context, if a government were to try to enforce work carried out by students in their own homes this might be seen to contravene legislation associated with parental rights and entitlements, as well as the rights of young people.

Gladman (1885) stated that the point of homework was for recapitulation, preparation, independent work, useful evening employment, preparation for inspection and the cooperation of parents. Similarly, in 2004 Hallam included promotion of academic learning, developing generic skills, benefiting schools and promoting communication with home. In 2014 the schools involved in the current study stated that the point of homework was to consolidate learning, extend learning, prepare for classwork, develop independent learning and study skills and cover the curriculum. Claims about efficacy continue to be made, therefore, without, it seems, schools carrying out any evaluation of whether the rhetoric matches the reality.

Although important reasons were stated for setting homework from all groups, it is highly significant that there are differences between those in schools who support the public discourse and other groups who state that it should not be set. School documents outlined that homework was set to support students in developing independent learning skills, including organisational, study and research skills in preparation for future study and work skills. However, in some important ways, reports, particularly those of the students and their families, of the reality of undertaking the homework differ from those of the school policy makers and those who set the homework. There were important differences also between responses from families, teachers and governors at the higher achieving schools in comparison with the rest about whether homework should be set, whether it improves grades and whether it is a valuable aid for learning. Really important are issues of:

- whether public perceptions of a school would be damaged if it were to discontinue setting homework;
- whether homework really is needed to ensure curriculum coverage, or whether this could be done another way;
- whether other advantages attributed to homework could be achieved in a different way;
- whether and how teachers are able to set homework that is meaningful to students, is differentiated, and formative feedback given in a timely manner;
- the degree of stress caused by homework, in particular with students in the higher achieving schools finding homework more stressful than other students;
- how schools can encourage or persuade families that their children should complete homework when some did not have the resources, for example computer and Internet access, that teachers seemed to assume they would have, some reported that they did not have the time or confidence to help their children, and the majority saw it as damaging to family life and activities.

Pragmatically it seems that there is much schools themselves can do to make the setting and completion of homework much more meaningful, manageable and conducive of higher student achievement. If homework is set:

- to support learning it can be set to either reinforce the work carried out in class or in preparation for future classwork. When setting homework the resources needed to complete the work must be considered, taking into account the fact that not all pupils have access to the same resources and even though the school may offer a homework club, not all pupils who should be accessing it are able to or want to access it. Also, there is an important question here of differentiation in general terms. The students can only complete the work satisfactorily if they have understood it in class, which implies that the materials and/or the homework activities should be differentiated to relate to the attainment levels of the students, but, as has been discussed, this was not always the case;
- for families to work together then this work cannot be assessed as there is no indication of what is completed by adults and what is completed by the students;
- to make sure the curriculum is covered, then questions need to be addressed as to why the curriculum cannot be covered in class time. There may be an implication that the curriculum is too crowded if work has to be completed at home;
- and homework is essential to curriculum coverage, then those students who do not complete it will be disadvantaged in comparison with those who do. Schools where there is less homework set to complete curriculum coverage and where there is less support from families may well do less well on league tables of student performance;
- as all the teachers, student and family groups reported, it may well cause stress. The highest stress levels reported by students were to be found in the highest achieving school. This may well reflect the pressure that is put on them by the schools to achieve well on the academic league tables, and by the students

themselves in an endeavour to gain good examination grades in the hope of finding suitable well-paid employment or going on to further study. A further issue was that there were times when homework from different subjects was given all at the same time. Although schools had homework timetables they were not always adhered to.

## Conclusion

It is essential that families see value in the homework that is set. This will only happen if they see their children achieving. In turn this requires attention to be given to meaningful work that fits what the young people are already engaged in and that is manageable and achievable. Consideration therefore needs to be given to the difficulty level of the work and adequate differentiation so that it is compatible with the attainment level of the student, and the resources required to complete particular types of homework, both human and physical. The question about space available to students has been an issue since it was reported by Crichton-Browne in the *School Guardian* (1884), when children found it difficult to complete their work due to overcrowding in the home and social conditions. In some homes children had to help their parents, which is still the case today with children looking after siblings while their parents are at work. Those schools taking the home environment into consideration do make allowances by making resources available during the school day or in homework clubs or by giving extra time for the work to be completed. The provision of homework clubs does not appear to be sufficient in itself, however, because few students in the study used them. Perhaps what is provided in these clubs, when they are available, and the status given to them need to be investigated, together with the way in which they are viewed by the students. The low status of provision predisposes to disregarding and devaluing what could be an important resource for students (Wearmouth, 1997), particularly for those with few resources at home.

The current study suggests that students' opposition to the setting of homework relates, at least in part, to: the amount of time it takes up; difficulty in understanding the work in the first place; in some cases, a disjunction between activities in class and the homework that is set; and, sometimes, lack of timely and constructive feedback so that students can learn from their mistakes. All these issues have clear implications for teachers in terms of ensuring the intelligibility of homework and also for considering the time demands. In short, schools need to look at what is set, when it is set and whether all pupils need to undertake it in the same way.

## References

Black, P. & William, D. (1998) *Inside the Black Box: Raising standards through classroom assessment.* London: London School of Education, King's College.
Board of Education. (1937) Homework educational pamphlet no. 110. London: HMSO.
Department for Education (DfE) (2013) Home-schools agreements. Guidance for local authorities and governing bodies. London: DfE.

Department for Education (DfE) (2014) Statutory policies for schools. Advice on the policies and documents that governing bodies and proprietors of schools are required to have by law. September 2014. London: DfE.
Department for Education (DfE) (2017) Governance handbook. For academies, multi-academy trusts and maintained schools. London: DfE.
Department for Education and Employment (DfEE) (1998) Homework: Guidelines for Primary and Secondary Schools. London: DfEE.
Department for Education and Science (1987) Education observed 4: Homework. Report by Her Majesty's Inspectors. London: HMSO.
Elementary Education Act (1870) (33 & 34 Vict c. 75) Available at: www.educationengland.org.uk/documents/acts/1870-elementary-education-act.pdf (accessed: 30 January 2018).
Elementary Education Act (1880) (43 & 44 Vict c. 23) Available at: www.educationengland.org.uk/documents/acts/1880-elementary-education-act.pdf (accessed: 30 January 2018).
Gladman, F. (1885) *School work*. London: Jarrold and Sons.
Gordon, P. (1980) 'Homework: Origins and justifications', *International Journal of Research & Method in Education*, 3(1), 27–46.
Hallam, S. (2004) Homework: The evidence, Bedford Way Paper 21. London: Institute of Education/University of London.
Hansard (1934a) House of Lords official report 5th series, vol. 289 col. 427–548, 16 June 1884.
Hansard (1934b) House of Lords official report 5th series, vol. 291, col. 1779, 3 July 1934.
Hansard (1934c) House of Lords official report 5th series, vol. 296, col. 205, 11 December 1934.
Hattie, J. (2009) *Visible learning; a synthesis of over 800 meta-analyses relating to achievement*. London: Routledge.
Higgins, S., Katsipataki, M., Kokotsaki, D., Coleman, R., Major, L. E., & Coe, R. (2014) *The Sutton Trust-Education Endowment Foundation Teaching and Learning Toolkit*. London: Education Endowment Foundation.
MacBeath, J. & Turner, M. (1990) Learning out of school: Homework, policy and practice. A research study commissioned by the Scottish Education Department. Glasgow: Jordanhill College.
Martin, C. (1979) *A short history of English schools 1750–1965*. Hove: Wayland.
Office for Standards in Education (Ofsted) (2015) *School inspection handbook*. Manchester: Ofsted.
Prime Minister's Office (2014) Speech: David Cameron on Families, Delivered at the Relationships Alliance Summit, 18 August 2014 at the Royal College of GPs, part of Support for families and Looked-after children and adoption.
*School Guardian* (1884) Home lessons, 20 September 1884, p. 646.
Sharp, C., Keys, W., & Benefield, P. (2001) Homework: A review of recent research National Foundation for Education Research (NFER). Slough: NFER.
Wearmouth, J. (1997) 'Pygmalion lives on', *Support for Learning*, 12(3), 122–126.
Weston, P. (1999) *Homework: Learning from practice*. London: The Stationery Office.

# INDEX

Note: page references in italics indicate figures; bold indicates tables; 'n' indicates chapter notes.

academies 7, 11, 145, 152, 155
Advanced Skills Teachers (ASTs) 123–37
Al-deen, T. J. 186
Alton-Lee, A. 83
Arnold, T. 3
Australian Institute for Teaching and School Leadership 126
autism 191–94; *see also* special educational needs (SEN)

Bachelor of Education (BEd) 159, 164
Ball, S. 111, 161, 163, 167, 168
Bauer, E. 186
Beck, C. 161, 164
behaviour management, student teachers on 116–17
Bell, A. 3
Berryman, M. 80
Bhatti, G. 187
Bilingual Creative Writing Clubs 55–74, *62*, *65*, *71*
bilingual students' voice: Bilingual Creative Writing Clubs 55–74, *62*, *65*, *71*; Bulgarian-English 64, *65*, 72; Polish-English 33–54; South Asian with non-English speaking parents 172–88
Bitan, K. 167
Black-Hawkins, K. 165
Blair, T. 10
Blake, D. 162

Bloom, A. 8
Blunkett, D. 209, 212
Bolam, R. 152, 155
Bourdieu, P. 112–13, 184
Boyson, R. 6
Brember, I. 168
Brown, M. 168
Brown, P. 6
Browne, L. 165
Brundrett, M. 162
Bruner, J. 17
Bubb, S. 141, 142, 143, 144, 146, 147, 148, 151, 152, 153
Bulgarian-English bilingual students 64, *65*, 72
bullying 2–4, 204
Bush, T. 152
Butler Act (1944) 5
Byrne, B. 172

Cameron, D. 218
Carter Review (2015) 167
Case, H. 8
Centre for British Teachers, The 129
change 146, 150
Chapple Report (1997) 78
Charmaz, K. 159
Chartered College of Teaching 136
children's voice *see* students' voice
Citizenship Education Longitudinal Study 11

class, social 2–3, 4, 173, 185, 188
climate, school, for teacher training 167–68; *see also* environment
coalition government (2004) 11
coalition government (2010–15) 111
Coleman, J. S. 184
Coleman, M. 152
community: as resource in Bilingual Creative Writing Clubs 72; and South Asian non-English speaking parents 174
comprehensive schools 5, 9
Conservative government (1979) 6, 111
Conservative government (2016) 7
Cook-Sather, A. 119
Cooper, C. L. 149
Coulthard, M. 161
Courtney, S. 168
Crichton-Browne, Dr 208–9, 221
critical thinking skills, student teachers' 160, 165–66, 169
Crosby, S. 95
cross-cultural learning 58–59
Crozier, G. 173, 185, 191
Cummins, J. 57, 73, 74
Curry, W. B. 8

Dakin, J. 57–58
D'Angelo, A. 34, 48
Davies, J. 173, 185
Davis, G. H. 5
Dawes, R. 4
Dewey, J. 18, 93
Dimmock, C. 141, 146, 151, 152
Direct Grant Funding 173
discipline 2–3, 4, 5, 9
Draper, J. 152
Drury, R. 34, 36, 47

Earley, P. 141, 142, 143, 144, 145, 146, 147, 148, 151, 152, 153
Early, M. 57, 73, 74
Early Years Keyworkers 201
Education Act (1980) 6, 10
Education (No.2) Act (1986) 6
Education Health and Care Plan (EHCP) 179–80
Education Reform Act (1988) 6–7, 216
education system, impact on Māori students' voice 77, 78–79
Educational Psychologists 203
'Effective Teaching Profile' framework 82
Elementary Education Acts (1870/80) 207
English as an Additional Language (EAL) 39, 55, 56, 172, 173, 213; *see also* bilingual students

environment: classroom, literacy learning identities and 100; home, for homework 214–15; *see also* climate
equity: homework policies and 217; in teacher training 163–64
Ethnic Minority Achievement Grant (EMAG) 173
Eversley, J. 34
*Every Child Matters* (ECM) initiative (DfES, 2003) 10

families' voice xiv–xv; on homework 207–21; South Asian non-English speaking 174–75; *see also* parents' voice
feedback 26; failure 36–37
Flintham, A. 149
Florian, L. 165
Forster Act (1870) 4
Fox, A. 115
free schools 8–9, 11, 151
Frost, D. 18, 22

Gabarro, J. J. 144
Gallimore, R. 19, 23, 28, 29, 30
*Gardiner v. Bygrave* (1889) 4
Garmarnikow, E. 185
Gay, G. 81
General Teaching Council (GTC) 123
Gipps, C. 18
Gittins Report (Central Advisory Council for Education, 1967) 5
Gladman, F. 207, 219
good practice 162–63
Goodall, J. 173, 187
Gordon, P. 208
Gove, M. 158, 159, 163, 209, 212
Graduate Teacher Programme (GTP) 158
Grandin, Temple 192
Green, A. 185
Greening, Justine 7
Grover, K. L. 152

Hadow Report, *The Education of the Adolescent* (1927) 5
Haep, A. 167
Hagger, H. 165
Hall, D. 117
Hall, E. 167
Hallam, S. 207, 218, 219
*Handbook of Suggestions for the Consideration of Teachers and Others Concerned in the Work of Public Elementary Schools* (1905) 7–8
Hanley, V. 162
Hargreaves, D. 166
Hargreaves, E. 18

Harris, R. 162–63
Hattie, J. 160
Haya, I. 110
headteachers' voice: experiences, challenges, successes of new headteachers 139–55; on school's roles in teacher training 158–69
Highly Accomplished Teachers (HAT), United States 125
Hobson, A. 141, 145, 146, 147, 148, 150, 151, 152–53, 154, 155
Hoegaerts, J. 3
homework: economic factors 217; educational factors 218–19; effectiveness 212–14; historical context 207–9; home environment for 211–15; political factors 216–17; purpose 211–12; social factors 218
Hopkins, E. 22
Hughes, Thomas, *Tom Brown's School Days* 2, 3

indigenous students' voice, Māori 76–89
Individual Education Plans (IEP) 41–42
Initial Teacher Education (ITE) 15, 17, 28, 31; *see also* student teachers; teacher training
Institute for Fiscal Studies 166
integration, social 35–36, 72, 172, 176, 187
inter-/intrapersonal space 24–25, 29
interthinking 24, 28–31, *30*
Isaacs, Susan 8
Ishikawa 18, 22
isolation, professional 148, 153

Jackson, N. 58

Kelly, M. 149
Kershner, R. 17
Klin, A. 192
Kontopoulou, K. 115
Kosnik, C. 164
Kyriacou, C. 161

Labour government (1964) 5
Lamb Enquiry (2009) 191, 192
Lancaster, J. 3
Lauchlan, F. 46, 47
Learning Support Assistants (LSAs) 201–2
Levin, B. 10
literacy learning: identities in New Zealand 92–108, *96, 101, 102, 104, 105*; through Bilingual Creative Writing Clubs 55–74, *62, 65, 71*
Littleton, K. 29
local education authorities (LEAs) 5–7, 129, 151, 152, 155

Lofthouse, R. 167
Lopez-Rodriguez, M. 34, 48
Lord, P. 152

Macbeath, J. 18, 22
Major, J. 6
Makaton signs 198, 200, 205n3
Male, T. 164, 165
Mangan, J. A. 3
Mansell, W. 165
Māori students' voice 76–89; education success as Māori (study 2) 85–87; in Te Kotahitanga Phase 5 (study 1) 82–84
McCallum, B. 18
McGinity, R. 117
McIntyre, D. 15, 18, 165
McMichael, P. 152
mentors/mentoring: for new headteachers 150, 152–54; for students teachers 16–19, 20, 22, 25–30, *26*, 164–65, 167–68
Mercer, N. 17, 29
metacognition 16–18, 22, 24, 27
metalanguage 18
meta-learning 24, 26
monoculturalism 55, 74
monolingualism, norm of 34–35, 55, 74; *see also* bilingual students' voice
Monsour, F. 152
Montgomery, C. 173, 187
morale 150
More Knowing Other (MKO) *see* mentors/mentoring
Morgan, N. 7
Murphy, V. 56
Murray, J. 164, 165

Naqvi, R. 56
National College of Teaching and Leadership (NCTL) 112, 158
National Curriculum 9, 163, 218
National Professional Qualification for Headship (NPQH) 144, 151
National Student Survey 11
Neddam, Fabrice 3
Neill, A. S. 8
Nevill, A. 162
New Labour government (1998) 10, 11
New Zealand education system 77; Māori students' voice in 76–89; positive literacy learning identities in 92–108, *96, 101, 102, 104, 105*
Newly Qualified Teachers (NQTs) 27, 164; *see also* student teachers' voice
Nunn, T. P. 8

Office for Standards in Education, Children's Services and Skills (Ofsted) 7, 112, 126, 129, 144, 145, 149–50, 154, 155, 159, 166, 168, 210, 216
Oral and Written Language Scales (OWLS-II) 38, 40, 45, 49
Ozga, J. 168

Panek, R. 192
Parent Teacher Associations (PTAs) 5
Parents' Charter (1991) 7
parents' voice xiv–xv; development of 'voice' in education 4–7; Polish-English bilingual students 33–54; South Asian non-English speaking 172–88; the special educational needs (SEN) system 191–205, *195*, *196*, *198*, *199*, *200*; in students' Bilingual Creative Writing Clubs 70–72, *71*; *see also* families' voice
pedagogical tools 22–23; classroom observation 23; special educational needs (SEN) 194–99, *195*, *196*, *198*, *199*, *200*; student teacher' reflective logs 23; 'Talking Stones' 95, *96*, 103–5, *104*, *105*; 'The Thinking Fish' scaffold 22, 22–26, *24*, 31; *see also* literacy learning
pedagogy 16–19; culturally responsive 81; reciprocal dialogic 82
Pedder, D. 15, 18, 22
Picture Education Communication System (PECS) 198, 205n2
Plowden Report (1967) 5–6, 8, 9
Pocklington, K. 152
Polish-English bilingual students 33–54; case study 1, Kamila 38–41, **52**; case study 2, Lila 41–43, **53**; case study 3, Marek 43–45, **54**
Post Graduate Certificate in Education (PGCE) 159, 164
pre-service teachers *see* student teachers
primary schools: headteachers' views on schools' roles in teacher training 158–69; South Asian non-English speaking parents' voice in 172–88; special educational needs (SEN) in 191–205, *195*, *196*, *198*, *199*, *200*
public schools 2–4
punishment, corporal 2–4
pupils' voice *see* students' voice
Putnam, R. 184

Qualified Teacher Status (QTS) 109, 161, 163

Rafferty, F. 163–64
Ralph, S. 168

Raynor, S. 162
Reay, D. 172, 191
recruitment and retention 112, 124, 129, 145–48, 150, 154
Reid, J. 165
Rhodes, C. 162
Rojas, S. 110
role models *see* mentors/mentoring
Ross, G. 17
Rudduck, J. 15, 18
Rudney, G. L. 173
Ryan, L. 34, 48

Safford, K. 34, 36, 47
Sales, R. 34, 35, 47, 48
scaffolding 17–19, 22, 27, 28, 30, *30*, 97, 98–100; 'The Thinking Fish' 22, 22–26, *24*, 31
scheduling, visual 198, 205n4
school councils 11–12
School Councils (Wales) Regulations (2005) 11
School Direct Salaried route (SDS) 111–12, 159, 164
School Guardian 208, 221
Scottish Chartered Teacher Scheme 125
Second Hadow Report (Board of Education, 1931) 8
Seidman, I. 159
self-confidence, students' 46, 104–5
self-determination, students' 83, 89
self-esteem: students' 33, 40, 46, 49, 56–58, 70, 73, 74, 192; teachers' 134, 143, 152
self-evaluation 133
Senior Leaders in Education (SLE) study 135–36
Sharp, C. 152–53
silence, students' 2–4
Sleeter, C. E. 81
social capital 184–86
social constructivism 16–18, *24*, *26*, 26–28, 31, 92
social media interactions, student teachers' voice in private 109–21
Sockett, H. 160
South Asian non-English speaking parents' voice 172–88
special educational needs and disability co-ordinators (SENDCo) 200, 201, 202, 204
special educational needs (SEN) system, parents' voice in 191–205, *195*, *196*, *198*, *199*, *200*
Speech and Language Therapists (SALT) 202
Steins, G. 167

stress xxv, 48, 133, 148–49, 152, 154
student teachers' voice: habitus 112–14; in private social media interactions 109–21; reflective logs 23, 24–26, *25*; use of students' voice in teaching practice 15–31, *20, 21, 22, 24, 25, 26, 29, 30*; *see also* mentors/mentoring; teacher training
students' voice xii–xiii; Bilingual Creative Writing Clubs 55–74, *62, 65, 71*; development of 'voice' in education 7–10; headteachers' views on schools' roles in training 158–69; on homework 207–21; Polish-English bilingual 33–54; positive literacy learning identities in NZ 92–108, *96, 101, 102, 104, 105*; South Asian with non-English speaking parents 172–88; in the special educational needs (SEN) system 191–205, *195, 196, 198, 199, 200*; student teachers' use of in teaching practice 15–31, *20, 21, 22, 24, 25, 26, 29, 30*
Susinos, T. 110
Sussman, F. 194–96
Sutton Trust and NFER report (2018) 11

'Talking Stones' pedagogic tool 95, *96*, 103–5, *104, 105*
Taubman, P. 161
Taylor, C. 158, 163
Taylor Report (1977) 6, 9, 10, 11
teacher training, headteachers' views on schools' roles in 158–69
Teachers' Standards (2011/12) 15–16, 27, 28, 31, 161, 163, 169
teachers' voice xv; communication with South Asian non-English speaking parents 177–79; on homework 207–21; on positive literacy learning identities in NZ 92–108, *96, 101, 102, 104, 105*; professional advancement and Advanced Skills Teachers (ASTs) 123–37; *see also* headteachers' voice; student teachers' voice
*Teaching Excellent and Student Outcomes Frameworks* (2017) 11
Tharp, R. 19, 23, 28, 29, 30

Thatcher, M. 6
'Thinking Fish' scaffolding tool *22*, 22–26, *24*, 31
Tillman, L. C. 81
Training and Development Agency for Schools 128
translation services, non-English speaking parents 177, 178, 180, 182–87
Tripartite System 5
'Trojan Horse' controversy, Birmingham (2016) 11

uniforms 9
unions, teacher 123
United Nation (UN), *Convention on the Rights of the Child* (1989) 10
universities 10, 11–12; and teacher training 166, 169
university students' work in Bilingual Creative Writing Clubs 55–74, *62, 65, 71*

'voice' in education xii–xv; developments towards 1–12; *see also* families' voice; headteachers' voice; parents' voice; students' voice; student teachers' voice; teachers' voice
Vorhaus, J. 187
Vygotsky, L. 15–16, 19, 28, 93–94

Warnock Report (1978) 6
Warwick, P. 17
Webb, M. 167
Weindling, D. 141, 146, 151, 152
Wenger, E. 112, 116
Wenger-Trayner, E. 167
Wesley, J. 2
Whitty, G. 10–11
Wilshaw, M. 163
Windle, J. 186
Wisby, E. 10–11
Wood, D. 17
writing *see* literacy learning

Zone of Proximal Development (ZPD) 16–17, 18–19, 25, 27, 28, 29, *30*

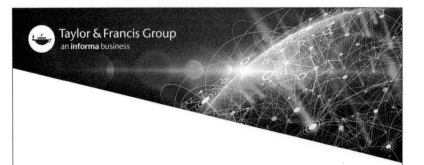